OPTIONS

A Personal Seminar

OPTIONS

A Personal Seminar

Scott H. Fullman

NEW YORK INSTITUTE OF FINANCE

Library of Congress Cataloging-in-Publication Data

Fullman, Scott H.
    Options : a personal seminar / Scott H. Fullman.
       p.   cm.
    Includes index.
    ISBN 0-13-643578-5
    1. Stock options. I. Title
    HG6042.F85   1992
    332.63'228--dc20   92-19109
                                           CIP

This publication is designed to provide accurate and authoritative information in regard to the subject matter covered. It is sold with the understanding that the publisher is not engaged in rendering legal, accounting,
or other professional service. If legal service or other expert assistance is
required, the services of a competent professional person should be
sought.

*—From a Declaration of Principles jointly adopted by a
Committee of the American Bar Association and a Committee
of Publishers and Associations*

Printed in the United States of America

10 9 8 7 6 5 4 3 2 1

ISBN 0-13-643578-5

New York Institute of Finance

For
Deborah M. Taylor-Fullman

Contents

Acknowledgments

I would like to thank the following people and groups for their help and assistance:

* All-Quotes, Inc. for the supply of stock and option data. This data was used in providing price information for strategies and graphs. All-Quotes is a supplier of stock and option information as well as supporter for the Best Options Strategy Selection computer program. All-Quotes can be reached at 212-425-5030 or by writing their main office at 40 Exchange Place, New York, N.Y. 10005.

* Harrison Roth, senior options strategist at Cowen & Co. Sitting next to Harry has provided great insight as well as a different way of looking at things. Harry also provided some insight into certain strategies including the use of repair strategies.

* Joseph Dunn, partner and Al Napolatano, trader at Cowen & Co. Joe and Al have been great partners to work with, showing a superior level of expertise and professionalism.

* Paul McQuarrie, NYIF Corp. Paul has given me the opportunity to express the use of option strategies through the teaching of advanced strategies at the NYIF. In addition, it was Paul's idea for writing the book.

* Sheck Cho, Simon & Schuster. Sheck has provided great insight and assistance in writing this book. His help as well as understanding and patience have been a great asset.

* Ed Herbst and the partners of Cowen & Co. for recognizing the great advantage of having an area to assist in the formation of strategies using options.

Preface

Options: A Personal Seminar was written for the individual investor, but is not limited to the individual investor. This book focuses on the development of different strategies, with a concentration on maximizing profit and limiting potential risk. The comparison of different investment techniques using puts and calls can allow the investor to make an educated selection of the appropriate strategy. To aid in the strategy selection, *Options* contains many suggested guidelines as well as worksheets and graphic illustrations.

All of the strategies illustrated are not meant for all investors. Some of the strategies are given to help the investor understand how option professionals utilize different techniques while they also demonstrate the pricing of options contracts and the efficiency of the options markets.

Option strategies are built on one another, and this book uses a method of building blocks to explain different strategies. Starting from the simple purchase of an options contract and building up to options arbitrage, *Options: A Personal Seminar* explains many of the different option strategies and how they are used to achieve desired results.

The use of option contracts as a means of repairing stock and option positions is also explained in this book. Chapter 19 focuses on some of the techniques used by professionals to reduce losses to break-even situations. While the stock may not always cooperate, the use of a repair strategy helps to avoid the use and risk of additional capital.

Because high technology is the focus of many investors, Chapter 21 will focus on some of the methods in which computer programs can be used to evaluate and search out potential investments. Sample screens have been provided to show the amount of information which is available to the user of such programs.

In addition to the use of puts and calls, *Options* discusses the use of longer-term option contracts known as LEAPS™ (Chapter 18) and CAPS™ (Chapter 24). Futures and the use of futures/stock arbitrage explain one use of systematic program trading. At the end of the book, Chapter 22 discusses some of the uses of options in managing portfolios.

While this book intends to detail as much information as possible with respect to the different strategies, the responsibility to evaluate risk is on the person who uses the strategy. It is inconceivable for a book to detail every single risk on every strategy or even to detail every strategy. The best attempts have been made to cover as much about the strategies as possible. It is important that people fairly new to using options carefully evaluate any action and use small amounts of contracts until they are comfortable with determining the risk on any trade which they do using that strategy.

Options will help both the personal investor and the professional evaluate the benefits of various option strategies through the use of guidelines, illustrations, examples, and worksheets. Almost every worksheet has a box at the top, with spaces for such information as name of stock, rating, yield, expiration date, interest charges, and so on. Versions of the same box are used for all of the worksheets, and a line is placed in an information area that is not necessary to the calculations of the particular worksheet.

In addition, a chapter has been dedicated to the follow up of trades on a wide group of strategies. While it is very important to follow-up on winning strategies, it is equally if not more important to follow-up on strategies which may not be doing so well. It is highly suggested that the user of options carefully maintain the status on all positions and that a periodic review, which should be daily, be utilized to keep fully informed on the outlook of using both options as well as stocks. While certain strategies may not have as much risk as others, there might be an occasion for the investor or trader to take advantage and adjust positions which could lock in profits, allow additional time or to take profits or losses. It is also suggested that positions be closed before expiration and not held to the last minute. It is possible for losses to become bigger or even for gains to become losses in a short period of time. Waiting till the last minute to close a position can put unnecessary risk, frustration and pressure on a position which could be avoided if acted on in a timely fashion.

1
Options:
An Introduction

All investment decisions hold a certain degree of risk. The failure of savings and loans as well as other banks has proven that no matter where you invest your hard-earned dollars, there is always the possibility that something will go wrong, leaving you holding the bag—an empty bag. While the chance of losing your money is always a possibility, it is unlikely that every bank will fail. Many people have invested in the real estate market, buying second homes or rental properties, only to see that those investments did not do as well as they had hoped. Other investors put capital into "high risk, high yield" instruments, also known as junk bonds. Unfortunately, some of these people found that there was more risk than yield and lost thousands of dollars because of something that was "never going to happen."

The stock market does have certain pitfalls, as well. Many small investors as well as large investors were severely hurt during the market crash of 1987, as they rushed to sell their holdings in a panic, as the market bottomed. The fear of a further market decline led many investors to abandon ship and then left them out in the cold as the market recovered. The loss of capital kept many investors out of the market for several years. The fear of another market crash has continued to keep many away from Wall Street, and those who have returned have done so cautiously.

For years, the use of option contracts has enabled investors and traders to position their holdings to reduce risk or even increase risk for the opportunity of increasing reward. Option professionals have

1

constructed many strategies which can be used to offset, limit, or reduce the potential risk associated with trading stocks. The use of option contracts has allowed investors to hedge positions or create similar positions while increasing profit potential and lowering the amount of risk associated with such trading. Strategists have developed simple as well as sophisticated techniques for achieving goals which allow for less capital expense, less dollar risk, and greater return. In addition, strategies have been developed which allow the user to profit even if the price of the underlying stock is static during a certain period of time. Other strategies allow for the benefit of large stock movements regardless of the direction of the movement.

Before the various strategies involved in trading options are discussed, it is important to understand the background and fundamentals of option contracts.

Options have traded for many years, but in 1973 the first exchange was formed with the exclusive function of trading option contracts. The Chicago Board Options Exchange (CBOE) was formed by members of the Chicago Mercantile Exchange (CME) and the Chicago Board of Trade (CBOT), which trade commodities. Many traders from these exchanges became market-makers on the CBOE, establishing the standardization of listed option contracts. As the option market continued to expand, four more exchanges joined the world of listed options:

American Stock Exchange

Philadelphia Stock Exchange

Pacific Coast Options Exchange

New York Stock Exchange

Since the standardization of listed option contracts, new option products have developed, such as options on indexes, interest rates, commodities, treasury securities and even longer-term option contracts on equities. The expansion of the options universe has also been evidenced through the creation and expansion of sophisticated computer hardware and software, some of which have become prototypes for stock trading. Other changes, such as the rise in stock volume, and improvement in market making on stocks, have also been attributed to the popularity of options trading.

What Is an Option?

Option contracts have become standardized by the rules of the five option exchanges:

American Stock Exchange (ASE)

Chicago Board Options Exchange (CBOE)

New York Stock Exchange (NYSE)

Pacific Stock Exchange (PSE)

Philadelphia Stock Exchange (PHLX).

In conjunction with trading options, the five exchanges have formed and are members of the Options Clearing Corporation (OCC). It is the responsibility of the OCC to guarantee and back the value and properties of all the listed option contracts.

An option is a contract in which there are actually three parties. The first party, the purchaser, pays a consideration for the right, but not the obligation, to take a certain action, at a specified price, until a certain date. The second party, the seller (also known as the writer), agrees to perform the action which is specified in the option contract, at the specified price, until the date that the contract expires. For taking on the burden of performing that obligation, the writer collects the consideration from the buyer. The third party, the OCC, guarantees and ensures that the action which the option contract specifies, will be performed according to the agreement between the two parties.

There are two types of option contracts. The most popular type of contract is known as the *call*. The call is a contract in which the writer agrees to sell the stock which the contract represents to the buyer, if the buyer decides to exercise the right to purchase the stock. The stock will be purchased by the buyer of the option and sold by the writer of the option at the exercise price, also known as the strike price. Therefore, as the value of the stock appreciates, the value of the call will also appreciate since the contract states that regardless of what price the stock is, the writer would have to deliver that stock to the purchaser, upon the demand of the purchaser. Conversely, if the price of the stock depreciates, so will the value of the call option. If the stock remains unchanged, the value of the option will also depreciate by a certain amount. This topic, known as the *time premium* will be discussed shortly.

The second type of option contract is the *put*. The purchaser of the put is purchasing the right to sell the stock which the option represents (the underlying stock) at the exercise price, regardless of the value of the stock. As the value of the underlying stock depreciates, the value of the put contract will appreciate, even if the stock drops to zero. However, if the value of the stock appreciates, the value of the put contract will be worth less since it would not be as advantageous to sell a stock lower through the put than it could be sold on the open market. The stock/put price relationship is inverse. As the price of the stock rises, the put drops and as the stock drops, the put rises.

The exercise price, also known as the strike price, is the value at which the stock will be exchanged by the buyer and the writer. If the buyer of the option contract decides to take action on that contract, a notice of exercise is sent to the OCC. The OCC will inform a writer (not necessarily the original writer of the contract) that the contract has been exercised and that according to the terms of the contract, the writer is *assigned* to perform the action which is specified in the contract. In this case, the writer of the call would be obligated to deliver or sell the underlying stock to the buyer of the contract at the exercise price. If the contract were a put, the writer would be obligated to purchase the underlying stock from the buyer of the put at the exercise price. Once that contract is exercised, it no longer exists and the writer is under no further obligation, and the contract between the parties no longer exists.

Unless the stock is adjusted for a split, distribution, or other special type of dividend, the option contract will represent 100 shares of the underlying stock. Should the option contract be exercised, 100 shares of the underlying stock would be exchanged by the parties for each contract which is exercised. If the option contract is adjusted for a split, the adjusted amount of shares which the contract represents will be exchanged upon exercise.

The amount of shares which the contract represents is known as the *multiplier*. The multiplier has a function aside from that of the exercise quantity. Since the standard option contract represents 100 shares of stock, the quoted price of the option is multiplied by 100 or the multiplier. Therefore, if the price of the option contract is 1¼ points, the dollar value of that one contract which represents 100 shares of stock would be $125.00 (1¼ × 100). If an investor purchased 100 calls, he has purchased the right to buy 10,000 shares of the underlying stock. The writer of the 100 calls would be obligated to deliver 10,000 shares of the stock to the buyer at the exercise price.

It was stated that the option may be exercised until a specific time. Every option contract has a term or life span. The expiration date is defined in the description of the contract by the month in which it expires. The last day for trading an option is the third Friday of the month in which it expires. The earliest date in the month in which a contract will stop trading is the 15th of the month and the latest the contract can trade will be the 21st of the month. In the event that the third Friday of the month is a market holiday, the last day for trading will be the business day before. All option contracts, which are American style options, can be exercised up until and including the last day of the life of the contract. Some contracts, representing index options, are European style options, which may only be exercised on the last day of trading.

The purchaser of an option is not required to exercise the contract. The contract may be sold out by the purchaser, closing the position at current market price for the contract. In the same way that the purchaser of an option can liquidate the position, the writer may repurchase the option contract if the contract has not been already assigned against him. The option writer may go into the market and repurchase the contract at the current market price. Since option contracts are standard, a buyer may sell the contracts which were previously purchased to another purchaser in the market, or to a writer who is looking to repurchase a contract previously written.

Option exercise prices are also standardized. Except for contracts which are adjusted for splits or other distributions, the exercise prices for option contracts are set in intervals. Those intervals are dependent on the price of the underlying stock and can be seen in Table 1-1. Options on products other than stocks have different strike price intervals, and do not conform to the table.

TABLE 1-1. Equity Option Exercise Price Intervals

Exercise Interval	Stock Prices
2½ Points	5 – 25
5 Points	25 – 200
10 Points	205 – up

TABLE 1-2.   Option Expiration Month Codes

Month	Call	Put
January	A	M
February	B	N
March	C	O
April	D	P
May	E	Q
June	F	R
July	G	S
August	H	T
September	I	U
October	J	V
November	K	W
December	L	X

Option Symbology

Obtaining a quote on an option contract is as easy as entering the ticker symbol on a stock plus a few extra codes. Most quote systems require the following information to obtain a quote on an option contract:

Stock ticker symbol

Option expiration month code (see Table 1-2)

Option exercise price code (see Table 1-3)

Option exchange code (see Table 1-4)

Most computer systems will either display all of the options available on a stock with the press of a key or require that the investor enter the necessary information into the system. For example, to retrieve a quote on the IBM January 90 call, the investor would enter the following on a Quotron System:

IBMAR.CO

where **IBM** is the ticker symbol, **A** is the code for January calls, **R** represents the 90 exercise price, and **.CO** is the exchange designation for the Chicago Board Options Exchange. Systems other than Quo-

TABLE 1-3.   Exercise Price Codes

Code		Value (Exercise Prices)		
A	5	105	205	305
B	10	110	210	310
C	15	115	215	315
D	20	120	220	320
E	25	125	225	325
F	30	130	230	330
G	35	135	235	335
H	40	140	240	340
I	45	145	245	345
J	50	150	250	350
K	55	155	255	355
L	60	160	260	360
M	65	165	265	365
N	70	170	270	370
O	75	175	275	375
P	80	180	280	380
Q	85	185	285	385
R	90	190	290	390
S	95	195	295	395
T	100	200	300	400
U	7½			
V	12½			
W	17½			
X	22½			

TABLE 1-4.   Option Exchange Codes

Exchange	Possible Exchange Designation Codes*		
American Stock Exchange	AO	AQ	
Chicago Board Options Exchange	CO	WQ	
New York Stock Exchange	NO	NQ	
Pacific Coast Stock Exchange	PO	PQ	
Philadelphia Stock Exchange	XO	XQ	PHQ

*Various quote services use different exchange codes.

TABLE 1-5.   Sample Option Display

C-Bid	C-Ask	C-Last	C-Volu	Series	P-Bid	P-Ask	P-Last	P-Volu
6⅛	6⅜	6½	2	Jan 40	½	⅝		
2⅜	2⅝	2⅜	48	Jan 45	1⅞	2	1¹⁵⁄₁₆	65
¼	⅜	¼	14	Jan 50	5¾	6	5⅞	3
6½	6¾	6⅝	22	Feb 40	¾	¹⁵⁄₁₆		
3½	3¾	3½	62	Feb 45	2¾	2⅞	2¹¹⁄₁₆	29
⅞	1⅛			Feb 50	6½	6⅝	6⅝	37
7¼	7½			Apr 40	1⅛	1³⁄₁₆		
4¼	4⅜	4⅝	40	Apr 45	3⅞	4	4	1
1⁷⁄₁₆	1½	1⁷⁄₁₆	35	Apr 50	7¼	7⅜		

tron may have slightly different formats. Some systems allow the investor to view information on all of the options on an underlying stock by pressing one key (See Table 1-5). Vendors carrying stock and option pricing information use different formats to display information. Some vendors offer more services than others, while other vendors offer the ability to customize the output for the user's needs. See Chapter 21 for a discussion on computer systems and trading options.

The market data that the user views on the screen usually carries some important information. For example, most vendors display the last trading price of the options contract, which might not even be today's trade. In addition, if the contract has traded on the date that the user is viewing, the net change for the day will be displayed. Additional information includes the bid price, the offer price and the volume traded for the day. The bid price is the highest price that someone is willing to pay for that option contract, while the offer price (also known as the asking price) is the lowest price which someone is willing to sell that option contract for. Other information which might be displayed includes the high of the day, the low of the day, open interest, theoretical value and hedge ratio (see Chapter 20).

Options Pricing

The option contract price is known as the **option premium**. The option premium is a value which encompasses two major segments pertaining to the value of the underlying stock. The first value is known as the *intrinsic value*, while the second value is known as the *time premium*.

The intrinsic value is the amount which the option is worth, should the contract be exercised. The measurement of the intrinsic value is the amount that the contract is considered to be **in-the-money**, or the real worth of the option contract. A call is considered to be in-the-money if the price of the underlying stock is above the exercise price of the option contract. A put is considered to be in-the-money if the price of the stock is below the exercise price of the options contract. For example, if a stock is at 88 and an investor had purchased a call option with an 85 exercise price, the position would be 3 points in-the-money. In this case, the holder would realize a price of 3 points ($300 per option) if the call were to be exercised and the stock was sold in the immediate market, at a price of 88. If the investor had purchased a put with an 85 exercise price, the put would be out-of-the-money, since exercising the put would be useless since the underlying stock might be sold for a higher value at expiration. A put and call with the same exercise price cannot be both in-the-money or out-of-the-money, at the same time.

The intrinsic value of the call is calculated using the following formula:

Intrinsic Value of a Call = Stock price − Exercise price subject to the Stock price being greater than the Exercise price.

The intrinsic value of the put uses the following formula:

Intrinsic Value of a Put = Exercise Price − Stock Price subject to the Stock price being less than the Exercise price.

If the price of the stock is less than the exercise price of the call option, the option has no intrinsic value, while if the price of the stock is greater than the exercise price of the put option, the option has no intrinsic value.

The value of the time-premium is made up of many smaller parts. Time is not the only factor which determines the time premium of an options contract. To calculate the time-premium, simply subtract the intrinsic value from the option premium. The amount which is left is the time-premium. Therefore, if an option contract is trading at 6½ and the contract has an intrinsic value of 4 points, the time-premium would be 2½ points, which applies to both puts and calls.

The relationship of the exercise price of an option to the price of the underlying stock is a major contributor to the value of time. The further the option is from being at-the-money or in-the-money means that there is less probability that a purchaser of an option contract will be able to exercise that contract, therefore the less opportunity of the contract being profitable. Option contracts which are at-the-money have the greatest amount of time value and usually have the greatest amount of trading volume. An option contract which is closer to being in-the-money will have a greater value to investors and traders compared to contracts which are further away, and their interest in those contracts will help to add time value to the option.

Interest rates also play a major role in option pricing. As interest rates rise, the time premiums of option contracts, particularly calls, also rise. Writers of option contracts, especially those writing calls against stock (covered call writing, see Chapter 3), demand higher premiums in order to take the risk and obligation associated with writing options. If interest rates rise and premiums do not, option traders will elect to put their capital into, what is termed as "risk-free," interest bearing instruments, such as Treasury bills or Treasury bonds. A goal of option writers is to achieve gains above those earned through the purchase of interest bearing vehicles.

The value of time contributes to the valuation of the option price. Which option contract would you rather purchase: a contract with one month until expiration; a contract with two months until expiration; or a contract with six months until expiration? If all three of these contracts had the same price, you as the purchaser would probably choose the contract with six months until expiration, giving you the greatest time to be correct about your assumption. Since the longer contract gives the greatest amount of opportunity, the time value of this contract reflects it. In addition, the writer of an option would choose the contract with one month until expiration, since the risk of writing the contract would be limited to only one month. In exchange for the added risk involved with writing an option contract with a longer period until expiration, the writer demands additional compensation. Option writers are very careful about the amount of risk which they are willing to be subject to, and will quantify that risk based on time, which is reflected in the option's time premium.

The price of the underlying stock is a determinant factor with regards to the options time-premium. The higher the price of the stock, the greater time-premium of the option contract. Options on stocks which are trading above $100 will have a greater time value than a stock which is trading below $20. Two stocks, which trade at significantly different prices, will have different price movements if the market moved 10 percent, and both stocks moved 10 percent.

For example, assume that ABC stock is trading at 120 per share, and that XYZ stock is trading at 20 per share. If the values of both stocks rose 10 percent, ABC will have a 12 point gain while XYZ will only have a gain of two points. To add to the value of this example, assume that a call on ABC was purchased with an exercise price of 125 and a call on XYZ was purchased with an exercise price of 25. Both options are five points out-of-the-money, yet if both stocks rose 10 percent, the value of the contracts would be substantially differ- ent. If ABC were at 132 (120 + the 12 point gain), the intrinsic value of the 125 call would be seven points (132 − 125). If XYZ rose to 22 (20 + the two-point gain), the intrinsic value of the call with the 25 exercise price would still be zero. In such a case, it would be more advantageous for the purchase of the ABC call. Since there is an added benefit to purchasing a call on a higher priced stock, the time- value of the call will reflect it.

For the writer of an option, the risk of an out-of-the-money option becoming in-the-money is significantly higher on a stock with a greater price. In the prior example, the writer of the ABC call has a much greater risk if the stock rises 10 percent than the writer of the XYZ call, since the XYZ call would still be out-of-the-money if the stock rose 10 percent. Because there is a greater risk to the writer of an option with a higher stock price, the writer demands a higher premium. If there is not a higher premium on the higher priced stock, the writer would have no incentive to writing the option and would therefore find a lower priced stock to take risk in.

Dividends also play a role in evaluating the value of an option. As noted, the purchaser of an option contract does not collect any dividends paid to stock holders. Some investors find this a disadvan- tage to purchasing an options contract. The fact is, the dividend paid by the corporation which issued the stock has another effect on the price of the options contract. When a corporation declares a dividend, three dates are set which have a bearing on whether the investor will collect that dividend. The first date is the date of payment, which is the date that the checks are actually mailed to stockholders. The second date is the date of record. On the date of record, all stockholders of record (stock has already settled) will be eligible to collect the dividend paid. The last date, which chronologically takes place first, is the ex-dividend date (ex-date). The ex-date, symbolized as XD, is the date after the trade date which would allow the investor to be a holder of record on the date of record, since it takes five business days for the stock to settle in the investors account after being purchased. On this date, any stock which is purchased will *not* be permitted to collect the dividend. At the opening of business on the ex-dividend date, the specialist (listed stocks) will reduce the price of the stock by the amount of the dividend, rounded upward to the nearest ⅛ of a point (12½ cents). This devaluing of the stock reflects the dividend paid to stockholders. This adjustment is figured into the time-value of the options contract. Dividends tend to raise the value of the put contract slightly while lowering the value of the call contract.

There is another reason why dividends affect the price of the option contract. The covered call writer (see Chapter 3) requires less time-premium for a profitable position if the underlying stock pays a high dividend. In addition, the purchaser of a put in conjunction with a stock position (see married put, Chapter 5) will be able to pay additional time value from the proceeds received from the dividend, without affecting the potential outcome of the strategy.

Industries that customarily pay high dividends, such as utilities, tend to have lower option premiums than those industries which pay lower dividends. Another reason is that stocks which pay high dividends usually have less stock movement, also known as volatility, than those of other industries. Therefore, the chance that the stock will have a significant move is lower, lowering the opportunity for the purchaser of an option contract as well as lowering the risk to the writer of a contract. A stock such as Niagara Mohawk Power Corp. (Figure 1-1) as well as other electric utility stocks pay significant dividends and have very low stock movement.

The upward and downward movement of a stock is a major contributor to the value of time on an option contract. The movement of value of the stock is called **volatility**. The greater the price fluctuations of a stock, the more frequently the stock moves. The volatility of a stock is determined by the violent price movements.

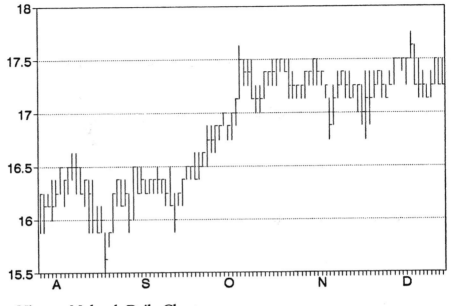

FIGURE 1-1. Niagara Mohawk Daily Chart.

Mathematicians have quantified this price movement as a percentage of standard deviation. The greater the volatility of a stock, the greater the price movements. A stock which rises 10 points over a period of two months may have a lower volatility than a stock which has moved up five points and then down five points and up five points during the same period. The volatility reading of both stocks will be different since the second stock had a more violent type move than that of the first stock, even though the actual price move was less than the first stock.

The greater the volatility, the higher the time-premium. A stock with a greater volatility has a greater chance of trading through the exercise price of an option, going both in-the-money and out-of-the-money. In addition, this violation of the exercise price may be frequent, raising the opportunity for profit or loss to both the buyer of the option as well as the writer. This possibility of greater opportunities and greater risks to both the purchaser of an option and the writer of an option requires an increase in the premium of the option contracts.

Expectations on the price of the stock will also show a discrimination on the price of the option contracts. If many investors believe that the price of the stock will rise, such as in the case of a takeover rumor, the call option premiums might rise significantly, and the value of the puts may drop. Conversely, if a company is expected to report significantly lower earnings or cut its dividend, the value of the puts will appreciate, while the calls will depreciate. Note that in this case, the value of the calls may not have an impact on the value of the puts, and vice versa. Stock expectations are influenced by earnings, legal decisions or filings, new products, corporate accidents, takeovers, competition, dividends, stock listing, corporate meetings and events, death of a chairperson, political events, world events, public opinion, and even events occurring to other corporations. For example, if McDonnell Douglas loses a contract with the Navy, not only does that affect that firm but any company that has been hired as a subcontractor. While this event may hurt McDonnell Douglas, it might benefit another corporation, such as rival Lockheed or Boeing. In addition to expectations about an individual corporation, events which happened in an industry may lead to expectations on another stock in that industry. Many believe that if a company in a certain industry is part of a takeover, other companies in the same industry will be the focus of raiders.

Option activity is both a direct result of the time-premium as well as a contributing factor. The greater the activity in the option contract, the easier it will be for the purchase and sale of the contract. Option activity is not only measured in daily volume, but in **open interest**. The open interest is the amount of contracts which have been created and not liquidated. The higher the open interest, the easier it would be to purchase a larger quantity of contracts, or write them for that matter. This is known as increased liquidity. Higher open interest allows for easier liquidation of a position. Vendors providing option pricing information may also provide the amount of contracts outstanding. If you are unable to obtain the open interest yourself, most brokers are able to obtain that information directly from their quote machines.

Market sentiment and direction have a direct bearing on the price of many stocks. If it is believed that the market will have a major gain or correction, the movement of a majority of stocks will reflect that ideal. Since the stocks are reflecting the anticipated movement in the market, so will the options. If market opinion is focused upon a major gain, the time value of most call options will increase while the time value of the puts will decrease. An anticipated bullish move in the market is believed to have a bias in favor of the call buyer while being a disadvantage to the writer of the call, since the call writer has a greater chance of having the underlying stock called. If market opinion shows a bearish view of the market, the put purchaser will be in favor, while being a put writer will be a disadvantage. The same response will be seen in stocks in certain industries when favorable or unfavorable conditions exist in those industries.

Some industries tend to buck market trends. In times of distress, when the market would be subject to a severe downturn, certain areas will benefit. For example, in an oil crisis, market sentiment will be extremely bearish. Although the market sentiment will be negative, two groups that would probably show gains are oil stocks, which benefit from higher oil prices, and gold stocks, which tend to rise during times of higher inflation. Investors should pay special attention to trading stocks in certain industries which might buck the trend of the rest of the market, for the anticipated action of stocks in those industries might not make the movements which are anticipated.

Finally, with respect to the time-premium on options is the economic reality of supply and demand. The more contracts which are bid for, the greater the support of the price of that contract. Conversely, the greater amount of contracts being offered, the greater the resistance of the option rising. If the market on a particular option contract is 2¼ bid to 2½ offered with 50 contracts bid for, and 200 contracts being offered, there is a greater chance of the contract dropping below the 2¼ price than rising above the 2½ price at that moment. The sizes of markets change very quickly and therefore cannot be used as a complete rule of thumb. However, if the purchaser of an option is willing to pay the higher price, and others decide to follow, the value of the option might rise without a change in the last sale of the stock.

What Is Time Worth?

While this is only a preliminary look into the pricing of options contracts, understanding what goes into the value of time is important when constructing an options strategy. The higher the time value of an option contract, the greater the appeal that contract will have to a writer, while the less appeal that contract will have to the purchaser. Lower time-premiums have a low incentive to the writers of option contracts, since it may subject the writer to less profit potential and greater risk.

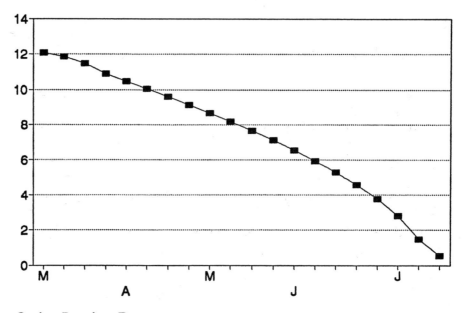

FIGURE 1-2. Option Premium Decay.

Knowledge of option pricing is very important to anyone trading options contracts. For additional information about the pricing of options and how certain variables affect the value of a contract see Chapter 20, which analyzes the impact of certain variables on the value of an option contract.

Earlier in this chapter it was stated that the time to expiration has an effect on the pricing of an options contract. The longer the period till expiration, the greater the time-premium of the options contract and therefore an option which is expiring in six months would have a higher time-premium than a contract which is expiring in one month. As the contract gets closer to expiration, the time-premium of that contract decreases. This is known as the **time decay factor.** The closer to expiration the contract gets, the more the time-premium will decline and the greater the rate of that decline. An option contract will lose more during the last month than during any other time during the life of the contract, assuming that all of the other variables that contribute to the price of the contract remain equal. Figure 1-2 shows the decay of an options contract. The closer the option gets to expiration, the greater the loss of time value. Therefore, the writer of an option will benefit from the decay of time more in the last month than any other time. This is how time works in favor of the writer of an option while it works against the purchaser of an option contract. Many option professionals are willing to take less time-premium in dollars for a contract which is expiring in less than a month, than to gain more dollar premium but be subject to holding the contract for two or three months which does not provide as much economical advantage as the final month does.

Entering Option Orders

When placing an order on an option contract, certain information must be specified to execute and process the order efficiently. As option strategies are discussed further, you will see that entering orders will get more complicated as more information is added. It is important that not only the order be entered correctly but also that the order clerk, trader or broker has taken your instructions correctly. Most brokers and order clerks will repeat the order back, attempting to ensure that the instructions are accurate. If the order is not executed correctly, the investor placing the order may lose money on the order entered as well as miss the opportunity on the order which should have been executed. While one may argue who is in the wrong, if the order is repeated back to the person placing it, that person is usually responsible if the mistake is not caught and corrected.

The correct format for entering an option order is as follows:

Verb:	Buy or Sell
Opt Type:	Put or Call
Quantity:	Amount of Contracts
Stock:	Corp Name or Symbol
Month:	Option Expiration Month
Exercise:	Strike Price
Price:	Market, Limit, or Stop/Stop Limit
Position:	Open or Close Customer
Account:	Your Account Number

For example:

Buy Call 10 IBM Jan 95 at 2⅛ to Open for my account.

The verb and the option type are self-explanatory. The quantity is the number of contracts and *not* the number of shares. In this example, the 10 calls would represent 1000 shares of IBM stock. The stock, month and exercise price are also self-explanatory.

The price of the order can take several forms. An order entered "at the market" (MKT) instructs the person taking the order to purchase the contracts immediately at the next available trade, regardless of the price. A limit order, such as the sample order shown, instructs the person taking the order to pay any price up to and including the limit of 2⅛. If the order was a sell order, the limit would be to sell the contracts at any price down to and including the limit price. If the order is a stop order (STP), this tells the trader to execute a market order once the option reaches the stop price (buy) or a market order once the option drops to the stop price (sell). The difference between a stop order and a stop limit order is that once the stop price is reached, the order becomes a limit order at that price. Some brokerage firms will not accept stop orders because the different option exchanges have different rules with regards to stop orders. Investors planning orders using stops and stop limits should take special note of the difference between exchanges.

The position designation of open or close is very important when entering orders for option contracts. If a position is being initiated or added to, the open designation would be used. If the position is being liquidated or reduced, then the close designation would be the appropriate position designation. The position designation is used by the OCC to determine the amount of outstanding contracts as well as which positions are subject to exercise and assignment. Entering the incorrect position limit can lead to a loss of money if a position is not accurately represented to the OCC.

Options Eligibility

Option contracts may not be suitable for everyone. Trading options can subject the investor/trader to great amounts of risk which may not meet the needs and goals of the investor. Most brokerage firms will ask an investor to complete and sign an agreement of suitability, verifying that the investor understands the risks associated with trading options and that the current positions and assets meet the requirements for options trading. While the investor may meet the requirements for trading puts and calls, not every strategy would necessarily be suitable for that investor. Brokerage firms reserve the right to limit the use of such strategies which do not meet the investment goals of the investor or would be considered inappropriate based on the experience or assets of the investor.

Many brokerage firms only allow the investor to perform a select group of strategies in certain account types, such as IRAs, KEOGH, trusts, and even custodial accounts. By limiting the types of trades which the investor may execute in these accounts, the brokerage firm attempts to limit undue risk which would not be suitable for those account types.

Before any option transaction is done, the investor should obtain from the brokerage firm or one of the option exchanges the risk disclosure booklet, *Characteristics and Risks of Listed Options* (published by the option exchanges and the OCC). This booklet explains the risks involved in trading options. It is required that a copy of this booklet be mailed to the customer by the brokerage firm before an order is entered on any option contract. The investor should take the time to read this document.

2
Purchasing Options

Investors and traders use many different strategies when purchasing options. The most popular strategy, option contracts, is also the simplest to enact, monitor, and maintain. The buyer of an options contract attempts to take advantage of using a lower priced instrument which is anticipated to return a higher percentage gain. This is known as leverage. By choosing this strategy, a certain amount of risk must also be assumed. It is important to weigh the potential risks versus the potential rewards. While the possibility exists for tremendous returns, there is equally as much chance that a total loss might be realized. Remember: an option is a wasting asset, and time works against the buyer.

The main reason the purchase of option contracts is so popular is that a great amount of leverage may be applied. Most option premiums trade at a small percentage compared to the price of the underlying stock. Although these premiums are small, the profits that may be achieved are relatively large, which may give the option purchaser a substantial percentage return. It is important to remember that options may only be purchased for cash, requiring that 100 percent of the purchase price be paid by the settlement date, usually the next day of business. Many brokerage firms, also known as broker/dealers, require that the funds for the transaction be in the account before an option is purchased. Stocks, unlike options, may be purchased in a margin account, requiring only a portion of the purchase price be paid, usually 50 percent. A margin account is the type of account which allows the purchaser of stock to pay for part of that purchase while borrowing the balance of the funds from a bank through the brokerage firm. In exchange for borrowing the funds, the investor agrees to repay the loan when the stock is sold and to maintain a certain level of equity by putting up additional cash if the stock declines in value.

Bullish Stock Opinion

In exploring the purchase of option contracts, the purchase of calls must first be analyzed and then the purchase of puts. Since calls gain value when a stock rises in price, the purchaser of a call must be bullish. The next step is choosing the option contract which will meet the investment objective. Many investors and traders tend to lose money because they fail to purchase a contract which best meets the investment objective. There are many cases when the purchaser of a call may be correct in the assumption about the direction of a stock, but chooses the wrong option contract, resulting in a loss.

The most important fact to remember in selecting an options contract is that time works against the buyer of an option. Should the stock fail to move in any direction and remain stagnant, the option purchaser will probably realize a loss as time depreciates the value of the options contract. Therefore, it is suggested that purchase of an options contract with more than 45 days is advisable. Once the option has less than 30 days left until expiration, the contract should be sold, as the value may quickly be eaten away by the clock. Recall that the time decay curve in Figure 1-2 showed how quickly the premium erodes during the expiration month (also known as the spot month).

Another mistake made by many call purchasers is in choosing the exercise price. Many traders purchase a call with an exercise price which is more than four points out-of-the-money. The reason for the choice of an option with an out-of-the-money exercise price is because of the very low dollar cost per contract compared to a call which is at-the-money. Since these contracts are so inexpensive, the trader tends to purchase a larger quantity. Purchasing a substantial amount of these contracts unnecessarily subjects the investor to a great deal of risk and little probability of profit. Even if the call buyer is correct and the stock does rise, the option may still lose value. It will take a greater move in the underlying stock for the option contract to gain value and become profitable.

Purchasing short-term calls which are out-of-the-money tends to

TABLE 2-1.   Comparative Example of Call Purchases

	XYZ Stock Price	Call with 55 Exercise	Call with 50 Exercise
Today	50	½ point	2 points
At Expiration	55	-0-	5 points
Gain	5 points	−½ point	3 points
Return	10%	−100%	150%

be the greatest cause of option losses for purchasers of option contracts.

Choosing the exercise price should not be difficult. The goal of purchasing a call should be to double the value of the option (100 percent gain) with the underlying stock appreciating only 10 percent. This is the advantage to leverage. Computing the value of a call is accomplished by assuming that the rise in the underlying stock is made by expiration of the call. At expiration, the value of the call option will be merely the intrinsic value, with no time value left.

See Table 2-1 for a comparative example of how to choose the more profitable exercise price. Assume that the XYZ stock is currently trading at 50. A call option with two months left until expiration and an exercise price of 55 is trading at ½ point ($50 per call), and that another call representing the same stock trading in the same month but has an exercise price of 50 is trading at two points ($200 per call). In evaluating which contract would be the better purchase, lets assume that the stock appreciates 10 percent. Now, let us compare these two contracts and see which makes the better investment decision.

As can be seen in the evaluation, the underlying stock gained 10 percent during the two-month period. The call option with the lower exercise price (50) realized a gain of three points or 150 percent while the call with the higher exercise price (55) lost 100 percent of its value. The purchaser of the call with the 55 exercise price needed the stock to be at 55½ just for the value of the call to break-even. Computing the break-even point for a call at expiration is accomplished using the following formula:

Stock Price for Break-even   =   Exercise Price +
of Call At Expiration   Premium Paid for the Call

While the profit potential on the purchase of any call is virtually unlimited, the risk to the purchaser is always 100 percent of the purchase cost of that call. In the preceding example, the purchaser of the call with the lower exercise price of 50 could suffer a total loss of $200 per contract or 100 percent of the purchase price (not including commissions or other transaction fees). It is important to keep this risk in mind when evaluating different strategies. The purchaser of the out-of-the-money call with the 55 exercise price would suffer a 100 percent loss as long as the stock remained under 55.

Many traders feel that purchasing 100 calls at ½ point, which would cost $5000 and has a limited $5000 risk, is a great opportunity since the position represents 10,000 shares of stock (100 calls × 100 shares of stock per call). If the trader purchased an equal *dollar value* of the calls with the at-the-money exercise price (50), the dollar risk would be equal, but the break-even point would be much lower. In addition, the investor would enjoy a greater opportunity of realizing a profit. Should traders follow this suggestion, they would purchase 25 calls with the lower exercise price for the same dollar value and same risk. This would lower the break-even point by 3½ points on the underlying stock, or 7 percent.

Purchasing calls provides greater leverage than the purchase of stock in a margin account. If an investor were to purchase XYZ on margin, an initial requirement of 50 percent of the value of the purchase might be necessary. Since only half of the purchase price is actually paid when the position is enacted, a return of almost double that of purchasing the stock for cash might be realized. While this might be an impressive return, the purchase of the call option would probably still realize a greater percentage return. Purchasing stock on margin also requires that interest be paid on the remaining debit balance, since it is a loan.

Risk is a key concern when making any purchase. The risk of purchasing an options contract might be total loss (100 percent) over a short period of time. Although this is a substantial risk, the dollar risk of purchasing a call might be far less than that of purchasing the stock, if the stock were sold for a loss. For example, if XYZ declined 10 percent to 45, the loss to the buyer of the calls with the 50 exercise price would be two points ($200 per call) or 100 percent. The loss to an investor who purchased XYZ stock at 50 might be five points ($500 per 100 shares) or 10 percent, if the stock were to be sold at that point. The call buyer may risk all of the investment but would sustain less of a dollar loss than the stock purchaser. The disadvantage to purchasing the call instead of purchasing the stock is time.

When purchasing a call, a method of limiting risk is to purchase a quantity of calls which is equivalent to the amount of shares the investor or trader could purchase on the stock. For example, if an investor were to purchase 2000 shares of stock, a quantity of 20 calls (20 calls × 100 shares per call) would be prudent. By purchasing an equivalent amount of calls, the risk to the buyer remains limited to a small dollar amount. It can be very dangerous for the buyer to purchase a multiple equivalent dollar value of calls, and defeats one of the primary reasons for utilizing calls over purchasing the underlying stock.

Further benefits can be achieved by purchasing calls as an alternative to buying the underlying stock. Purchasing calls, as stated previously, costs the buyer less capital, thereby putting less at risk. The balance of this capital can be invested in lower risk Treasury bills, Treasury bonds, certificates of deposit (CDs) or money market funds. This action would enable the purchaser to benefit from lower risk investments with capital which would have been invested. This not only lowers the investment risk, but adds to the profitability through purchasing calls rather than stock. This also assumes, however, that the call buyer is correct about the movement in the underlying stock during the holding period. The Three Case Scenario in Table 2-2 demonstrates that buying calls provides a greater return than purchasing the underlying stock in either a cash or margin account.

The use of calls also has its limitations. It can be self defeating for an investor to purchase calls on stocks with a low trading price. The purchase of a call on a $7 stock should be avoided, since the low price of the issue provides for little additional leverage. As an alternative, the investor or trader may wish to purchase the stock in a margin account, allowing for a greater return. Once the stock is purchased, the investor may wish to periodically write covered calls against the stock (see Chapter 3).

The potential value of a call at expiration is the intrinsic value of the call, or how much the call will be in-the-money. The value of the call is zero when the stock is at 60 or below, but rises as the price of the stock rises above the exercise price. Figure 2-1 illustrates the profit and loss based upon the intrinsic value of the call at expiration of that contract, if it were originally purchased at 1½ points. As can

TABLE 2-2.   Three Case Scenario

On November 20, Chevron (CHV) could be purchased for $69 per share. At the same time, Chevron March 70 calls (expiring on March 16—116 days later) could be purchased for a premium of 3½ points ($350 per call).

Investor "A" purchased 100 shares of CHV for cash.
Investor "B" purchased 100 shares of CHV on margin.
Investor "C" purchased 1 CHV March 70 call for cash.

	"A" Purchase 100 Shares for cash	"B" Purchase 100 Shares on Margin	"C" Purchase 1 Call for cash
Value of Transaction	$6900	$6900	$350
Cash Required	$6900	$3450	$350
Interest Charge till expiration at 10%	-0-	$ 109.64	-0-
Dividends earned till expiration	$ 77.50	$ 77.50	-0-

Stock Price on March 16	Value Profit/Loss	Value Profit/Loss	Value Profit/Loss
60 down 9 pts. or 13%	$6000.00 −822.50 −11.9%	$6000.00 −932.14 −27.0%	-0- −350.00 −100.0%
65 down 4 pts. or 5.8%	$6500.00 −322.50 −4.7%	$6500.00 −432.14 −12.5%	-0- −350.00 −100.0%
69 unchanged or 0.0%	$6900.00 +77.50 +1.1%	$6900.00 −32.14 −0.9%	-0- −350.00 −100.0%
74 up 4 pts. or 5.8%	$7400.00 +477.50 +6.9%	$7400.00 +367.86 +10.7%	$400.00 +50.00 +14.3%
79 up 9 pts. or 13%	$7900.00 +977.50 +14.2%	$7900.00 +867.86 +25.2%	$900.00 +550.00 +157.0%

Value = Value of stock (or call) without dividends or fees.
Profit/Loss includes interest fees (margin) and dividends.
To simplify this comparison, commission charges are omitted.

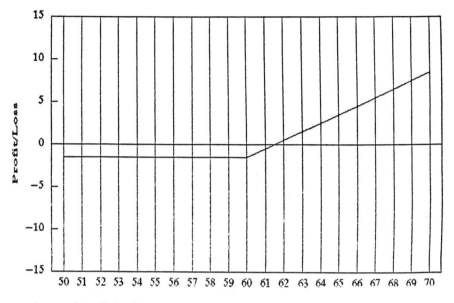

FIGURE 2-1. Purchase of Call Options.

be seen, the break-even point of this call is where the stock is at 61½ points.

Bearish Stock Opinion

Having a bearish opinion on a stock can have its merits as well as its profits. A trader or investor who believes that a stock is going to drop in price will usually attempt to sell the stock *short*. Selling short stock is a common strategy in which a person borrows the stock of a company from someone who owns it, and sells it now with the intent of repurchasing the stock at a later date, at a lower price. There are six disadvantages to selling a stock short.

1. When selling short, the borrower of the stock may have to pay a rebate to the party from whom he borrowed the stock. This fee might be about one percent of the value of the stock. Even before the stock is sold, the short seller may be losing money, as the rebate would have to be accounted for in the computation of profit or loss.

2. When executing a short sale order, New York Stock Exchange regulations require that short sale orders be identified as such and that short sales only take place on an **up-tick**, or at a price which is higher than that of a previous sale. This can make selling the stock short a bit of a nightmare, if not impossible. Because of this rule, the

short seller may not be able to execute the order at a desirable price, if at all. In fact, the short seller may not be able to execute the order at all. Long sellers of the stock may step ahead as the ticks change. This rule is effective on all stocks trading on the NYSE and the ASE and is currently pending on stocks traded on the NASDAQ.

3.   The short seller is required to keep the proceeds of the sale in a special margin account, known as the short account. In addition to keeping the proceeds in the account, a good-faith deposit or margin requirement must be met, which is usually 50 percent of the value of the stock. This requirement may be met with other securities or bonds. The margin requirement is meant to protect the investor and the brokerage firm in case the stock should rise in price. In addition to the initial margin requirement, the short seller may have to put up additional capital or assets to meet maintenance requirements. A maintenance requirement would be required, should the stock rise in price. As the price of the stock rises, the equity in the account decreases as the difference between the current market value and the short sale price would become a liability.

4.   The short-stock seller is required to pay out any dividends which the holder of the stock would be entitled to during the period in which the short position is held. The dividend will be charged by the brokerage firm to the account of the short seller. Should the stock pay a special dividend or a spinoff of stock, the short seller would be required to deliver the additional cash or stock. This delivery may be required at the time when the stock goes ex-dividend (trades without the dividend) or when dividend is actually paid. In addition, any dividend which is paid while the short position is held may be required from the short seller by the brokerage firm.

5.   The sale of a short position does not have all of the rights of owning stock. The decision to close the short position may not be that of the short seller. If the individual who loaned the stock to the short seller decides to sell the shares which he owns, the short seller would be required to replace the shares. This is known as being **bought-in**. The short seller will either have to borrow shares from another stock holder or to repurchase the shares and return them to the holder of the long stock, from whom the stock was borrowed.

6.   The short seller faces a number of obstacles in just initiating and maintaining the position. This is all before taking into account that the short seller faces unlimited risk. If the stock which the investor sold short rises dramatically in a short period of time, the short seller could face a substantial loss which would not be limited

to the initial capital requirement, as it would be in purchasing the stock.

The answer to all of the problems of selling the stock short is the alternative of purchasing puts. The put contract will rise in value as the stock drops in price. The same investment goal might be met by purchasing the put without the disadvantages of selling the stock short.

The put buyer may realize a loss, should the stock rise or stay at the same level, however, the loss would be limited to the purchase price of the put (plus commissions and other transaction charges). The maximum amount of the loss is fixed at the time the investment decision is made, and there is no danger of losing additional capital. Just as in purchasing a call, the maximum loss to the put buyer is 100 percent of the investment.

The put buyer does not face the regulatory requirements that the short seller must encounter. The buyer of a put is not subject to the "up-tick" rule and does not have to maintain a margin requirement. The put buyer does not have to worry about being bought-in and will not suffer an additional unforeseen risk should the dividend be increased or a special type of dividend be declared or paid during the holding period. In fact, the payment or declaration of a dividend may favor the put buyer as the stock might usually fall or be adjusted lower by the amount of the dividend, subject to the rules of the exchange.

Just as there are several factors which influence the purchase of calls, there are also factors in making decisions to buy puts. As with calls, put purchases should not be made if there are less than 45 days until expiration. A minimum of six weeks is suggested when initiating any option purchase. It is important to avoid purchasing an option contract which can depreciate rapidly as the result of time.

Once again, it is suggested that a put be purchased which is not considered to be out-of-the-money. For the same reason as buying a call, the put buyer might be correct in the assumption that the stock will drop in price, but may still realize a loss if the stock does not drop substantial amount. It is suggested that an exercise price be chosen that would enable a double in the price of the option by expiration, if the stock were to drop by 10 percent of its value.

The amount of puts purchased should be limited to the amount of stock that the investor would be able to sell short. Purchasing additional puts might defeat the purpose of using the put to limit risk, and

TABLE 2-3.   Example of Put Purchase

Stock = 62
Put with 60 Exercise Price = 2¼

Put with 60 Exercise Price is Purchased at 2¼ with 3 months until expiration. At expiration, the stock can be at any level in the first column below. The value of the put is calculated in column 2, while column 3 shows the dollar profit/loss of the put.

Stock at Expiration	Value of the Put	$ Profit/$ Loss
40	$2000	$1775
45	$1500	$1275
50	$1000	$775
55	$ 500	$275
60	-0-	<$225>
65	-0-	<$225>

put additional capital in jeopardy of an unlimited loss, should the assumption about the deterioration in the value of the stock be incorrect.

Let us assume that QRS is a stock trading at 72 and that a put with an exercise price of seventy and three months till expiration has a premium of 1½ points ($150 per put). If the stock dropped 10 percent to $63 per share, the put option would be worth an intrinsic value of seven points for a gain of 5½ points ($550 per put) or 367 percent. If the put buyer had purchased a put with a lower exercise price of 60 in the same month for a ¼ point premium, the option would expire worthless, and the put buyer would realize a 100 percent loss. For an example see Table 2-3.

The use of put options provides plenty of leverage and relatively little risk, especially compared to selling the stock short. Put buyers enjoy the comfort in knowing that while 100 percent of the cost of the puts is at risk, the amount is limited to a fixed, and what should be low, dollar amount. Figure 2-2 shows the profit and loss of a put based on the intrinsic value which assumes that the put was purchased at 2¼ points. The short seller has unlimited risk and may suffer a severe dollar as well as percentage loss, if the stock rises in value.

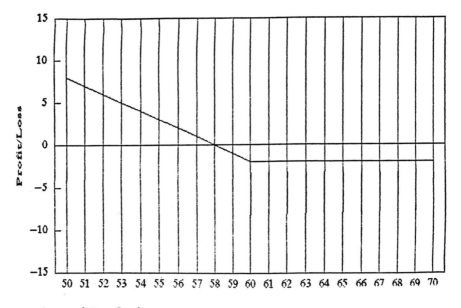

FIGURE 2-2. Purchase of Put Options.

Put buyers may also invest the unused proceeds in safer instruments, such as bonds, CDs, or money market funds. By doing so, greater returns may be achieved with capital which is not being used at that moment to maintain other positions.

The purchase of puts and calls should be made with great care. Discipline is a key ingredient in the success of all investment transactions, but holds special meaning when dealing in option contracts. While profits are the goal of all investors and traders, capital should be protected. It is suggested that a mental stop-out point be selected when an option is first purchased. There are two methods of setting a stop point. The first is to decide that if the contract drops to a certain point that the position be closed. The second method states that a position should be liquidated if the underlying stock moves a certain amount against the desired direction. If the stock is moving in the direction which the option buyer desires (higher for calls, lower for puts), these stop-out points should be adjusted to reduce the amount of potential loss and to protect profits which may be accumulating. Once a stop point is violated, the position should be closed. No rationalization makes it worth risking additional capital or profits. Just as it is important to know when to purchase and what to purchase, it is equally as important to realize when to close out a position; profit or loss.

TABLE 2-4.   Suggested Guidelines for Option Purchases

1. Purchase options with 45 or more days till expiration.
2. Purchase contracts which will have an intrinsic value of double the purchase price if the stock moves 10 percent.
3. Only purchase a quantity of contracts equivalent to the amount of stock which you would be able to purchase.
4. Set stop loss points, and stick to them.
5. Evaluate *all* outstanding option contracts and compare the price with the amount of time till expiration. An additional month or two may be purchased for a small premium.
6. Once the option contract doubles, take some action.
7. Carefully monitor the progress of both the option and underlying stock.
8. Close or roll option position when the option has less than thirty (30) days of life left. Don't wait until the last minute.

Table 2-4 outlines eight suggestions for the investor purchasing options. This list will aid in the decision making process of purchasing both puts and calls. While there are many advantages and some disadvantages to purchasing options over trading certain stock positions, the use of an alternative can provide for greater opportunity. The advantages and disadvantages associated with the purchase of an options contract in lieu of purchasing the stock or selling the stock short, are found in Table 2-5.

Following up on an option purchase is important in managing a portfolio. It is suggested that if an option doubles from the original price paid, action should be taken to protect the profits and limit losses. There are several methods to following up on an options position.

If the option which is purchased doubles, and the buyer is still confident that a further move is underway, half of the position should be sold. By closing half of the position, the holder of the option ensures that the initial capital which was invested has been removed and that a loss cannot be sustained. In the worst case, the investor will break-even, even if the option should drop in price and expire worthless. The second half of the position should be sold in steps, on a time basis. A position should not just "left to ride." Stop points should also be used to protect unrealized profits.

Another suggestion for maintaining a position is to sell the exist-

TABLE 2-5. Advantages and Disadvantages of Purchasing Option Contracts

Buying Calls v. Buying Stock

Advantages	Disadvantages
Greater leverage	No dividend collected
Lower dollar risk	Options are wasting assets
Flexibility of choice	

Buying Puts v. Selling Short Stock

Advantages	Disadvantages
No borrowing stock	Options are wasting assets
No up-tick rule	
No margin requirement	
No margin maintenance	
No dividend risk	
Risk is limited to put price	
No rebate to paid for borrowing stock	
No risk of short-squeeze	
No risk of being bought-in	

ing contracts, if they are more than four points in-the-money and purchase the same amount of at-the-money contracts with a longer period till expiration. In taking this action, the buyer takes capital out of the position and purchases a new position for less capital and more time, providing for further and greater opportunities. The initial capital outlay (in the first purchase) should be removed from the position, regardless of time.

Spreading a position can also prove to be beneficial once the price of the option doubles. Spreading involves selling one option contract (of the same type) against the purchase of another contract. Spreading is a topic which will be highlighted in Chapter 6 and should be looked at carefully.

If the stock on which the option was purchased has a substantial move, the option holder may wish to purchase a contract of the opposite type (call versus put). This purchase should be made to protect the existing position in case of a sudden reversal in the stock.

TABLE 2-6.   Suggested Strategies for Maintaining Long Option Positions

1. Sell half of the option position if the premium doubles.
2. Sell an out-of-the-money option against the long position, creating a spread (see Chapter 6).
3. Purchase an option with the opposite type (put versus call or call versus put) to protect against a sudden turn in the movement of the underlying stock.
4. Sell the entire option position and take a position in the underlying stock.
5. Sell the entire option position and purchase another option with additional time and an exercise price which is now at-the-money. This will allow some capital to be removed while continuing to hold a position.
6. Close out the entire position and take the profit.
7. Combine two of the above strategies (such as 1 and 2).

Special attention should be paid to the exercise price in relation to the current value of the stock.

Remember, even if the choice is correct, the underlying stock can suddenly move, wiping out any gain, and turn a winning strategy into a loser. Don't be fooled into losing everything. A loss of opportunity is better than a loss of dollars. Table 2-6 summarizes these valuable strategies in managing long option positions.

Summary

1. The purchase of call options can provide high leverage and substantial returns while limiting dollar risk.
2. The purchase of put options can provide high leverage, lower dollar risk, and greater advantages to selling stock short.
3. Short stock sellers have many disadvantages and the chance of unlimited loss.
4. Purchasing options requires important investment decisions and a lot of discipline.
5. Option positions should be carefully maintained and monitored. If an option doubles, action should be taken. Stop-points should also be used to limit losses.

3
Writing Calls

Purchasing puts and calls can return large profits with little risk, as compared to purchasing the stock. While the risk is limited, there is still the possibility of losing 100 percent of the investment. While someone might be willing to buy an options contract, there must be another who is willing to sell that contract to the buyer. Since the underlying corporation does not issue options, another trader or investor must be willing to sell the contract without ever owning it. This is known as **writing** the contract.

Writing an options contract is similar to selling a stock short, since the contract is sold leaving the writer with a short position. Unlike the short seller, the writer does not have to borrow the option from someone. The writer actually creates the contract at the time it is written. Writing an option contract can have many benefits but is not without its risks either. This chapter will focus on the use of writing call options while Chapter 4 will concentrate on the use of writing put contracts.

The writer of a call is obligated to sell the buyer of the call 100 shares of the underlying security at the exercise price by expiration. In exchange, it was noted that the buyer of the call will pay the writer a premium as a consideration for agreeing to sell the stock in the future at the exercise price. The call writer must understand the obligation of delivering the stock when requested to do so by the purchaser of the call. Since the obligation is on the writer of the call, the writer may select one of several methods of handling this risk. Two of these methods will be discussed in this chapter: (1) naked call writing and (2) covered call writing.

Uncovered Call Writing

The naked call writer is an investor or trader who writes the option with no hedge against the position. If requested to deliver the stock by the call buyer, the writer would have to purchase the underlying stock in the open market and deliver it to the buyer of the call. If the stock is much higher than the exercise price, the cost to the call writer could be substantial, leaving the writer with a large loss.

The investor who writes naked calls expects that the underlying stock will decline in price or remain at the same level until expiration. Time is usually on the side of the call writer since as the time moves on, the value of the call should depreciate. As the call depreciates the writer may wish to repurchase it at a lower price or allow it to expire worthless. If the stock depreciates in price, the call should also lose value, allowing the writer to repurchase the option even sooner and realize a profit from the difference.

If the stock rises in price, the call writer would most probably be faced with either repurchasing the call for a loss or delivering the underlying stock to the buyer. If the stock appreciates only a small amount and the time depreciation is greater than the upward move in the stock price, the call writer may still realize a profit. In addition, if the call is out-of-the-money, the writer may have a cushion between the price of the stock and the exercise price.

The risk to the naked call writer is that if the stock makes a large move during a short period of time, the writer may face a loss which can be beyond what the investor is thinking at the time when the strategy is initiated. The naked call writer is therefore said to have an unlimited liability or unlimited risk during the holding period. For example, during October 1989, UAL Corporation, parent of United Airlines, was the subject of takeover and buy out stories and rumors. During the months which followed, the stock rose from a level of 100 to a high of $280 per share. The writer of a call with an exercise price of 110 would have the responsibility of delivering 100 shares of UAL Corp. at 110 and might have to purchase that same stock in the open market at $280. If the naked writer received five points when the call was written, a loss of 175 points or $17,500 per call might be realized.

To protect against unlimited losses, brokerage firms are required to collect collateral or margin on the writer of naked calls. The margin may be deposited in cash, securities, or bonds. Currently the industry standard for a naked option margin is:

Margin Requirement = 20% of the Underlying Stock Value
— the out-of-the-money amount + the option premium subject to a minimum of 10 percent of the value of the underlying stock.

This requirement is the minimum which may be charged by the brokerage firm. Many firms have requirements which exceed this standard. The margin required is updated everyday and will change on a daily basis as the stock moves higher and/or lower. The higher the stock moves, the greater the margin requirement to the naked call writer. As the stock drops, the lower the margin requirement which would be required.

As noted earlier, the writer of naked calls expects that the underlying security will decrease in value or remain at the same level until expiration, allowing time to deteriorate the value of the option premium. Refer back to Figure 1-2, which shows the deterioration of option premium based on the movement in time. As can be seen, the greatest amount of time decay occurs during the final month of the life of the option contract. During that final month, the greatest percentage depreciation occurs. It is important to realize that while this might be the case, it might be beneficial to repurchase the call before expiration. Should the stock make a sudden move to higher ground, the risk could out weigh the potential reward.

The maximum profit which can be obtained will require that the underlying stock's price remain below the exercise price. If this occurs, the option will expire worthless, allowing the writer to keep the entire premium. Should the stock rise above the exercise price, the profit would begin to deteriorate and might even turn into a loss.

One of the most important aspects of developing an options strategy is pinpointing the potential break-even point. This allows the investor to predetermine risk. In the case of writing naked calls, the break-even point will be at the exercise price plus the option premium received (not including commissions or other transaction fees). The higher the break-even point, the greater advantage to the

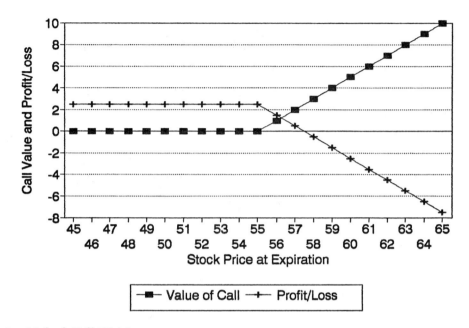

FIGURE 3-1. Naked Call Writing.

naked call writer. Figure 3-1 shows the value of a naked call with an exercise price of 55 as well as the potential profits and losses based upon different prices in the underlying stock at the expiration of the call.

Another reason the writer of a naked call might wish to re-purchase the contract, is that it frees up the margin requirement. This will allow the naked call writer to establish other positions with the money which is being tied up to satisfy the margin.

The naked call writer should establish two parameters before initiating this strategy. The first parameter is the correct time to repurchase the option contract. This is a goal for establishing profits. While it might be tempting to ride the wave and hope the contract will expire worthless, it is *not* practical. Stocks tend to make sudden movements which could turn a nice profit into a loss in a short period of time. Since the potential loss in unlimited, the call writer should pay serious attention to this fact.

The second parameter should be a stop point where the naked call writer would be willing to repurchase the contract and take a loss. Since the potential loss is unlimited, this second parameter would help to limit the loss which the call writer might realize. If the price of the call does depreciate, the stop point should be lowered to further limit losses and possibly to ensure profits. While nothing is a guarantee, and no one knows if a stock will have a gap opening at some point, the use of stop points can help to protect investments and provide for good investment habits.

Once one of the parameters has been violated, the naked call should be covered. In addition, it is important to realize that profits can turn to losses very quickly and that trying to squeeze out ⅛ of a point could put the naked writer in more jeopardy than it is actually worth.

The naked call writer may also face the risk of being called away just before the stock begins to trade without its dividend or ex-dividend. Should the call be in-the-money and the time premium is less than or equal to the value of a dividend, there is a very strong chance that the stock would be called away, which might leave the naked writer short the underlying stock. If this does happen, the naked writer might be liable to deliver the dividend on the stock, should the stock position be short on the ex-date for the dividend. Many naked call writers will repurchase the call before the stock goes ex-dividend, especially if the call is in-the-money.

In addition to the parameters discussed, a predetermined profit should be established as a goal. Since writing naked calls is a risky strategy, the writer should attempt to capture the most premium possible. A guide to determining the amount of premium is that the potential return should be approximately four times the riskless interest rate (rate which would be paid on government bonds or T bills). To determine the return on writing naked calls use the formula:

$$\text{Potential Return} = \frac{\text{Optional Premium}}{\text{Margin Requirement}}$$

Naked call writers should maximize the use of time and the rate of deterioration by writing short-term calls, those with less than three months until expiration. This allows the naked call writer the ability to take advantage of the rapid premium deterioration during the final month of the options life as well as the ability to write another call, should the first employment be successful.

The writing of naked calls is an aggressive strategy which can lead to high profits or high losses. The movement of the underlying

TABLE 3-1.   Naked Call vs. Short Stock vs. Long Put

Stock = 46
Call with 50 Exercise Price = 2
Put with 45 Exercise Price = 2

Position Capital Req.	Naked Call −1 call with 50 Exercise Price $520		Short Stock −100 shares $2300		Long Put +1 put with 45 Exercise Price $200	
Stock at Expiration			*Profits and Losses*			
35	$200	or 38.5%	$900	or 39.1%	$800	or 400%
40	$200	or 38.5%	$600	or 26.1%	$300	or 150%
42	$200	or 38.5%	$400	or 17.4%	$100	or 50%
45	$200	or 38.5%	$100	or 4.3%	<$200>	or −100%
48	$200	or 38.5%	<$200>	or 8.6%	<$200>	or −100%
50	$200	or 38.5%	<$400>	or 17.4%	<$200>	or −100%
52	-0-		<$600>	or 26.1%	<$200>	or −100%
55	<$300>	or 57.7%	<$900>	or 39.1%	<$200>	or −100%
Max Profit	$200		$4600		$4300	
Max Loss	Unlimited		Unlimited		$200	
Break-even point	52		46		43	

stock should be considered as well as the possibility for developing situations which might change the opinion or the stability of the stock. Table 3-1 compares the use of a naked call to the selling short of the underlying stock, to the purchase of a long put contract.

The Naked Call Writers Worksheet (Worksheet 3-1 at end of chapter) has been provided to aid in the decision making of writing naked calls. This worksheet was designed to show the investor the potential profit as well as the price of selling the stock short should the call be assigned against that writer.

Covered Calls

Covered call writing is a strategy which holds less of a reward with a lower amount of risk. The covered call writer has a differing opinion on the stock from the naked call writer and also has a much different view of risk. The naked call writer is an investor who believes that the underlying stock will move higher or remain the same until expiration. In most cases, the covered call writer favors the bullish side but does not expect a substantial move in the underlying stock.

The covered writer is a strategy in which an investor purchases the underlying stock and writes a call against those shares purchased. In purchasing the stock, the covered writer has taken the risk out of delivering the shares should the stock at a future date be called away (i.e., the writer is forced to sell the stock at the exercise price). If the stock makes a dramatic move, the covered writer, unlike the naked call writer, would not have to go out and buy the stock in the open market.

When the call is written against the stock position, the cost basis of owning the underlying stock is reduced, providing the investor with a small cushion in the event that the stock drops in price. Should the stock rise, the investor realizes that the maximum profit which can be realized is limited to the level of selling the stock at the exercise price. Should the stock remain below the exercise price until expiration, the call would expire worthless, leaving the investor to either sell the stock, hold the stock, or write another call and collect additional premium.

The risk to the covered call writer is less than if the stock was merely purchased. The option premium received lowers the break-even point for the investor and therefore also lowers the risk. Many covered writers use the calls to lower the cost of the purchase and are not expecting to be called away. If not called away, calls may be written indefinitely, offsetting the cost of stock and eventually lowering the cost to a point where the stock might be owned for no cost. While this might take years, many covered call writers have been known to achieve this goal.

Another use of covered call writing is taking advantage of the movement of time. Should the underlying stock price remain unchanged, the covered call writer would collect the entire premium, and if the option is out-of-the-money, the call writer would keep the stock. The option premium would gradually decrease, just as it did for the naked call writer. As the premium decreases, the writer could repurchase the call and write another call or allow the call to expire worthless. The stock may be purchased for either cash or margin, with no affect on the call.

The maximum profit for the covered call writer occurs when the stock is at or above the exercise price. The maximum profit is calculated in the following manner:

Profit if Called = Exercise Price + Dividends + Option
Proceeds − Stock Purchase

In most cases, the covered writer will also realize a gain if the stock is unchanged to expiration. If the stock is in-the-money, the profit would be the same as the profit if called. If the stock is out-of-the-money, the profit would be calculated as follows:

Profit if Unchanged = Current Stock + Dividends + Option
Proceeds − Stock Purchase

One of the great functions of the covered write is that it provides a small cushion in the event that the stock depreciates during the holding period. This gives the covered writer a lower break-even point. The break-even point is calculated as follows:

Break-Even Point = Stock Price − Dividends − Option Proceeds

The three calculations, including commissions and interest charges (if the stock is purchased in a margin account) can be calculated easily using the Covered Call Writers Worksheet (see Worksheet 3-2 at end of chapter). This worksheet provides a comparison between various option contracts. In addition, the worksheet will provide a comparison for using margin or cash to purchase the stock. In general, but not always, returns are almost double since only half of the investment must be made immediately. One disadvantage to using margin is that the interest charge will lower the dollar profit to the covered writer.

Maximum profit for the covered call writer usually occurs with the stock above the exercise price. If the stock is higher than the exercise price, it will be called away from the covered writer (sold at the exercise price). Should the stock close just under the exercise price at expiration, the covered writer would be free to write another call.

The covered call writer also enjoys the possibility of realizing a profit, even if the stock is unchanged to expiration. This return can be substantial, making the covered write even more attractive. Should the stock remain static to expiration, the profit would be computed as follows:

$$\text{Profit if Static} = \text{Current Stock} + \text{Option Proceeds} + \text{Dividends} - \text{Stock Cost.}$$

The return would be computed as follows:

$$\text{Return if Static} = \frac{\text{Profit if Static}}{\text{Capital Required}}$$

Figure 3-2 shows the profit if called, profit if unchanged and break-even points on the covered write. Table 3-2 shows a profit comparison between the covered write and just owning the stock without writing the call, as well as purchasing the call by itself. As can be seen, the profit potential of the covered call writer is limited to the stock being sold at the exercise price, but the covered call writer enjoys greater opportunity to profit, even if the stock is unchanged.

The covered call writer should also set certain guidelines for investment. The following guidelines will help in the decision making process, and provide guidance in choosing the proper call.

The potential return if the stock is called should be approximately twice the amount of investing in riskless instruments such as T bonds. If the stock is unchanged to expiration, a return equal to the T bond rate should be used as a minimum.

Another guideline should provide the covered call writer with some downside protection. This downside protection should give a cushion of at least 3 percent. Should the stock decline, the covered call writer has some protection, which the purchaser of the stock does not have.

The option should have at least 30 days until expiration, although many professionals prefer at least 60 days. It is suggested that

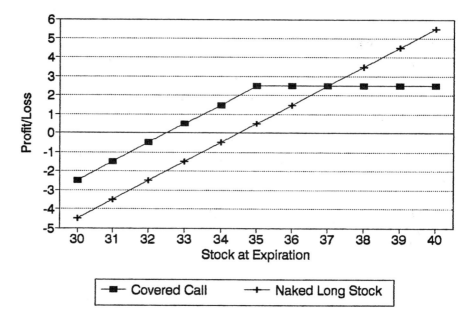

FIGURE 3-2.   Covered Call versus Naked Stock.

the covered writer not use a contract with more than 180 days, as
this may limit the opportunity to write another contract in the future.
In addition, the longer the term till expiration, the less liquid the
option contract and the more difficult it will be to execute the
strategy. The difference between a call expiring in 4 months and a
call expiring in 6 months may only be ½ or ¾ of a point, however,
the open interest (amount of contracts which are already outstanding) in trading the calls might be very great.

The covered call writer should also calculate all returns using
commission. Should the commission charged be too high, the profit
may be eaten up leaving the covered writer in a situation which might
be worse than just purchasing the stock outright.

Many brokerage firms do not allow the trading of option contracts in restricted accounts such as IRAs and KEOGHs. Most restricted accounts, however, do allow the writing of calls which are
covered through the ownership of stock.

While writing calls might be favorable, the use of these strategies
should not be the only choice. There are many different types of
strategies, many of which follow in subsequent chapters. Some of
these different uses for options may be coupled with the writing of
calls. It is suggested that *all* of the possibilities be analyzed in con-

TABLE 3-2. Covered Call Writing vs. Stock Purchase vs. Long Call

Stock = 72 Dividends Till Expiration = .90/share Days Till Expire = 70
Margin Interest Rate = 9% Call With Exercise of 75 = 2½

Type	Covered Call Writing Cash	Covered Call Writing Margin	Long Call Purchase Cash	Long Stock Purchase Cash	Long Stock Purchase Margin
Position	+100 Shares −1 Call	+100 Shares −1 Call	+1 Call	+100 Shares	+100 Shares
Debit	69½	69½	2½	72	72
Capital Req.	$6950	$3350	$250	$7200	$3600
Stock @ Exp.					
65	<360>	<422.14>	<250>	<610>	<672>
	−5.2%	−12.6%	−100%	−8.4%	−18.7%
69½	90	27.86	<250>	<340>	<402.14>
	1.3%	0.8%	−100%	−4.7%	−11.2%
72	340	277.86	<50>	90	27.86
	4.9%	8.3%	−20%	1.3%	0.8%
75	640	577.86	250	390	327.86
	9.2%	17.2%	100%	5.4%	9.1%
80	640	577.86	750	890	827.86
	9.2%	17.2%	300%	12.4%	23.0%

junction with the expectation (the anticipated direction of price movement) of the stock as well as the investor's view of risk, reward, and market expectation.

Summary

1. The writer of a call is obligated to sell the underlying stock at the exercise price of the call until expiration.
2. The writer of a naked call is speculating that the price of the underlying stock will be below the exercise price of the call until expiration.
3. In exchange for delivery of the stock, if called out, the writer of a call receives a consideration, the premium.

4. The writing of a call while owning the underlying stock is known as covered call writing.

5. Covered call writers agree to deliver the shares which they have already purchased if the stock rises above the exercise price.

6. In exchange for a predetermined return if called, the covered call writer agrees to allow someone else the opportunity for an unlimited return.

7. The premium received for writing a covered call helps to lower the break-even point on the stock and increase the return if the stock is static until expiration.

Naked Call Writers Worksheet

STOCK			SHARES	PRICE	—52 WEEK—		RATING	PIE RATIO	YIELD
					HIGH	LOW			
OPTION CONTRACT			CONTRACTS	PREMIUM	EXPIRATION DATE		DAYS TILL EXP.		
QUART DIVID	DIVIDS TO EXP	TOTAL DIVID COLLECT		DEBIT	REG. T RATE		MARGIN INT RATE		
							TODAY'S DATE		

REQUIRED CAPITAL

Stock Price. . . . .

Option Margin Requirements . . . . ×

Amount Out-of-the Money. . . . . −

Margin Result. . . . . =

Option Margin Requirement Minimum. . . . . ×

Margin Minimum. . . . . =

Greater of Value. . . . .

Equiv. Amount of Shares . . . . ×

Option Commission. . . . . +

Required Capital. . . . . =

MAXIMUM PROFIT

Stock below Exercise Price of . . . .

Option Premium. . . . .

Equiv. Amount of Shares . . . . ×

Option Commission. . . . . +

Profit. . . . . =

Return (Profit ÷ Req. Capital) × 100 . . . .

*Ann. Return (Return × 365 ÷ Days). . . . .

COST OF STOCK SOLD SHORT IF CALLED

Exercise Price . . . .

Option Premium. . . . . +

Equiv. Amount of Shares . . . . =

Option Commission. . . . . −

Commission of Stock @ Exercise Px . . . . −

Total Cost . . . . =

Equiv. Amount of Shares . . . . ÷

Sale per Share . . . .

Current Stock Price . . . .

Difference (Sale − Current). . . . .

% Difference (Diff ÷ Current) × 100 . . . .

*Annualized returns may only be used if holding is over 60 days.

WORKSHEET 3-2:

Covered Call Writers Worksheet

STOCK		SHARES	PRICE	—52 WEEK— HIGH | LOW	RATING	PIE RATIO	YIELD
OPTION CONTRACT		CONTRACTS	PREMIUM	EXPIRATION DATE	DAYS TILL EXP.		
QUART DIVID	DIVIDS TO EXP	TOTAL DIVID COLLECT	DEBIT	REG. T RATE	MARGIN INT RATE		
INTEREST CHARGES:		INT RATE | DAYS × ÷ 365 ×	DEBIT BAL | $ =		TODAY'S DATE		

REQUIRED CAPITAL

		CASH	MARGIN
Stock Price................................			
Amount of Shares........................	×	00	00
Stock Commission	+		
Stock Cost	=		
Reg T Rate	×		
Equity Required	=		
Option Premium........................			
Amount of Shares........................	×	00	00
Option Commissions	−		
Option Proceeds	=		
Required Capital (Equity Required-Option Proceeds)...	=		

RETURN IF CALLED

		CASH	MARGIN
Strike Price.............................			
Amount of Shares........................	×	00	00
Commisson	−		
Dividends Expected	+		
Interest Charges	−		
Debit Balance	−		
Required Capital........................	−		
Profit................................	=		
Return (Profit ÷ Required Capital)..............			
*Annualized Return (Return × 365 ÷ Days)			

STATIC RETURN

		CASH	MARGIN
Current Price..................................			
Amount of Shares........................	×	00	00
Dividends Expected	+		
Interest Charges	−		
Debit Balance	−		
Required Capital........................	−		
Profit................................	=		
Return (Profit ÷ Capital Required)..............			
*Annualized Return (Return × 365 ÷ Days)			

NOTE: If call is in-the-money, use return if called.

BREAKEVEN POINT

		CASH	MARGIN
Capital Required.............................			
Debit Balance	+		
Interest Charges	+		
Dividends Expected	−		
Subtotal	=		
Amount of Shares........................	÷	00	00
Breakeven...................................			

*Annualized returns may only be used if holding is over 60 days.

48

4
Writing Puts

Call writers and put writers may not hold the same view on a stock but the one ideal which they do share is that time should work in the favor of the writer. As with calls, the premium on a put deteriorates as expiration nears, with the greatest decay realized during the final month. The decay factor can make put writing an appealing strategy for an investor who is bullish on a stock as well as a great hedge for an investor who sold the stock short.

Writing Naked Puts

Before analyzing the strategy of writing naked puts, it is important to remember that the writing of naked options is subject to a good faith deposit, also known as margin. Throughout these pages we will utilize the industry margin requirement for writing naked options, which is the minimum margin requirement used on equity options. Many brokerage firms have higher requirements.

Margin Required on Naked Puts = Stock Price × .20 − amount
out-of-the-money + option
premium
(subject to a minimum of Stock Price × .10)

Selling naked puts requires that the investor has confidence that the stock price will rise. Should the stock rise in price, the put writer would claim victory as the strategy would prove to be a success. If the writer of a put is incorrect, the loss may not be that great and may actually prove to be beneficial in the long run.

The put writer achieves maximum profit if the stock is above the exercise price and the stock is not put to the writer during the holding period. If the stock remains above the exercise price, the put writer is entitled to keep the entire premium (less commissions and other transaction costs). If the stock is lower than the exercise price, the put writer would be required to purchase the stock at the exercise price. The premium which the put writer received when the put was written would offset the cost of purchasing the stock, which may still leave the put writer with a profit.

The writer of a naked put would not realize a loss unless the price of the stock dropped below the break-even price. The break-even price is the exercise price of the option less the put premium received. For example, if a put with an exercise price of 30 was written for $1\frac{7}{8}$ points, the break-even point would be $28\frac{1}{8}$. If the stock dropped below $28\frac{1}{8}$, the naked put writer would then begin to realize a loss. If the stock remained above the $28\frac{1}{8}$ level, the writer of the naked put may realize a small gain. Once again, for simplicity, the commission charges and other transaction costs have been left out of this example.

The writer of a naked put is usually an investor or trader who has a positive opinion of the underlying stock. If the stock declines in price, the put writer would not mind owning the stock, at a lower level. Since the cost of owning the stock would be less, the writing of puts can provide the investor with a unique opportunity. Many investors wish to own a stock but like to wait for the price of the stock to drop to a certain level. Sometimes this level is never reached and the opportunity of owning a good stock is lost. The writer of a naked put can realize some profit if the stock rises in price. This allows the investor the opportunity to be right, even if the stock does not drop to the level where the investor would have purchased the stock. If the stock drops, the naked put writer may achieve the desired purchase price on the stock, even if the stock does not drop to that level. Therefore, the put writer has many advantages over the would-be stock buyer.

In addition to these advantages, the naked put writer has an additional advantage. Should the stock remain unchanged to expiration, the naked put writer would realize the benefit of time premium decay while the would-be buyer of the stock *may* only realize a dividend payment.

TABLE 4-1. Naked Put versus Long Stock versus Long Call

Stock = 93
Put with 90 Exercise Price = 3½
Call with 95 Exercise Price = 4¼

Position	Naked Put −1 put with 90 Exercise		Long Stock +100 Shares		Long Call +1 call with 95 Exercise	
Capital Req.	$1560		$9300		$425	
Stock at Expiration			*Profits and Losses*			
85	<150> or	−9.6%	<$800> or	−8.6%	<$425> or	−100%
87	$ 50 or	3.2%	<$600> or	−6.5%	<$425> or	−100%
90	$350 or	22.4%	<$300> or	−3.2%	<$425> or	−100%
93	$350 or	22.4%	-0-		<$425> or	−100%
95	$350 or	22.4%	$200 or	2.1%	<$425> or	−100%
97	$350 or	22.4%	$400 or	4.2%	<$225> or	−52.9%
100	$350 or	22.4%	$700 or	7.5%	$ 75 or	17.6%
Max Profit	$350		Unlimited		Unlimited	
Max Loss	$8700		$9300		$425	
Break-Even point	96½		93		99¼	
Cost of Stock	96½		93		99¼	

The use of naked puts instead of the purchase of the stock or a call is portrayed in Table 4-1. As can be seen, if the stock drops a small amount, the writer of the naked put may still realize some profit, from the time value collected, where the stock purchaser as well as the call buyer outright lose. However, if the stock does rise in price, the naked put writer has a limited gain while the stock purchaser and call buyer have unlimited opportunity. The comparison of the writing of a put and the purchase of the underlying shares of stock is further illustrated in Figure 4-1.

As with the writing of calls, put writers should follow certain guidelines when initiating this strategy. The first is that the opinion of the investor upon the stock should be favorable and that the put writer would not mind owning the underlying stock, if it were put to

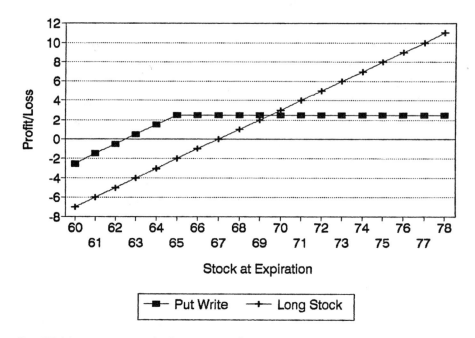

FIGURE 4-1. Put Writing Versus Naked Long Stock.

them. If the opinion of the stock is negative or neutral, writing naked puts may not be a desired strategy.

The naked put writer should write puts that offer some downside protection should the stock drop in price. The put writer should allow for a cushion before he is obligated to purchase the stock or repurchase the put for a loss. It is suggested that a put with an exercise price which is at least 4 percent out-of-the-money and a premium of at least 1 percent of the stock value be used. This will provide the put writer with some protection should his opinion of the stock be incorrect.

The writing of naked puts should be done on a short-term basis. This allows the put writer to take advantage of the decay of time premium which is usually greatest during the final month of the life of an option. It is suggested that puts with a time value of no more than three months be utilized for this strategy.

Writing puts can be a very attractive strategy, however, it is cautioned that writing an excessive amount of puts can place the investor into a dangerous situation. Therefore, only an amount of puts which would be equivalent to the amount of shares the investor is able to purchase should be written. For example, if the investor can only afford to purchase 500 shares of the underlying stock, then only five put contracts should be written.

Should the premium of the put decline by 60 percent, then the put writer should repurchase the put and close the position. During the course of history, it has been illustrated that stocks can change direction very quickly. A strategy that might have been realizing a gain for several weeks may suddenly turn into a loss with a quick movement in the stock.

Puts should not be written on stocks which are the subject of rumors or other stories. History has shown that the writer of naked options, both puts and calls, can be severely hurt by using such techniques. Many put writers realized major losses by writing puts on "sure deals," such as UAL Corp, which was supposed to be taken over at $305 per share until the financing for the deal fell apart. It cannot be stressed enough that there is a significant risk of owning a stock at a much higher level than it might be trading during the next day.

If the stock begins to fall in price, defensive action should be taken to limit risk. Defensive action might be the repurchase of the put, the purchase of another put contract or even the selling short of the underlying stock. It is suggested that the put writer set a stop out point where the put would be repurchased if the strategy was not working out. This point should be maintained and only adjusted to a lower level which would help to lower the risk and possibly to preserve profits.

Stocks which have puts with excessive premiums should not be used for put writing. Nobody gives anything away, and there is usually a reason why premiums are so excessive. This might be an indication that there is high expectation that the stock will drop dramatically in price, during a short period of time. Caution should be used.

To aid the investor who wishes to write naked puts, the Naked Put Writers Worksheet (Worksheet 4-1 found at end of chapter) has been provided. This worksheet will show the investor both the maximum profit as well as the cost of owning the stock if the put is assigned against the writer. This worksheet is similar to the Naked Call Writers Worksheet (Worksheet 3-1).

Finally, as with all option positions, it is important to keep a very close watch on both the value of the put contract and the price of the stock during the holding period. The put writer's aim is to seize short-lived opportunities and limit the chance of a potential loss.

Writing Protective Puts

Writing puts against a short stock position can provide additional benefits and reduce risk to the short seller. The short-stock seller is an investor or trader who is bearish on the price of a stock. This view has led the short seller to borrow the shares of the stock from another investor who owns the stock and sell the stock with the intention of repurchasing the shares at a lower price in the future. In selling the stock short, many obstacles and disadvantages might be placed in the way of the short seller (see Chapter 2 for more information on purchasing puts). By writing puts against the short stock position, some of these disadvantages might be offset by the short seller.

When the put is written against the short stock position, the put writer is not obligated to put up an additional margin requirement. Since there must be a margin requirement maintained on the sale of the short stock position, the margin would be enough to cover the writing of the put. Second, should the stock be put to the writer (i.e., the writer is forced to purchase the stock at the exercise price), the purchase of the stock would be offset by the short sale, leaving the holder with a flat or no position in the stock.

By writing the put, the short seller would collect the premium, offsetting any cost in borrowing the stock. In addition, the short seller would achieve the advantage of the decay in time premium. If the stock remained unchanged to expiration and the stock is above the exercise price, then the premium would be captured as a complete profit adding to the potential profit on writing the stock short. Writing puts against the sale of short stock should not add any additional risk to the position.

If the stock is put to the short seller at the exercise price, then the difference between the price of the stock sold short plus the put premium less the exercise price plus any dividends for the period would be the profit realized by the investor (excluding commission and other transaction costs).

The maximum risk to this position is that the stock moves higher. However, the risk is slightly lowered by the premium received on writing the put. If the stock drops in price, and the put contract becomes in-the-money, then the stock would be repurchased. Repurchasing the stock at the exercise price may incur a loss of opportunity should the stock continue to decline. This is a disadvantage to using this strategy which the investor should realize before obligating the position to repurchasing the stock at the exercise price.

It is suggested that put contracts with between two and four months be utilized for writing against a short stock position. The put contract should have a premium of at least 1 percent of the value of the underlying stock with a premium of at least two points per contract. The two points should offset the loss of opportunity if the stock falls two points below the exercise price on the put.

For an investor who is very bearish on the stock, it is suggested that puts only be written on ratio basis. For example, if there are 4000 shares of short stock held, 20 puts (equivalent to 2000 shares) should be written leaving the investor with the opportunity to have further downside participation or to write puts with a lower exercise price at a future date. There is no rule stating that puts must be written against the entire position.

If the stock rises in price, the investor may wish to repurchase the puts which were written and write puts with a higher exercise price. The investor should carefully weigh the use of such a strategy as to the addition of risk. If a put with a higher exercise price is used, then the repurchase price of the stock might be the difference in the exercise prices less the difference in the premiums (repurchase premium and the new put premium). At this point in time, the investor may also wish to change expiration months which might also have an effect on the value of risk.

The short seller must ensure that if the stock is repurchased in the open market that the puts are also repurchased. Should the puts not be repurchased, the investor would be left with a naked put position exposing the writer to purchasing the stock, which would give the investor a bullish position.

If the premium of the put declines significantly, the investor may look to repurchase the put and write another with a longer expiration period. This would allow the investor to further lower the risk of the position and again not take further risk on the position. It is highly suggested that puts not be repurchased to write other puts with a *shorter* expiration period, as this would probably add to the risk of the position.

Summary

1. Put writing is a bullish strategy which can provide an alternative to purchasing the underlying stock or a call.

2. The put writer can profit if the stock rises or remains above

the exercise price of the put while lowering the cost of owning the stock if the put is assigned to the writer.

3. Puts may be written against the short sale of stock, providing
   the writer with a repurchase level while allowing the investor
   to take advantage of the time premium of the options.

Naked Put Writers Worksheet

STOCK			SHARES	PRICE	—52 WEEK— HIGH	LOW	RATING	PIE RATIO	YIELD
OPTION CONTRACT			CONTRACTS	PREMIUM	EXPIRATION DATE		DAYS TILL EXP.		
QUART DIVID	DIVIDS TO EXP	TOTAL DIVID COLLECT		CREDIT	REG. T RATE		MARGIN INT RATE		
INTEREST CHARGES:		INT RATE ×	DAYS ÷ 365 ×	DEBIT BAL =	$		TODAY'S DATE		

REQUIRED CAPITAL

Stock Price.....................................

Option Margin Requirement .... ×

Amount Out-of-the Money..................... −

Margin Result..................'............. =

Option Margin Requirement Minimum.......... ×

Margin Minimum............................. =

Greater of Value.............................

Equiv. Amount of Shares .... ×

Option Commission........................... −

Required Capital................................. =

MAXIMUM PROFIT

Stock above Exercise Price of ....

Option Premium.............................

Equiv. Amount of Shares .... ×

Option Commission........................... −

Profit... =

Return (Profit ÷ Req. Capital) × 100 ....

*Ann. Return (Return × 365 ÷ Days)............

COST OF STOCK IF PUT

Exercise Price ....

Option Premium.............................. −

Equiv. Amount of Shares .... ×

Option Commission........................... +

Commission of Stock @ Exercise Px .... +

Total Cost .... =

Equiv. Amount of Shares .... ÷

Cost per Share .... =

Current Stock Price ....

Difference (Current − Cost per Shr) ....

% Difference (Diff ÷ Current) × 100 ....

*Annualized returns may only be used if holding is over 60 days.

*Note: Screened areas in respective boxes at the top of a worksheet indicate that these particular boxed areas do not need to be filled in when using the worksheet.

5

Protective Puts and Calls

Writing puts and calls provides a certain amount of protection. In addition, the investor is afforded the opportunity to take advantage of option premiums. The combination of both provides great flexibility in the decision making process. The purchase of puts and calls provides other methods for protecting positions: by purchasing options, the investor can limit losses to a fixed amount over the options holding period. This provides the investor with confidence and guards against the unexpected.

The covered call writing strategy, discussed in Chapter 3, illustrates that a limited amount of protection can be achieved while increasing potential return. Since the stock price is partially offset through the collected premium, the break-even price is lowered, giving the investor a cushion should the stock depreciate in price. Add to the premium the collected dividend and the covered call writer not only has a buffer but may realize a profit if the stock remains static to expiration or even drops by a small amount.

Four Strategies for Protecting Long Stock Positions with Puts

Put option contracts may also be used to lower the risk of owning a stock. Purchasing a put contract requires an additional outlay of funds, but can prove to be a great benefit to the buyer. There are four different strategies based on the purchase of a put in conjunction with owning stock. These strategies actually employ the same principle but are used at different times during the holding period of the underlying stock. By purchasing put contracts, losses can be limited and profits can be preserved during the holding period.

Many investors deal with risk in the investment arena very differently from the way they deal with it in their private lives: they may carry insurance on their homes, cars, and other assets, but fail to protect their stock and portfolio investments. Some people believe that potential profits will be offset by the cost of purchasing a put and therefore is not warranted. Others believe that if a stock is purchased, it must go up and that a decline in the price only provides opportunity to purchase additional shares.

The most ironic point is that an investor has a greater risk of losing money on an investment than having a car stolen or having a house burn down. Yet, most investors fail to see the need for protecting investment capital. This can prove to be detrimental to the investment goals and aspirations of the investor.

Married Puts

The purchase of a security and the simultaneous purchase of a put option contract is known as a **Married Put**. The term married put was created in the 1970s since, for tax reasons, the put contract was married to the stock which adjusted the stock price. The married put provides the investor with a limited amount of liability should the price of the stock drop in price. This allows the investor the knowledge of knowing what the maximum loss of owning the stock position at the time the position is initiated.

The purchase of a married put raises the initial cost of owning the position by the amount of the put (plus commission and any other transaction charges). This is the main reason investors do not utilize this strategy.

The maximum loss is the difference between the adjusted stock price and the put's exercise price. If the stock dropped way below the exercise price, even to zero, the investor would suffer only a limited loss. In the event that a dividend be paid during the holding period, the loss would be reduced by the dividend amount. As long as the stock position is held, the investor is entitled to collect any dividend which is paid, regardless of the stock price on the ex-date. The maximum loss can be calculated as follows:

$$\text{Max Loss} = \text{Stock Price} + \text{Put Premium} - \text{Dividend per Share} - \text{Exercise Price}.$$

The maximum loss, or the difference between the cost of the position and the exercise price, is similar to the deductible on an insurance policy.

While the amount of loss may be limited during the term of the option contract, the break-even point of owning the position is raised to the total cost of owning the stock and the put. Therefore, if the stock remains unchanged to expiration, the investor might realize a loss. The difference between the current stock price and the break-even point should be carefully analyzed before initiating the married put position. The break-even point can be calculated using the following formula:

$$\text{Break-Even Point} = \text{Stock Price} + \text{Put Premium} - \text{Dividend}$$

A loss realized to expiration if the stock remains unchanged is calculated as follows:

$$\text{Loss if Unchanged} = \text{Put Premium} - \text{Dividend Per Share}$$

These formulas, which can be used for stock purchases in a cash or margin account, can easily be calculated using the **Married Put Purchaser's Worksheet** (Worksheet 5-1 found at the end of the chapter). The worksheet includes commission charges as well as interest charges for stock purchased in a margin account.

When a married put strategy is initiated, it is important to define certain guidelines. These guidelines aid in the decision-making process. The first of these guidelines is to purchase a put which provides at least 30 days of protection. The longer the put can be purchased for, the greater opportunity that the investor has of being right. Should the stock decline, the loss would be limited to selling the stock at the exercise price. The additional cost of a put with extra time may prove to be minimal and reduce the cost if the put were to be purchased in the future.

When the put is purchased, the premium paid should be limited to 3 percent of the underlying stock. It is important not to pay an excess amount for the put as this would offset the opportunity for profit. In addition, if the put has too great a premium, the reason for utilizing the married put strategy might be self defeating. Excessive put premiums may also provide the investor with two additional pieces of information. If the premium is truly excessive, another investor or trader may believe that the stock is going to drop in price, perhaps substantially. Another clue of high put premiums is that there may also be high premiums in the calls, allowing the investor greater opportunity by writing covered calls. Both of these factors should *not* be overlooked.

The break-even point should be a maximum of 3 percent over the current price of the stock. The goal of using the married put strategy is to limit the risk of capital and not to interfere with the opportunity of achieving a profit. While there will be some interference, this too should be limited.

The maximum loss to expiration should be limited to 5 percent of the stock price. If the loss, after purchasing the put, is greater than 5 percent then the use of the put would be immaterial and it might be beneficial to purchase the stock of its own.

Protective Puts for Already Owned Stock

Purchasing a put while already owning the stock is very similar to using the married put strategy. The **Protective Put** is usually purchased while the stock is already being held, allowing the investor to continue holding the stock while reducing the risk of owning the position. This strategy is favored by investors when the outlook on the stock changes. The change in the outlook may be fundamental or may reflect apprehension of the market in general.

If the stock has already had a small move upward, the protective put may provide some security in limiting the risk to a zero dollar amount. At this point, the worst that the investor may realize is a break-even. This allows the investor greater chance to profit and reduces the reluctance and risk of holding the stock position.

As with the married put strategy, the same guidelines should be utilized. It is important not to pay excessive premiums to purchase the put, as this would defeat the purpose of using the protective put strategy. One difference should be noted by the investor. If the put price is excessive, and the investor has a fear that the stock price will drop, some action should be taken to protect the *already existing* position. The high put premium may confirm the fear which the investor is experiencing.

The maximum loss of utilizing the protective put strategy is as follows:

$$\text{Max Loss} = \text{Stock Price} + \text{Put Premium} - \text{Dividend} \\ - \text{Exercise Price}$$

Protective Puts When Stock Has Dropped

A third strategy is purchasing a protective put when the stock has dropped in price in order to limit further risk. Once this is accomplished, the investor may get a second chance at breaking even or realizing a profit, should the stock rise in price. It is strongly advised that the investor continue to have a bullish or favorable opinion of the stock.

Since the stock is trading at a lower price, the relative put premium will be higher. The investor should take this into account when deciding on which put to use and whether this strategy should be utilized at all. Purchasing a put when the stock has already dropped may limit against further losses, but it may also raise the break-even point. If the break-even point is too high, then use of the strategy is self-defeating and should be abandoned. An alternative to using this strategy is discussed in Chapter 19: Using Options For Repairing Damaged Positions.

Protecting Profits on Long Stocks

The fourth strategy which utilizes the purchase of a put in conjunction with stock ownership is known as **Profit Protection Using Puts.** Protecting profits can be beneficial, especially if the stock should take a sudden turn. An abrupt turn in stock price can be attributable to both individual stock and/or market conditions. If there is a sudden turn in the market, a profit can quickly be eroded and even become a loss. If the investor is still favorable on the stock, this profit protection strategy can prove to be very beneficial.

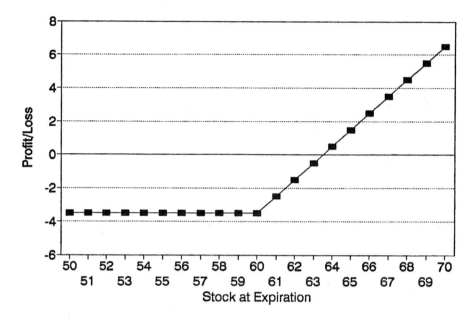

FIGURE 5-1. Married Put Purchase.

Premium paid to purchase the put should be limited to a small percentage of the profit. If the premium is too great, the profit could be eliminated if the stock drops to the exercise price. In addition, the distance between the current stock price and the exercise price should also be kept to a minimum. Should the distance between the stock price and the exercise price be too great, the profit may be entirely lost and the investor may realize a loss on the position. As an alternative, the investor may seek to write a call against the stock position.

Although the purchase of the put is intended to protect the profit, a certain amount of the profit would be lost if the stock dropped to or below the exercise price. The loss of profit is calculated as follows:

$$\text{Loss of Profit} = \text{Profit} + \text{Dividend} - \text{Put Premium} - \text{Difference}$$
$$\text{between Stock and the Exercise Price}$$

If the stock drops below the exercise price, this strategy would have protected a percentage of the profit plus the initial capital invested. If the stock continues to rise in price, the profit would be offset by the put premium paid. This protection could be very beneficial, costing the investor little opportunity while still allowing for a great advantage.

Figure 5-1, the Married Put Buyers Worksheet, has been provided to aid in both the use of married puts as well as protective puts. Figure 5-1 illustrates the profit and loss of using married puts. As can be seen, the potential loss in the stock is limited by the long put.

Protecting Short Stock Positions with Calls

Just as the put can protect a long stock position, a call can protect a short stock position. Since the properties which make puts and calls profitable are inverse, the same could be said for their uses in protecting stock positions. A call rises in value as the price of the stock rises, and a put rises in value as a stock drops. This allows the purchaser of an option to protect an inverse stock position, offsetting any risk once the exercise price is penetrated. This antithesis provides the investor with a tool to protect any position which is taken in the underlying stock.

One of the most agonizing positions which an investor or trader can be in is to be short a stock and watch the price of that stock climb higher and higher. For example, Figure 5-2 shows the trading of Microsoft. Microsoft is traded on the National Association of Securities Dealers Automated Quotation system (NASDAQ) and also trades puts and calls on the Pacific Coast Stock Exchange (PSE). As can be seen, the stock has risen 26 points or 52 percent in four months time (between January and May). This action could paralyze the investor who sold the stock short, leaving him with a large unrealized loss.

When contemplating the short sale of stock, the investor should also be evaluating and making other decisions that pertain to risk and reward as well as time. Options aside, the short seller of a stock has two immediate concerns when it comes to the clock. The first is that a margin requirement must be deposited with the broker at the time that the stock is sold short. This "good faith" deposit ensures the broker in case the stock should rise in value. Industry requirements state that 50 percent of the value of the stock sold must be kept in a short or margin account to guard against a rise in the value of the stock. This requirement is "marked to the market" or updated daily by the brokerage firm. While the industry standard is the minimum

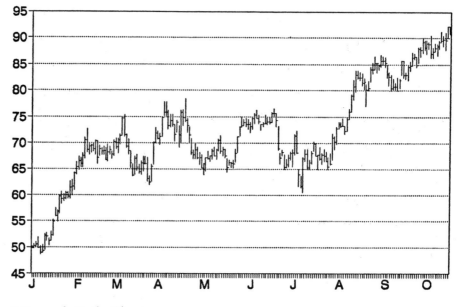

FIGURE 5-2.   Microsoft Daily Chart.

which a broker can charge, most do require additional capital. The capital requirement may be met with other securities or government bonds. While this may not bother some investors, it does bother others since a loss of opportunity might be realized if that capital requirement could be used elsewhere.

The second disadvantage dealing with time is the dividend. While not all stocks pay dividends, it is in the best interest of the stockholders if the company does pay a dividend. The short seller is obligated to pay any dividend which might come due during the holding period, which could realize a loss even if the stock does not move. The longer the holding period, the greater the potential loss due to payout might be. These disadvantages as well as other disadvantages of selling stock short were covered in greater detail in Chapter 3.

When the short sale position is initiated, the investor should determine at what price on the stock a profit should be taken, where a loss should be realized and how long the position should be kept on. While this may seem like an easy task, it is not always that way. When a stock is sold short, the investor is opening up the position to the possibility of an unlimited loss. Should some event arouse the stock, the short seller might be faced with a situation of taking a loss which should not be paid off. Just because the stock drops in price does not mean that the risk to the short seller is over. The price of a stock can rise just as fast as it declines. Therefore, the risk of selling a stock short can be overwhelming to the short seller.

The purchase of a call can protect the short seller from unlimited loss. If the stock rises in price, the unrealized loss will be partially offset with the rise in the value of the call. Should the stock rise in price, the short seller would be able either to sell the long call for a profit (versus a loss in the stock), or to exercise the call allowing the short seller to repurchase the stock at the exercise price, no matter how high the stock rises in price. The call acts as a type of short-term insurance against an unforeseen stock rise.

It is suggested that before a stock is sold short that an evaluation of potential call options be made. The first guideline in selecting a call for purchase is that the life of the call be at least as long as the short position is expected to be held. The call's life expectancy should not be even one day less than the expected holding period of the short stock position. If the holding period for the stock changes, the call should be sold and another should be purchased, giving the investor additional time.

The second guideline for purchasing a call is to choose an exercise price which is close to the price of the underlying stock. Purchasing a call which is in-the-money prevents the short sale from becoming profitable since the stock would have to drop a significant amount just to break-even. Purchasing a call which is more than 10 percent out-of-the-money can also be defeating as the protection might be insufficient. Should the stock rise more than 10 percent, the loss would be limited to 10 percent plus the call premium (excluding commissions, transaction charges and dividends).

The third guideline for utilizing the protective call is that the call not be overvalued. If the price of the call is too high, it might be a sign that interest in the call supports a belief that the stock will rise in price. In addition, if the call does have a high value, the dollar value of the loss would be greater, putting additional capital at risk.

As can be seen in Figure 5-2, Microsoft could have been sold short at $71 per share. In a period of less than four months, the stock rose from the level where it could have been shorted to over $90 per share. After an additional month the shares of Microsoft were trading at $110, leaving the short seller with an unrealized loss of 39 points (excluding commissions, dividends and other charges). With the stock up 55 percent, the short seller would realize a great loss if the stock were repurchased. If the same short seller also purchased a

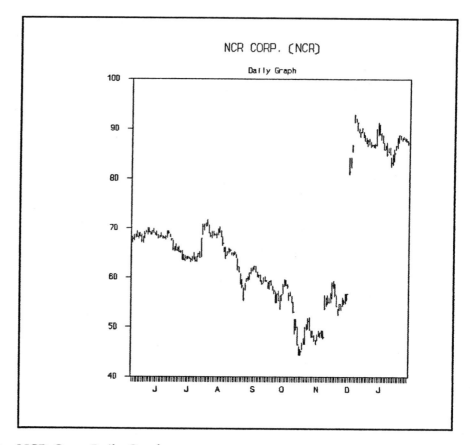

FIGURE 5-3. NCR Corp. Daily Graph.

six-month call with an exercise price of 75 for two points, the total maximum loss would be limited to six points, regardless of the price of the stock. This would result in a loss of 16 percent (excluding commissions and dividends) instead of a loss of 110 percent (using the industry margin requirement of 50 percent for a short sale). This is only one of many examples of how a protective call can protect the short seller against a sudden and substantial gain in the stock price.

During the summer of 1990, some investors became bearish on the value of NCR Corp. (NCR) and began to sell the stock short. The stock slowly dropped in value and the short sellers began to show a paper profit. To ensure the profits which they had not yet taken, the short sellers could have purchased a call which would have protected a portion of their profits and protected them against the possibility of loss. The investors who purchased the calls were very happy that they took such action because in December, AT&T (T) decided to pursue

TABLE 5-1. Protective Call versus Naked Short Stock

Stock = 43½
Call with 45 Exercise Price = 2⅛

Action	Protective Call −100 Shares +1 Call with 45 Exercise Price	Naked Short Stock −100 Shares
Credit	41⅜	43½

Stock at *Expiration*	*Profits and Losses*	
30	11⅜	13½
35	6⅜	8½
40	1⅜	3½
43½	<2⅛>	-0-
45	<3⅝>	<2½>
50	<3⅝>	<7½>
55	<3⅝>	<12½>
60	<3⅝>	<17½>
Max Profit	41⅜	43½
Max Loss	3⅝	Unlimited
Break-Even Point	41⅜	43½

the acquisition of NCR. The morning after the announcement to acquire NCR was made, the stock "gaped" on the opening more than 20 points higher (see Figure 5-3). This is just another example of how purchasing a protective call can benefit the investor. A comparison of using the protective call and holding a naked short stock position can be found in Table 5-1.

The same technique of selecting a call might be used if the short seller decided to purchase a call to protect unrealized profits in the stock. If the short seller is correct and the stock drops in price, protecting against a sudden turnaround in the stock price could provide to be a great advantage. Should the stock suddenly turn, unrealized profits may be lost and what was a profit might turn into a loss, in a very short period of time.

If the short seller of a stock does not purchase calls, an unlimited loss might be realized. If the stock starts to rise in price, the short seller might consider the purchase of a protective put, before the loss limit is reached. Once the loss limit is reached, the stock position should be closed. If the stock rises and the opportunity to limit the loss becomes available, the opportunity should be seized. Using derivative products to limit losses is a huge benefit. In addition, raising profit potential and limiting risk should be the focus of all investors.

This chapter has illustrated, the purchase of protective puts or protective calls can limit the potential for unforeseen dangers in both the underlying stock and/or the market as a whole. While the limit to risk may sacrifice some potential profit, the benefits far outweigh the potential drawbacks. Stock positions which are protected allow an investor or a trader the opportunity to be incorrect and still to keep a majority of the capital investment.

Summary

1. Options can be used as a means of protecting a long or short stock position.

2. Profits can also be protected through the purchase of puts and calls.

3. The purchase of a protective option contract does not limit profit potential but merely adds a safety net in case of the unwanted.

4. The purchaser of an option may give back a small portion of profits to protect the capital investment and the remaining profits if the stock has already had a desired move.

WORKSHEET 5-1:

Married Put Buyers Worksheet

STOCK			SHARES	PRICE	—52 WEEK—		RATING	PIE RATIO	YIELD
					HIGH	LOW			
OPTION CONTRACT			CONTRACTS	PREMIUM	EXPIRATION DATE		DAYS TILL EXP.		
QUART DIVID	DIVIDS TO EXP	TOTAL DIVID COLLECT	DEBIT		REG. T RATE		MARGIN INT RATE		
INTEREST CHARGES:	INT RATE	DAYS	DEBIT BAL	$			TODAY'S DATE		
	×	+365 ×		=					

REQUIRED CAPITAL

		CASH	MARGIN
Stock Price..................................			
Amount of Shares.............................	×		
Stock Commission	+		
Stock Cost..................................	=		
Reg T Rate	×	■	
Equity Required	=	■	
Option Premium..............................			
Amount of Shares.............................	×		
Option Commissions	+		
Option Proceeds	=		
Required Capital (Equity Required + Option Proceeds)....................	=		

MAXIMUM LOSS/MAXIMUM RISK

Exercise Price			
Amount of Shares.............................	×		
Commission @ exercise	−		
Dividends Expected	+	■	
Interest Charges	−	■	
Debit Balance	−		
Required Capital..............................	−		
Maximum Loss.............................	=		
Max % Loss (Loss ÷ Req Capital)..........			
*Max Ann Loss (Max % × 365 ÷ Days)			

STATIC RETURN

Current Price.................................			
Amount of Shares.............................	×		
Dividends Expected	+		
Interest Charges	−	■	
Debit Balance	−		
Required Capital..............................	−		
Profit ÷ Loss	=		
Return (Profit ÷ Capital Req)			
*Ann Return (Return × 365 ÷ Days)			

BREAKEVEN POINT

Capital Required.............................			
Debit Balance	+		
Interest Charges	+	■	
Dividends Expected	−		
Subtotal	=		
Amount of Shares.............................	÷		
Break-Even...................................			

*Annualized returns may only be used if holding is over 60 days.

6

Basic
Spread Techniques

Until this point, the focus has been on the use of option contracts in conjunction with stocks or as an alternative to trading stocks. Puts and calls have many different uses, and may be used in many different ways to profit from different investment panoramas. These views can be small upside or downward moves in a stock, the expectation of a major or minor move over time and even the inability to choose the correct direction which stock or the market is going to move. Option strategists have developed many different methods to take advantage of such circumstances. Depending upon the view the investor has with regard to the price and movement of the underlying stock and his approach to risk and reward, almost any objective can be met.

This chapter will focus on the use of option contracts to satisfy the needs of profiting on a stock which is expected to have a relatively small move over a short period of time. The objective of the investor will require the use of two option contracts at one time which will limit risk on the investment as well as limit profit potential. We will focus on four different option **spread** techniques.

The term spread refers to the use of two or more option positions and the relative difference between them. As will be seen in this chapter, the purchase of one option contract and the sale of another contract of the same type (put or call) can potentially achieve certain goals which may not be met by simply purchasing one option contract.

Bull Spread Using Calls

The first spread technique, is known as a **Bull Spread Using Call Options.** The bull spread implies that an upward bias in stock price is required to achieve a profit through the use of this strategy. While a bullish opinion is mandatory, the movement needed in the price of the underlying stock may not be that great. In addition, the bull spread allows the investor to offset some option premium cost with the sale of option premium.

The bull spread involves the purchase of one call option and the sale of another call option in the same expiration month, but with an exercise price which is higher than the exercise price for the call which was purchased. The difference between the premiums is known as the debit and is the maximum risk (excluding commissions, dividends, and other transaction charges) which the investor might realize. Since the call with the lower exercise price is purchased, the spread is considered to be **a covered spread,** and is not subject to any special margin requirements, except that it must be executed in a margin account. This is similar to a covered write strategy (Chapter 3) except instead of owning the underlying stock, the investor owns a call with a lower strike. Should the stock be called away, the investor may exercise the long call and deliver the stock, regardless of how high the stock moves. If the stock should gap open lower the day after being called, the investor might purchase the stock in the open market, still realizing no loss from the situation.

The maximum loss which the investor might realize is less than if the purchased call was bought without the sale of the call with the higher exercise price. If the stock is below the lower exercise price on the call which was purchased at the time of expiration, the maximum loss would be realized. If the price of the underlying stock is above the lower exercise price, a loss might still be realized but not one which is total.

The maximum profit for a bull spread using calls is when the stock is at or above the higher exercise price at expiration. The maximum profit is the difference between the two exercise prices minus the debit paid for the spread. The maximum profit will not get any higher, regardless of how high the stock should appreciate in price. During the holding period of the spread, no dividends will be collected unless the long call is exercised and possession of the stock is taken before the stock goes ex-dividend.

The break-even point of the bull spread using calls can easily be pinpointed by adding the spread's debit price to the exercise price of the long call. This is the juncture at which the difference between a loss and a profit takes place. The break-even point should not be too high as the chance to profit from the use of this strategy would greatly be diminished, and the chance to realize a loss would be very high.

Let us assume that Upjohn (UPJ) (Figure 6-1) is a stock trading at 41. The investor is bullish on the stock but believes that a maximum price rise in the stock would be limited to 4 points over the next three months. This investor decides to purchase a call option with three months to expiration with an exercise price of 40 and an option premium of 4⅛ points. In addition to purchasing this call, the investor decides to write or sell an equal number of calls with an exercise price of 45 in the same month, and collects a premium of 1⅞ points. The maximum loss to the investor occurs if the stock is below the 40 exercise price of the long call at expiration. If the stock is below the break-even point of 42¼ (the spread debit of 2¼ + the

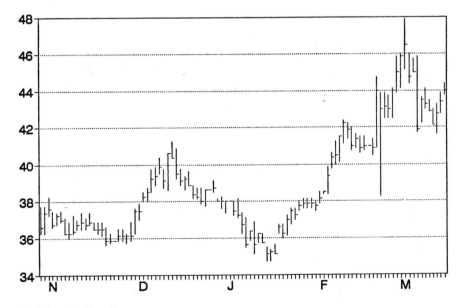

FIGURE 6-1. Upjohn Daily Chart.

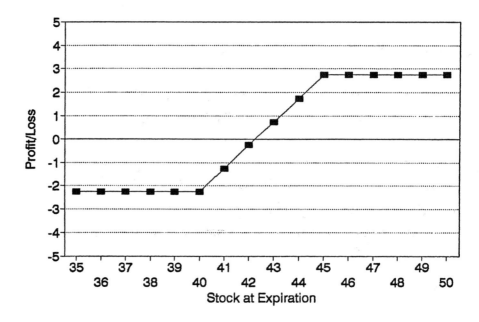

FIGURE 6-2.   Bull Spread Using Calls.

lower exercise price of 40), then some loss would be realized. If at expiration the stock is above the higher exercise price of 45, then a maximum profit of 2¾ points (difference in exercise prices of five— spread debit of 2¼) would be realized by the investor. If the spread achieved the maximum profit, then a return of 122 percent ((profit/ debit)*100) would be gained. Figure 6-2 evaluates the result of using the bull spread using calls in this situation.

Before initiating a bull spread using calls, certain guidelines should be observed to prevent a choice of the wrong spread or the wrong options. These guidelines can be found in Table 6-1. In addition, Worksheet 6-1 (found at end of chapter) will aid in the preparation of choosing the correct spread.

If the underlying stock rises above the exercise price of the short call, the investor should pay special caution to the dividend as the stock might be prematurely called if the company is about to pay a dividend to stockholders. If there is a fear of such a case, the investor should either close the spread, repurchase the short call or exercise the long call to protect against being short the stock on the day of record.

TABLE 6-1.   Guidelines for Bull Spread Using Calls
_____

1. The debit amount paid for the spread should be less than ½ the difference between the two exercise prices.
2. The spread should have a life expectancy of at least 45 days till expiration.
3. The stock should not have to gain more than 10 percent before the higher exercise price is violated.
4. The investor should not expect the stock to appreciate much higher than the exercise price on the call which was written.
5. The value of the call being written should be over ⅝ of a point.
6. If the stock rises above the higher exercise price, action should be taken.
7. If the value of the spread drops below ½ of the debit paid, the spread should be closed and the loss should be taken.
_____

Bear Spread Using Puts

Similar to the bull spread using calls is the **Bear Spread Using Puts.** This strategy has some of the same attributes of the bull spread, but has a negative price bias on the stock. The bear spread using puts allows the investor to speculate on a downside move on the price of the underlying stock with little risk. The investor must assume that the downside price movement will be limited. Since one of the puts which is being used is written, there will be no profit participation should the stock break below the exercise price of the short put.

The Bear Spread Using Puts also comprises the use of two option contracts. A put is purchased with an exercise price greater than the exercise price of the put which is written. Both put contracts utilize the same expiration month. Since the put which is purchased has a higher exercise price than that of the put which is sold, the spread is considered to be covered, and the only margin required is that the spread be kept in a margin account. The debit price must be paid for in full, just as it is in the Bull Spread Using Calls.

The goal of the investor in using this spread is that the stock will drop in price to or just below the exercise price of the put which is written. Once the stock drops below this level, the maximum profit would be reached, regardless of how much further the stock declined in price, even if the stock dropped to zero. The maximum profit (excluding commission charges and other transaction fees) would be the difference between the two exercise prices minus the debit paid for the spread.

If the stock dropped below the exercise price of the put which was written before expiration, and the stock was assigned to the investor, the investor might simply exercise the long put option, selling the stock to another investor or trader who wrote the put earlier. If the stock gap opened above the exercise price of the long put, the stock could be sold in the open market, still leaving the investor with no loss from this investment. Once the underlying stock is acquired through the assignment process, there is virtually no way the investor could lose, regardless of the price of the underlying stock between the time of assignment and expiration of the long option contract.

The maximum loss of this spread is if the price of the underlying stock is above the exercise price of the long put at expiration. The maximum loss is the debit paid for the spread (not including commissions or other transaction charges). If the stock is above the higher exercise price, a total loss or 100 percent of the investment would be realized at expiration. This loss would be less than if the long put was purchased with no option written against it. While this loss would be

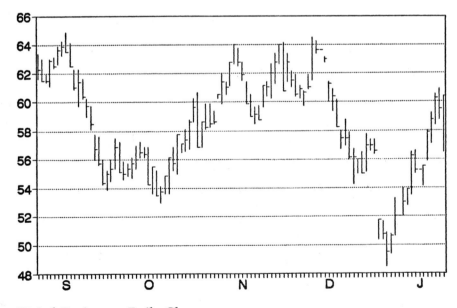

FIGURE 6-3.   Digital Equipment Daily Chart.

total, if the proper option contracts were used, then the dollar amount of the loss would be relatively low compared to that of purchasing a put outright or selling the stock short. In addition, the risks associated with selling stock short (Chapter 2) would also be avoided.

The break-even point in utilizing this strategy is the higher exercise price (on the put which was purchased) minus the debit paid to purchase the spread. If the stock is above this point at expiration, a loss would be realized. If the stock is below the break-even point, then a gain would be realized. If the break-even point is too close to the exercise price of the put which was written, then this strategy might not make sense.

The graph of the Digital Equipment (DEC) stock (Figure 6-3) shows of 15 points over 4 months. If a bear spread using puts was used, the investor might have done the following on DEC:

> Purchased 1 DEC JAN 60 put for 4½ and
> Written 1 DEC JAN 50 put for 1⅜ for
> a debit of.........................3⅛.

If the stock was below the exercise price of 50 (the put which was written) at expiration, a maximum profit of 4⅞ or 156 percent would be realized. If the stock was above the exercise price of 60 (the put which was purchased), then a loss of 3⅛ points or 100 percent of the investment would be lost. Table 6-2 illustrates a comparison between purchasing the bear spread using puts, purchasing puts, and selling stock short.

A graphic illustration of the bear spread using puts is shown in Figure 6-4 and a list of suggested guidelines for this strategy is found in Table 6-3. These figures should be analyzed until the strategy is fully understood. In addition, a worksheet has been provided (Worksheet 6-2) to help you calculate the benefits of this strategy.

In this chapter, we have shown how the purchase of one option contract and the sale (writing) of another contract can allow the investor the opportunity to profit from a relatively small move in the underlying stock, over a short period of time while not subjecting the investor to substantial risk. While the risk in using such a strategy is low, the investment may still double or yield to the investor a return of 100 percent. If the investor is wrong and the stock moves in the opposite direction, a total loss or 100 percent might be realized. This 100 percent loss may still hold less risk than if the investor would

TABLE 6-2.   Bear Spread Using Puts versus Long Put versus Short Stock

Stock = 82
Put with 80 Exercise Price = 3¼
Put with 75 Exercise Price = 1⅜

	Bear Spread	*Long Put*	*Short Stock*
Position	+1 Put with 80 Exercise −1 Put with 75 Exercise	+1 Put with 80 Exercise	−100 Shares
Debit/Credit	2⅛ Debit	3¼ Debit	82 Credit
Capital Req.	$212.50	$325.00	$4100

Stock at Expiration	*Profits and Losses*		
90	<2⅛>	<3¼>	<8>
85	<2⅛>	<3¼>	<3>
82	<2⅛>	<3¼>	-0-
80	<2⅛>	<3¼>	2
78	<⅛>	1¼	4
75	2⅞	1¾	7
70	2⅞	6¾	12
Max Profit	2⅞	76¾	82
Max Loss	2⅛	3¼	Unlimited
Break-Even Point	77⅞	76¾	82

have purchased an option or if a position in the underlying stock might have been utilized.

Bull Spread Using Puts

Not all option spreads are like the two which have been illustrated thus far. There are many different types and uses of option spreads. Some of those spreads may accomplish the same goals but not through the same means. In fact, at times there are spreads which provide a greater return to accomplish the same goals but also hold a

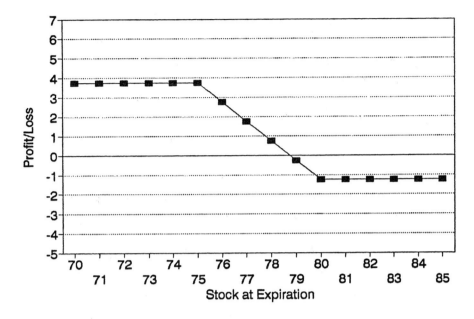

FIGURE 6-4. Bear Spread Using Puts.

greater amount of risk. This section illustrates two complements to the spreads already discussed. Just because the investor is subject to additional risk, there is no reason to completely rule out the use of these spreads before a proper evaluation of them is completed.

When evaluating the use of the Bull Spread Using Calls, the investor might become frustrated in that the spreads do not work out to the expectations of the investor. For example, a guideline which the investor utilizes to limit the debit amount to half of the potential value of the spread is not met, the investor might find it impossible to achieve the investment objective. An alternative to using that strategy might be using a spread technique known as **Bull Spread Using Puts.**

The Bull Spread Using Puts utilizes a technique which might assume some additional risk as well as the potential for profit, by using put option contracts and the use of a credit spread. This strategy is considered a short spread position and is subject to the following margin requirement:

Short Spread Margin Requirement = Difference Between Exercise
Prices + Credit Received

TABLE 6-3.   Guidelines for Bear Spread Using Puts

1. The debit amount paid for the spread should be less than ½ the difference between the two exercise prices.
2. The spread should have a life expectancy of at least 45 days till expiration.
3. The stock should not have to drop more than 10 percent before the lower exercise price is violated.
4. The investor should not expect the stock to drop much more than the value of the lower exercise price.
5. The value of the put being written should be over ⅝ of a point.
6. If the stock drops below the level of the lower exercise price, action should be taken.
7. If the value of the spread drops below half of the debit paid, the spread should be closed and the loss should be realized.

In addition, as will be demonstrated shortly, the user of this strategy is subject to an additional amount of risk over the use of Bull Spread Using Calls.

The use of this spread requires the purchase of a put option contract with a low exercise price and the sale (write) of a put contract with a higher exercise price. The difference between the two put premiums is known as the spread credit. The amount of the spread credit is also the value of the maximum profit of using this strategy. If the stock closes above the higher exercise price at expiration, and the stock is not prematurely put to the investor, then the maximum profit of the credit is earned. Therefore, it is desired that the underlying stock close above the higher exercise price. Regardless of how much the stock accumulates in value, once it is over the higher exercise price, the maximum profit will be achieved.

If the stock should decline in value, then the investor would realize a maximum trading loss with the price of the underlying stock at or below the lower exercise price. This maximum loss would be the difference between the two exercise prices less the credit received when the spread is initiated (not including commissions and transaction charges). Even if the price of the stock should decline to zero, the maximum trading loss the investor might realize would be the same as if the stock closed one point lower than if the stock was one point below the lower exercise price.

The break-even point in using this strategy occurs if the stock is at the price equal to the higher exercise price minus the credit received at expiration. If the stock is below the break-even point, then a loss would be incurred. If the stock is above the break-even point, then a profit would be realized. It is important to remember that the returns in such a calculation must be based on the margin requirement plus the premium paid for the long put, and not the price paid for the long put or the value of the spread itself. The profit and loss of the spread can be seen in Figure 6-5.

If the stock is prematurely put to the investor (usually after the stock has gone ex-dividend), then an additional risk might be assumed if the investor does not have the funds to purchase the stock. Therefore, it is strongly recommended that only a quantity of puts equivalent to the amount of stock the investor could afford to purchase should be used when using this strategy. If the stock is put to the investor, then a position equivalent to owning the stock and a protective put would be held. The cost basis for the stock would be the exercise price minus the credit received for the spread. There would be not cost for the long put. It is important to remember that in most cases the commissions paid on a stock position are much greater than those paid on an option position. This could put additional pressure on the investor.

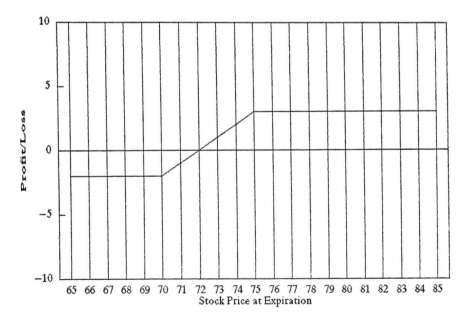

FIGURE 6-5.   Bull Spread Using Puts.

TABLE 6-4.   Bull Spread Using Puts versus Bull Spread Using Calls

Stock = 82
Put with 85 Exercise Price = 5
Put with 80 Exercise Price = 1
Call with 80 Exercise Price = 3½
Call with 85 Exercise Price = 1

Position	*Bull Spread Using Puts*	*Bull Spread Using Calls*
	+1 Put with 80 Exercise	+1 Call with 80 Exercise
	−1 Put with 85 Exercise	−1 Call with 85 Exercise
Credit/ Debit	4 pt Credit	2½ pt Debit

Stock at Expiration	*Profits and Losses*	
78	<1>	<2½>
80	<1>	<2½>
82	1	<½>
85	4	2½
87	4	2½
Max Profit	4	2½
Max Loss	1	2½
Break-Even Point	81	82½

TABLE 6-5.   Guidelines for Bull Spread Using Puts

1. The credit amount received for the spread should be more than ½ the difference between the two exercise prices.
2. The spread should have a life expectancy of no more than 60 days till expiration.
3. The stock should not have to gain more than 10 percent before the higher exercise price is violated.
4. If the stock rises above the higher exercise price, action should be taken.
5. If the value of the spread doubles the credit received, it should be closed and the loss should be taken.

While there is some additional risk in using the Bull Spread Using Puts technique over the Bull Spread Using Calls, the maximum profit, break-even point and maximum trading loss are known before the investor commits to using this strategy. Table 6-4 compares the use of the two different types of bull spreads. The use of puts over calls may become important if call premiums are too high or the objective as outlined through the suggested guidelines when using calls cannot be met. Worksheet 6-3 will help you calculate the benefits of the Bull Spread using Puts. Just as there were suggested guidelines for Bull Spreads Using Calls, there are also some suggested guidelines for Bull Spreads Using Puts, which can be found in Table 6-5.

Bear Spread Using Calls

The fourth strategy, **Bear Spreads Using Calls**, is similar to the Bear Spread Using Puts, but does have some differences. The most important thing to remember about use of this strategy, is that just as in using Bull Spreads Using Puts, the Bear Spread Using Calls technique requires that a naked margin requirement be met when the trade is initiated.

As the title implies, this spread requires a negative bias to the price of the underlying stock. The investor who utilizes this strategy will purchase a call with an exercise price which is higher than the exercise price of the call which is written (or sold). The difference in call premiums is the spread's credit. The credit received is also the amount of the maximum profit which might be realized. The maximum profit is achieved if the stock drops below the lower exercise price. If the stock is below that level, then both call options will expire worthless, allowing the investor to capture the entire credit received as profit.

The maximum loss when using this strategy occurs if the stock is above the higher exercise price at expiration. At that point, the spread would be worth the difference between the two exercise prices, with the loss being reduced by the amount of the credit. Therefore, the maximum trading loss is the difference between the two exercise prices minus the credit received.

The point at which this strategy would break-even is the lower exercise price plus the credit received. If the stock is higher than the break-even point then a loss will be incurred. If the stock is below the

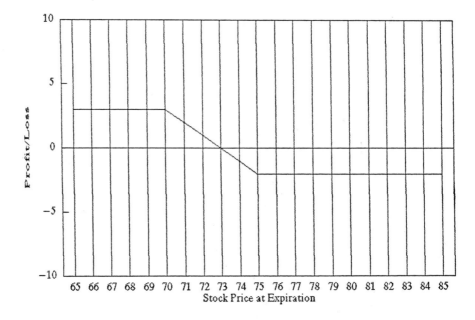

FIGURE 6-6.   Bear Spread Using Calls.

break-even point, then a profit will be incurred. Figure 6-6 illustrates the profit and loss of the bear spread using calls.

An important caveat that users of this strategy should remember is: if the stock is above the exercise price of the call which has been written, the investor is subject to being prematurely assigned. If the stock is called away prior to or on the ex-date of the stock paying its dividend, the investor would be responsible for paying out the dividend on the short stock position. It should also be realized that the position held after this point would be equivalent to that of a short stock with a protective call option position, as discussed in Chapter 2. Table 6-6 provides guidelines for this strategy. Table 6-7 compares the use of the Bear Spread Using Calls against the Bear Spread Using Puts. In addition, the Bear Spread Using Calls worksheet (Worksheet 6-4) will provide additional support for the investor.

The four option spreads outlined in this chapter are just the beginning of our study into the use of option spread techniques. Table 6-8 sets out a comparison of these four basic spreads. While there are many more spread strategies, which will be outlined in future chapters, it is important to understand the basics of using these techniques. The purchase of one option contract versus the writing of another allows the investor to take advantage of some of

TABLE 6-6.   Guidelines for Bear Spread Using Calls

1. The credit amount received for the spread should be more than half the difference between the two exercise prices.
2. The spread should have a life expectancy of no more than 60 days till expiration.
3. The stock should not have to drop more than 10 percent before the lower exercise price is violated.
4. If the stock drops below the lower exercise price, action should be taken.
5. If the value of the spread doubles the credit received, it should be closed and the loss should be taken.

TABLE 6-7.   Bear Spread Using Calls versus Bear Spread Using Puts

Stock = 84
Call with 80 Exercise Price = 5¾
Call with 85 Exercise Price = 1⅜
Put with 85 Exercise Price = 3
Put with 80 Exercise Price = ⅞

	Bear Spread Using Calls	Bear Spread Using Puts
Position	−1 Call with 80 Exercise Price	+1 Put with 85 Exercise Price
	+1 Call with 85 Exercise Price	−1 Put with 80 Exercise Price
Debit/Credit	4⅜ Credit	2⅛ Debit

Stock at Expiration	*Profits and Losses*	
87	<⅝>	<2⅛>
85	<⅝>	<2⅛>
83	3⅜	<⅛>
80	4⅜	2⅞
78	4⅜	2⅞
75	4⅜	2⅞
Max Profit	4⅜	2⅞
Max Loss	⅝	2⅛
Break-Even Point	84⅜	83⅞

TABLE 6-8.   Comparison of the Basic Bull and Bear Spreads

Spread Type	Use C/P	Db/Cr	Max Pft at	Max Loss at	B.E. Point
Bull	Calls +Lower −Higher	Debit	Higher Exercise Price	Lower Exercise Price	Lower Exercise Prx +Debit
Bear	Puts +Higher −Lower	Debit	Lower Exercise Price	Higher Exercise Price	Higher Exercise Prx −Debit
Bull	Puts +Lower −Higher	Credit	Higher Exercise Price	Lower Exercise Price	Lower Exercise Prx +Credit
Bear	Calls +Higher −Lower	Credit	Lower Exercise Price	Higher Exercise Price	Higher Exercise Prx −Credit

Use C/P Column: + means purchase   − means write

the benefits of being both the owner of an options contract and the writer. Along with these benefits also come the responsibilities involved in using such strategies. Through the use of the worksheets, figures and tables for each spread, the investor should be able to make a reasonable decision with respect to use of these strategies. Evaluation is the most important part of using spreads. The investor should pay special attention to profit potential and where the maximum profit might be achieved, the break-even point and its relation to the price of the underlying stock and the maximum loss and its level in relation to the price of the stock. In addition, while in theory the maximum profit might be the difference between two exercise prices minus the debit (in the first spreads), the actual profit received might be an ⅛, a ¼ or even ⅜ of a point lower, if the spread were to be closed out.

As with all strategies discussed and the ones to follow, positions should always be monitored. Losses should be taken as well as profits. While it is not always practical to completely close positions right away, not taking any action can also be very damaging to the investor. Before using any of these spread techniques, read Chapter

23 regarding maintaining positions and taking action on different strategies.

Spreads provide the investor with a great flexibility to achieve certain goals. This flexibility may come in the form of lower or higher risk, profits or cost. While this is all important, it is also important to remember that all investments hold the possibility of loss and the investor must be convinced about the expectation of the stock before entering into any transaction.

Summary

1. The purchaser of a bull spread using calls or a bear spread using puts reduces risk and capital.

2. The purchase of a bull spread using calls or a bear spread using puts limits profit potential while limiting risk and making the break-even point more favorable.

3. The sale of a bull spread using puts or a bear spread using calls provides the writer with a limited profit of the credit while limiting the risk of a naked position.

4. Basic spreads allow both the purchaser and writer to take advantage of expected but limited stock movement.

Bull Spread Using Calls

STOCK			SHARES	PRICE	—52 WEEK—		RATING	PIE RATIO	YIELD
					HIGH	LOW			
OPTION CONTRACT			CONTRACTS	PREMIUM	EXPIRATION DATE		DAYS TILL EXP.		
OPTION CONTRACT			CONTRACTS	PREMIUM	EXPIRATION DATE		DAYS TILL EXP.		
QUART DIVID	DIVIDS TO EXP	TOTAL DIVID COLLECT		DEBIT	REG. T RATE		MARGIN INT RATE		
INTEREST CHARGES:		INT RATE | DAYS | | DEBIT BAL | $					TODAY'S DATE		
		× ÷ 365 ×		=					

REQUIRED CAPITAL

Premium of Call Purchased		
Premium of Call Written	−	
Net Debit.	=	
Equiv. Amount of Shares	×	
Spread Cost.	=	
Commission on Call Purchased.	+	
Commission on Call Written	+	
Required Capital.	=	

MAXIMUM PROFIT

Stock at Higher Exercise Price.		
Value of Call Purchased		
Value of Call Written	−	
Equiv. Amount of Shares	×	
Commission of Long Call Sold	−	
Commission of Short Call Bought	−	
Returned Capital	=	
Required Capital.	−	
Profit.	=	
Return (Profit ÷ Req Capital) × 100.		
*Annualized Return		

BREAK-EVEN POINT

Required Capital.		
Equiv. Amount of Shares	÷	
Req. Cap. per Contract.	=	
Lower Exercise Price	+	
Break-Even Point per Share	=	

*Annualized returns may only be used if holding is over 60 days.

WORKSHEET 6-2:

Bear Spread Using Puts

STOCK			SHARES	PRICE	—52 WEEK—		RATING	PIE RATIO	YIELD
					HIGH	LOW			
OPTION CONTRACT			CONTRACTS	PREMIUM	EXPIRATION DATE		DAYS TILL EXP.		
OPTION CONTRACT			CONTRACTS	PREMIUM	EXPIRATION DATE		DAYS TILL EXP.		
QUART DIVID	DIVIDS TO EXP	TOTAL DIVID COLLECT		DEBIT	REG. T RATE		MARGIN INT RATE		
INTEREST CHARGES:		INT RATE DAYS	DEBIT BAL	$			TODAY'S DATE		
		× ÷365×	=						

REQUIRED CAPITAL

Premium of Put Purchased......................		
Premium of Put Written	−	
Net Debit.....................................	=	
Equiv. Amount of Shares	×	
Spread Cost..................................	=	
Commission on Put Purchased..................	+	
Commission on Put Written....................	+	
Required Capital..............................	=	

MAXIMUM PROFIT

Stock at Lower Exercise Price		
Value of Put Purchased.......................		
Value of Put Written..........................	−	
Equiv. Amount of Shares	×	
Commission of Long Put Sold..................	−	
Commission of Short Put Bought	−	
Returned Capital	=	
Required Capital..............................	−	
Profit..	=	
Return (Profit ÷ Req Capital) × 100...........		
*Annualized Return		

BREAK-EVEN POINT

Required Capital..............................		
Equiv. Amount of Shares	÷	
Req. Cap. per Contract........................	=	
Higher Exercise Price..........................	−	
Break-Even Point per Share	=	

---

*Annualized returns may only be used if holding is over 60 days.

WORKSHEET 6-3:

Bull Spread Using Puts

STOCK			SHARES	PRICE	—52 WEEK—		RATING	PIE RATIO	YIELD
					HIGH	LOW			
OPTION CONTRACT			CONTRACTS	PREMIUM	EXPIRATION DATE		DAYS TILL EXP.		
OPTION CONTRACT			CONTRACTS	PREMIUM	EXPIRATION DATE		DAYS TILL EXP.		
QUART DIVID	DIVIDS TO EXP	TOTAL DIVID COLLECT		CREDIT	REG. T RATE		MARGIN INT RATE		
INTEREST CHARGES:		INT RATE ╎ DAYS ╎ ÷365 ×	╎ DEBIT BAL ╎ =	$			TODAY'S DATE		

REQUIRED CAPITAL

Premium of Put Written		
Premium of Put Purchased	−	
Net Credit	=	
Equiv. Amount of Shares	×	
Spread Credit	=	
Commission on Put Written....................	−	
Commission on Put Purchased..................	−	
Difference Between Exer Prices × Equiv Shares ...	−	
Required Capital.............................	=	

MAXIMUM RISK

Stock at Higher Exercise Price..................		
Value of Put Written..........................		
Value of Put Purchased........................	−	
Equiv. Amount of Shares	×	
Commission of Short Put Bought	+	
Commission of Long Put Sold..................	+	
Capital Risk..................................	=	
Required Capital.............................	−	
Loss...	=	
Return (Profit ÷ Req Capital) × 100.		
*Annualized Return		

BREAK-EVEN POINT

Required Capital.............................		
Equiv. Amount of Shares	÷	
Req. Cap. per Contract........................	=	
Lower Exercise Price	−	
Break-Even Point per Share	=	

*Annualized returns may only be used if holding is over 60 days.

WORKSHEET 6-4:

Bear Spread Using Calls

STOCK		SHARES	PRICE	—52 WEEK—		RATING	PIE RATIO	YIELD
				HIGH	LOW			
OPTION CONTRACT		CONTRACTS	PREMIUM	EXPIRATION DATE		DAYS TILL EXP.		
OPTION CONTRACT		CONTRACTS	PREMIUM	EXPIRATION DATE		DAYS TILL EXP.		
QUART DIVID	DIVIDS TO EXP	TOTAL DIVID COLLECT	CREDIT	REG. T RATE		MARGIN INT RATE		
INTEREST CHARGES:		INT RATE | DAYS | | DEBIT BAL. | $				TODAY'S DATE		
		× ÷ 365 ×	=					

REQUIRED CAPITAL

Premium of Call Written . . . .

Premium of Call Purchased . . . . −

Net Credit . . . . =

Equiv. Amount of Shares . . . . ×

Spread Credit . . . . =

Commission on Call Written . . . . −

Commission on Call Purchased . . . . −

Difference Between Exer Prices × Equiv Shares . . . −

Required Capital . . . . =

MAXIMUM RISK

Stock at Lower Exercise Price . . . .

Value of Call Written . . . .

Value of Call Purchased . . . . −

Equiv. Amount of Shares . . . . ×

Commission of Short Call Bought . . . . +

Commission of Long Call Sold . . . . +

Capital Risk . . . . =

Required Capital . . . . −

Loss . . . . =

Return (Profit ÷ Req Capital) × 100 . . . .

*Annualized Return . . . .

BREAK-EVEN POINT

Required Capital . . . .

Equiv. Amount of Shares . . . . ÷

Req. Cap. per Contract . . . . =

Higher Exercise Price . . . . −

Break-Even Point per Share . . . . =

*Annualized returns may only be used if holding is over 60 days.

7

Spreads
Using Time

In Chapters 1 and 3, the value of time was addressed and it was shown that the clock favors the writer of an option while it works against the purchaser of an options contract. Also discussed was that the time value of an option decays at the greatest rate during the last 30 days of the life of an option. As shown in Figure 7-1, the time value of an option contract purchased with six months until expiration will realize the greatest percentage loss during the last month of the contract. This can be very dissatisfying to an investor who purchases this contract with less than two months till expiration. An investor who wrote this option will probably be very happy with the selection made, especially if the underlying stock remains at the same value until expiration.

While the purchaser of an option faces an obstacle with regard to time, the writer benefits from the passage of time. However, the writer of an options contract may also realize a great loss should the underlying stock move in the wrong direction and the position is not covered by the stock. While both the purchaser and the writer face some risk when the position is initiated, a combined strategy of purchasing and writing different option positions can provide a great advantage. Chapter 6 introduced the concept of bull and bear spreads, and this chapter will focus on the use of spread positions to take advantage of time using two different positions, known as **Time Spreads.**

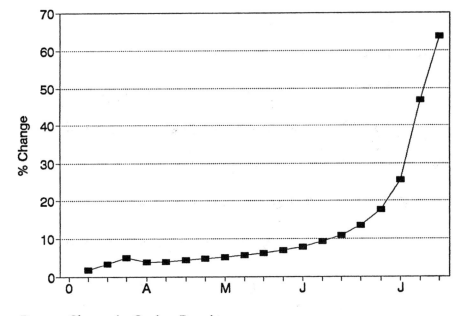

FIGURE 7-1.   Percent Change in Option Premium.

Horizontal Time Spreads

As the expiration of an option draws near, the value of the premium will decay until there is no time premium left. This may occur up to the last minute that the option can trade (depending on the stock and its volatility). Since the option will decline in time premium many investors feel that the risk in writing short term puts and calls holds relatively little risk. The common misconception is that people tend to forget that the underlying stock might move and a loss could be realized even if there is no time value left at all in the options contract. For example, an investor who writes a put with a $45 exercise price while the stock is trading at 47 might receive a premium of one point with 45 days left till expiration. At expiration, if the stock is trading below 44, the writer of the put would realize a loss if the put was repurchased or if the stock was put to the writer. Even though the time value of this put may be zero, the intrinsic value of the put would be the exercise price minus the price of the stock. This put writer might realize a substantial loss if the stock dropped dramatically.

If an investor who writes an option contract expiring in a short period of time also purchases a contract with the same exercise price with a life which is longer than the contract written, the investor has purchased a time spread. The time spread allows the investor to take advantage of the decay of time upon an options contract while limiting an unforeseen movement in the stock. Another use of the time spread is to purchase an option contract on a stock which is expected to move but may not move until after the expiration of the written contract.

During the holding period of the time spread, the option contract which is purchased will decline in value with the movement in time, but not nearly as quick as the option which was written. It should not be expected that the value of the long option would not decline at all during the life of the short option position. This is another common misconception among investors who try to utilize this strategy.

The use of the time spread does require some bias in regard to the direction of the stock. The expected movement in the stock does not have to be great for the investor to realize a gain, but should the stock move in the opposite direction, a loss might be realized.

A time spread using calls will allow the investor to purchase a call with several months until expiration and write a call with only several weeks until expiration. Both calls will probably utilize the same exercise price. Assume that the investor purchases a call with an exercise price of 60 with six months until expiration for an option premium of 3½ points with the underlying stock trading at 57. At the same time, the investor writes a call with one month until expiration for an option premium of one point. The position is purchased in a margin account but no margin requirement is necessary except for the spreads debit amount of 2½ points (3½ − 1). No additional margin requirement is necessary because the purchased option has a longer life than the written option, should the short contract be assigned, the long may be exercised allowing the investor to purchase the underlying stock at the same price as it was called away.

The maximum risk in the time spread is the debit cost (excluding commissions and other transaction charges) plus the possibility of any dividends paid should the stock be prematurely called just before the ex-date. If the stock is called, the investor may either exercise the long call option or sit with a position known as a synthetic put (see Chapter 12).

The break-even point for the time spread using calls is when the stock is trading at the exercise price plus the debit paid to initiate the spread. As long as the stock is not trading below this value (excluding dividends and transaction fees), the investor will not lose money. It is most beneficial that the stock not rise above the exercise price until after the short call expires. The difference between the exercise price and the break-even point represent the maximum trading loss. If the stock is called and the investor is forced to exercise the long call, a loss might be realized in this area. While the loss is limited to the maximum of the debit paid for the spread, the possibility of a loss does exist.

The ideal situation for the investor using this strategy is that the stock remain below the exercise price until the written call expires, allowing the investor to capture 100 percent of the premium written. After the expiration of the written call, the investor would hope for the underlying stock to make a bullish move making the purchased call even more valuable. In this situation, the investor would profit in both calls. The possibility of this situation happening all the time is small, but it does exist. This scenario has been seen in many take over stocks that receive bids after the expiration of the short call position. In fact, the announcement of a takeover or a new takeover bid has been known to happen just after the expiration of the short call. While this is the most perfect situation, it does not happen that often and investors should use extreme caution in attempting to duplicate such a move.

If the stock remains virtually unchanged till the expiration of the short call position, the investor may select at that time to sell the long call position. Even if the time premium on the long call has deteriorated, the loss will not equal that of the gain in the short call position, allowing the investor to realize a profit. Some investors will write another call option, which has a shorter life than the call which was purchased. This allows the investor the opportunity to duplicate the results of the previous month without any additional cost for the purchase of another call. If successful, the investor may duplicate the scenario for several months. While it is highly unlikely that the stock will remain unchanged or little moved during this period, substantial profits might be realized with little risk to the investor.

The investor who utilizes this strategy should be aware that once the written call expires, many option variations remain available and that duplicating the same strategy might not be the most advantageous. The investor might elect to write a call against the long call position, creating a bull or bear spread. This is only one of many possible situations. Chapter 21 discusses the maintenance and follow up of different option positions and might be very helpful in this situation.

The time spread might also be used for an investor with a slightly bearish bias toward the underlying stock. In such a situation, the investor would purchase a put option with several months until expiration and write a put option with the same exercise price with a shorter period till expiration. This is known as a **Time Spread Using Puts.** The long put (the option which was purchased) will protect the investor against any assignment which would force the purchase of the underlying stock from the obligation of the short put contract. Since the long put expires after the first put, there is no margin requirement (except for the payment of the debit and that the spread be maintained in a margin account). Unlike the call time spread, the put time spread is not subject to the payment of a dividend since the investor is only obligated to purchase the stock and not sell the issue short.

The maximum risk in utilizing this strategy is the debit amount (excluding commissions and other transaction charges). The investor utilizing the time spread using puts will benefit most if the stock remains above the exercise price until the short put position expires. If the stock declines after the expiration of the short put, the investor would realize maximum return from the written put plus appreciation of the purchased put as the stock moves lower. This is a twofold benefit, should the timing be correct. It is very difficult to enact a strategy which requires such precise timing for an exact movement. This should not be expected.

The break-even point for the use of the time spread using puts is realized if the stock is at a price equivalent to the exercise price minus the debit. If the stock is between the break-even point and the exercise price, a loss might be realized at the expiration of the short put. If the stock is put to the writer, the writer might choose to hold the position resulting in a married/protective put stock position, or the spreader might exercise the long stock position and sell the stock which was purchased.

The put spreader should not be too hasty to close the stock position through the exercise of the long put position. There are two reasons for this justification. First, the investor is not subject to any additional risk and might even lower the risk if a dividend is paid during the holding period. Second, a lower risk or possibility even a profit might be realized by selling both the stock and the long put option in the open market, allowing the investor to collect any

TABLE 7-1.   Forward Time Spread Example

Stock = 52
Put with 50 Exercise Price and 1 Month Till Expiration = 1
Put with 50 Exercise Price and 3 Months Till Expiration = 2½

Action: Purchase 1 Put with 3 Months till Expiration 2½
         Write 1 Put with 1 Month till Expiration 1
         Debit Cost 1½

Stock at Expiration of 1 Month Put	1 Month Put	3 Month Put	Profit/Loss
55	0	1	<½>
52	0	1¾	¼
50	0	2⅛	⅝
47	3	4¼	<¼>

If Stock Declines after Expiration of 1 Month Put	1 Month Put	3 Month Put	Profit/Loss
47	0	4	2½
45	0	5½	4
43	0	7¼	5¾

remaining time premium. Remember, once an option is exercised, the purchaser will only receive the equivalent of the intrinsic value and basically gives up all rights to the value of time.

Table 7-1 provides an example of the time spread using puts. As the table shows, if the stock is put to the writer, he will be in a better position to sell the stock and the put separately instead of exercising the long put. While this is only one scenario, as outlined, the investor is forced to make a decision. Note that this example excludes commissions and other transaction charges which might have a bearing on the investment decision.

Time spreads allow the spreader to take advantage of the time decay. The time decay allows the writer to profit on one side of the two sided transaction, should the stock basically remain unchanged till the expiration of the option which was written. While the idea of using such a strategy might be beneficial, a combination of the time spread and other spread positions might prove to meet the needs of the investor in a more appropriate fashion than if the time spread was utilized alone or in addition to other strategies. By combining two strategies into one, the spreader might lower the cost and increase the opportunity for profitability. These strategies are known as **Diagonal Spreads**. Diagonal spreads require that the spreader have an opinion which is more aggressive than the spreader utilizing the time spread strategy, since stock movement will be a very important part of the strategy.

The diagonal spread used for an investor who is bullish on a stock is known as the **Diagonal Spread Using Calls**. The use of the diagonal spread using calls allows the spreader to profit through an appreciation in the underlying stock and through the decay in the value of time. This strategy is a two part spread which gives the purchaser the best of two worlds. The diagonal spread using calls requires the investor to purchase a call with a lower exercise price and more time and the writing of a call with a higher exercise price and less time until expiration. Because the call which is purchased has a lower exercise price and expires after the call which is written, no special or naked option requirements are needed.

Since the call which is purchased has both a longer life and a lower exercise price, the spread will always be purchased for a debit. The debit is the maximum risk which the spreador might realize (excluding commissions and other transaction charges). The break-even in utilizing this strategy is the point where the stock is at the exercise price of the purchased call plus the debit paid for the spread. If the stock remains below this point until expiration, the spread purchaser will realize a 100 percent debit loss. If the stock is above this point at the expiration of the call, which was purchased, the spreader will realize a profit. Remember, since the call which was written expires before the call which was purchased, the investor might not realize this profit at the expiration of the written call unless the purchased call is sold.

To illustrate the use of this strategy, let us look at the stock of the Federal National Mortgage Association (FNM) also known as Fannie Mae. Assume the investor, on January 2 purchased 1 call of the FNM Jun 30 call (4½) and wrote 1 FNM Feb 35 call (1¼) for a debit of 3¼. Like the bull spread using calls (see Chapter 6), if the stock rose above the higher exercise price of 35 by the February expiration, the maximum profit till the first expiration would be 1¾ points. If the stock remained below 35 until February expiration, the investor could allow that call to expire and would simply be left with the long Jun 30 call. If the stock stayed above 33¼ until June expiration, the investor would not lose any money since this is the break-even point (lower exercise price + debit). If the stock rose after the expiration of the call which was written, maximum profit potential would be unlimited. If the stock declined below the break-even point, the investor could realize a loss. The maximum loss which the investor might realize is 3¼ points (the spread debit).

The investor should not wait until the last minute to sell the purchased call. As with the written call, the time premium will decline especially if the position is held into the last or spot month. In addition, if there are several months until expiration of the purchased call, the investor may wish to duplicate the diagonal spread by writing another call which expires before the purchased call with an exercise price which might be equal to or greater than that of the purchased call. The writing of this call might even be with an exercise price higher than that of the first call written, especially if the value of the stock has appreciated. Many different possible investment scenarios are available to the investor. All possibilities should be considered and no rash decisions should be made. The investor should also consider the opinion of the stock and re-evaluate the expectation of the stock and the overall market. Expectations and conditions can change during the holding period and a new view on the stock might influence the decision of the investor to possibly close out all positions and move on to something new.

Time spreads can provide the best of two worlds in allowing the investor to profit from the options time premium decay as well as a movement in the underlying stock in the correct direction. While the investor might have a substantial opportunity as well as potential profit, it should be understood that a loss might still be realized should the stock take a quick and decisive move in the direction opposite to what is desired. Furthermore, the investor should take careful interest in the position and not forget about the purchased option once the written contract expires. Forgetting to monitor any option position could prove to be detrimental to the investor's financial well being and might turn a profit into a loss over a very short period of time.

While the investor should take careful notice of any outstanding positions, note that once the written option contract expires, a variety of opportunities may become available to the investor which were not available before. The investor should, however, not allow the long contract to remain completely unhedged. If this were the case, the investor would probably have purchased the contract outright and not written any other option contract against the long position.

Diagonal Time Spreads

The use of time spreads is similar to a covered write. Instead of owning the underlying stock, the investor owns another option contract on the same security with a longer life cycle.

Time spreads can be very versatile when combined with other spread positions. For example, it is possible to combine a bull spread using calls with a time spread using calls. This would be known as a **Diagonal Time Spread Using Calls.** The diagonal time spread is a spread in which the investor buys a call with a lower exercise price in a further out month and writes a call with a higher exercise price in a near-term month. Should the stock begin to move higher immediately, the investor would still realize a profit should the position have to be closed by the time the first call (near-term) expires.

Diagonal spreads can also be very favorable to an investor with a bearish opinion of a stock. This is known as a **Diagonal Spread Using Puts.** Similar to the diagonal spread using calls, the investor purchases a put contract with several months till expiration and an exercise price near the current stock price (higher exercise price) and writes another put contract with an exercise price which is out-of-the-money (lower than the put which was purchased) and is expiring in a short period of time. Should the underlying stock depreciate in price before the expiration of the put which was written, the investor should still realize some profit. While this profit might not be as much as if the move happened post the first expiration, the investor should still realize a profit.

The example of this strategy uses L.A. Gear (LA). An investor purchased an LA Apr 17½ put for 3 and wrote an LA Mar 12½ put for 1¼. The maximum risk to the investor of 1¾ points would only be realized if the stock closed above 15¾ until expiration of the March contract. The investor realized a maximum profit till expiration of the first put since the stock dropped below the 12½ exercise price of the put which was written. The maximum profit (excluding commissions and other charges) of 3¼ points per spread was realized by the investor for a return of 185 percent till expiration. While this result may have not been the goal of the investor, the result was more than pleasing.

The user of a diagonal spread should be limited to a debit of less than 60 percent of the difference between the exercise price. If the investor pays more, the opportunity for profit is limited. In addition, the break-even level should not require that the stock move more than 5 percent of the value, since this would defeat the purpose of writing the option contract for time decay. Once the short option position expires, the investor should consider the writing of another out-of-the-money option. Options may be written right until the month in which the long option contract expires. The ultimate position *might be* a bull spread using calls or a bear spread using puts. If the options are written for several months the ultimate cost of owning the long option position might be very little or even a credit.

Four strategies which involve time and two different positions have now been examined. These spreads can prove to be very beneficial given the right situation and might fit the needs of most investors. While these spreads provide little risk to the investors, positions which are similar yet turn the positions around can also be beneficial. The next four spread strategies may not be for all investors because they put the investor at unlimited risk. While these strategies might not be for you, understanding these spreads can help you understand the options market and other strategies which will be examined in future chapters.

Horizontal Reverse Time Spreads

Before identifying the next four strategies, it is important to note that *all* of these spreads are subject to the option naked margin requirement. If you are not familiar with the naked margin requirement or have forgotten it, take this opportunity and review it in Chapter 3.

The first spread is known as the **Reverse Time Spread Using Calls.** This strategy involves the purchase of a call which expires in a short period of time and the writing of another call with the same exercise price but which has a longer time period until expiration. The reverse time spread using calls is for the investor who believes that the price of the underlying stock will decline before the expiration of the written call. The purchase of the short-term call is to protect the investor in case the stock moves in the wrong direction short term. Some investors believe that if a stock does not move against them in a short period of time, then their assumption is correct.

Let us consider the L.A. Gear example once again. Assume that the investor purchases a Feb 15 call and writes a Apr 15 call for a credit of two points. If the stock declines, and remains below the exercise price until expiration in April, the investor will realize a profit of two points (the amount of the credit). If the stock rises dramatically during the holding period of the long call, the investor can exercise the call position and turn a bearish position into a covered write. If the investor decides not to exercise the call, the spread position could be closed out for a debit which would probably realize a small loss.

Should the stock make a sharp move to a higher price, the investor could be assigned on the written call. This would leave the investor with a short stock position and subject to the risk as a outlined in Chapter 2.

After the expiration of the long call, the break-even point for the investor would be the exercise price plus the original credit received. The investor should pay attention to the naked call position as the risk to the investor is unlimited. If the stock suddenly rises, the investor could face serious financial risk. If the stock remains unchanged for some time, the investor should consider the premature closure of the naked option position.

The investor may also decide to hedge the short call position by purchasing an out-of-the-money call with a higher exercise price, creating a bear spread using calls.

The second reverse time spread is the **Reverse Time Spread Using Puts.** Similar to the call spread, this spread has the investor writing an option contract with a longer period till expiration than the put which is purchased. This strategy is for an investor who is bullish on the underlying stock and is willing to take risk. The risk involved could have the investor purchasing the underlying stock at the exercise price less the credit received for the spread position. The risk of owning the stock was previously outlined in Chapter 2.

The best situation for this investor would be for the stock to rise. In that scenario, the investor would realize a maximum profit of the credit received. If the stock stopped before the expiration of the purchased put, the investor might choose one of two strategies. The investor may exercise the long put and become short the underlying stock. This would leave the investor with a short stock position and short a put. If the investor is assigned on the put which was written, the stock position would be flat. The investor should pay attention to any dividends. This position is known as a synthetic call position and is discussed in Chapter 12.

The break-even point for this strategy is the exercise price less the credit received. Should the stock drop below this level after expiration of the long put, the risk to the investor would be unlimited to the point that the stock could only go to zero. Therefore the maximum risk is the difference between the break-even point and zero.

The reverse time spreads are similar to the writing of naked options but use the purchase of a shorter-term contract to hedge the naked option position. Option positions are frequently used to protect other option positions especially when a naked position is employed. It is important to realize that once the short-term option position (which was purchased) expires, the investor will have a naked short option position. This position can subject the investor to unlimited risk.

Diagonal Reverse Time Spreads

The use of **Reverse Diagonal Time Spreads** are used by some traders and investors to take opportunity in anticipation of sudden changes in stock activity, also known as trend changes. Some traders believe that once a stock reaches certain parameters in pricing, a quick change in reversal may take place. These parameters which the trader uses might be part of some school of technical analysis. Technical analysis is the study of price movements in an effort to predict future price movements of a stock, commodity, or index. This analysis might set a target price for the stock, violation of a price trend or channel. In such instances, reverse diagonal time spreads can prove to be an advantage.

The **Reverse Diagonal Call Spread** can be accomplished in two different methods. First, the trader might purchase a call option which expires before the call which is written. The purchased call may give extra protection and possibly even a profit if the call utilizes an exercise price which is lower than that of the call which is written. If the stock rises short term, the purchased call could be sold for a quick profit, leaving the investor or trader with a naked call position. If the trader or investor believes that the stock will have a quick short-term rise, and then begin to decline in price, this strategy could be most beneficial. If the stock drops in price first, the purchased call will probably drop and might expire worthless. This loss should be partially offset as the value of the written call should also decline, allowing for the call to be repurchased at a profit. The investor/trader should not wait for the written call to drop to zero before buying the call back. At this time, the investor might wish to write another call in the same month, but with an exercise price which is lower. This strategy should employ plenty of caution as the price of the underlying stock might quickly reverse.

A second method of using the reverse diagonal call spread involves the purchase of a call which expires before the call which is written, with the purchased call utilizing a higher exercise price. If the price of the underlying stock rises dramatically before the expiration of the purchased call, the trader/investor has a liability which is limited to the difference between the two exercise prices. The maximum loss before the expiration of the purchased call is the difference between the two exercise prices less the credit received, if the purchased call is exercised. It is not possible to compute the potential maximum loss if the spread is simply closed out, since it is impossible to accurately predict the time value of the call which was written. The reason for the lack of accuracy will be evident in Chapter 20 which discusses in greater detail the pricing of options contracts.

The difference between the two reverse diagonal call spreads can be seen as we examine the following illustrations. It is important to realize that one strategy is not better than the other, but that the stock expectation and the degree of risk on which the choice should be based will determine the correct strategy for the user. The difference between each strategy being profitable can merely be the difference in the stock movement over a short period of time.

The stock of Time-Warner (TWX), shown in Figure 7-2, has a high volatility as can be seen in the upward/downward movement in the stock. Assume that there are two investors. The first investor believes that the price of the underlying stock will quickly rise and reverse direction once the trend line is touched. The second investor believes that the price of the underlying stock will drop, but wishes to hedge the position in case the stock rises before it falls. Both of the investors can be correct as we explore further.

The first investor purchases a call with the lower exercise price of 85 for November and writes the January 90 call with a premium of

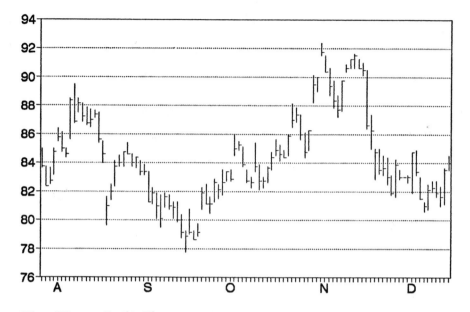

FIGURE 7-2.   Time-Warner Daily Chart.

2⅜. This investor has a 3⅝ debit. In addition to the debit, the investor/trader must deposit cash or securities equal to $1200, the margin required for the written call. The total initial investment for *this* spread, using one contract on each side, is $1800.

The second investor/trader purchases a call with a higher exercise price of 90 for December and writes the January 85 call with a premium of 7¼. This investment has a 4¼ credit. There is also a margin required for writing the call of $1700 which must be deposited. The total initial investment for *this* spread, using one contract on each side, is $2000.

Both of these strategies employ the writing of the *same* option contract, but the purchase of different calls. The difference between the calls is simply the exercise price as both contracts expire in the same month.

Similar to the reversal diagonal spread using calls is the **Reverse Diagonal Put Spreads.** The use of puts merely changes the opinion of the anticipated price movement. The use of reverse diagonal put spreads also holds the risk of being naked put options in the future. The investor/trader, therefore, should be willing and able to own the underlying stock in the future if he intends to have an unhedged position once the purchased put expires. In addition, once the put which was bought expires, an evaluation of further hedges might be prudent.

Summary

1. Horizontal time spreads allow the investor or trader to take advantage of the decay of time value on an options contract with little risk.
2. Diagonal time spreads can be used like bull or bear spreads, allowing the user to take advantage of price movement and time.
3. Reverse spreads allow for short-term price movement with limited liability.
4. The use of time spreads can allow the investor to hedge positions already being held.

8

Combining Puts and Calls

This chapter will focus on the use of options for investment when a major move in the underlying stock is anticipated, but the direction of the move is unclear. The opposite use of these strategies will also be examined. In essence, this chapter will tackle some of the strategies associated with stock volatility.

There are two basic strategies which when expanded into four strategies can handle most situations involving volatility. These strategies will be evaluated based upon expected high volatility and expected low volatility.

Purchasing Straddles

In Chapter 2, the purchase of puts and calls was examined. The purchase of a call is a strategy in which the investor expects the price of the stock to rise over a short period of time. The purchase of the put is used when there is an expectation that the value of the underlying stock will depreciate during a short period of time. But what if the stock is expected to move one way or the other over a short period of time? The purchase of call would not be profitable should the stock fall. However, the purchase of a put would not be profitable if the stock should rise in price. The use of spreads, as evaluated thus far, would not satisfy the need of the investor either. However, the investor might wish to purchase a put and a call in the

111

same expiration month, using the same exercise price. This strategy is known as buying a **Straddle**.

Straddles employ the use of both put and call option contracts for the investor unsure of the direction of the underlying stock, but expects that the move will be sizable. The use of straddles entails a larger capital requirement than that of purchasing an option, since two different options will be purchased. Both of the contracts used must be paid for in full at the time of purchase. A margin requirement is not necessary. The maximum risk to the purchaser of a straddle is *100 percent of the total investment*. The chance of losing 100 percent is slim, but the possibility is there and is real.

The investor using the straddle must assume that the stock will move more than the total debit price from the exercise price before expiration. Naturally, the greater the volatility of the underlying stock, the higher the option prices. The higher the option prices, the more difficult it will be for the straddle to become profitable. Therefore, if the stock has a history of high volatility, the use of the straddle may not be beneficial to the investor, since the cost of employing such a strategy might be greater than the possibility of reaching the break-even point.

The straddle has two break-even points. The first break-even point known as the **upper break-even point** is the exercise price plus the total debit paid for the straddle. The second break-even point is known as the **lower break-even point**, which is the exercise price minus the total debit paid for the straddle. If the stock remains between the two break-even points, a loss would be realized at expiration. If the stock expires at the exercise price, and the position is held till expiration, the loss to the investor would be total.

The maximum profit on the purchase of a straddle is unlimited on the upside. That is, as long as the stock keeps rising above the upper break-even point, the investor will continue to accumulate profit. This is similar to that of purchasing a call. The maximum profit on the straddle to the downside is only limited by the fact that the stock could not drop below the zero (0) value. The profit will accumulate as long as the stock drops below the lower break-even price until the stock hits zero.

Figure 8-1 illustrates the profit, loss and breakeven points as they relate to the purchase of the straddle. If the profit/loss value is equal to zero, then the strategy is considered breakeven. Between those two breakeven points, the strategy yields a loss, with the maximum loss at the exercise price (in this case $60). Above the breakeven points, the

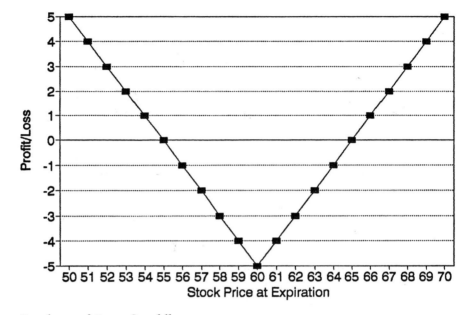

FIGURE 8-1.   Purchase of Long Straddle.

strategy realizes a profit. Up until now, each of the strategies which we have examined had only one break-even point. Once the stock moves out of the triangle of loss, the profit is unlimited.

As with other strategies, certain guidelines should be used when purchasing a straddle. Among the first guidelines, just as in the purchase of an option contract, there should be at least 45 days left until the expiration of the contracts. As previously shown (Figure 1-2), the time decay of an options contract has the greatest effect during the final month. Since both a put and call are purchased with the same exercise price, the time decay will have a greater effect on the investment as both contracts lose value at the same time, even if the price of the underlying stock does not move. The longer the potential holding period till expiration, the greater potential for profit as well as the greater the opportunity to profit.

The break-even level for the underlying stock should be no more than a five percent (5%) move from the exercise price. If a move of more than 5 percent is needed to break-even, the chance of even reaching the break-even level will make the opportunity of profit unachievable. The reason for the 5 percent move is that while the move might be in either direction, *there is a risk of the additional capital* paid for the opposing contract. Remember, one of the reasons for using option contracts is to limit potential dollar risk, not to increase the risk.

If one of the option contracts becomes profitable, it is advisable to sell a portion of the profitable contracts as well as *all* of the opposing contract. The investor should try to take the original investment out of the strategy, protecting against the possibility of loss. Usually, if the move in the underlying stock is made in a short period of time, there will be some value left to the contract which is not favored. If the value of the total position doubles (100 percent profit), the entire straddle position should be closed. Remember, as quick as a profit can be made, in most cases there is a strong possibility for that gain to turn into a loss.

Once the original investment is removed, several mental stop out points should be established. These points should be established on a time and price basis. Do not just allow the balance of the position to expire worthless. Remember, time continues to work against the purchaser of a straddle. Stop points can be established based on time, dollar value or a combination of the two. The combination may be placed on a sliding scale, adjusting time and price together. What ever choice the investor makes, the methodology should provide that the entire position be closed before expiration. The methodology used should also provide a logical scale which can easily be monitored.

Purchasing a Combination

The purchase of a straddle can provide the investor with an opportunity for great reward, regardless of which direction the stock should move. A problem of purchasing a straddle can be that the premium on a straddle can put the investment out of the reach of the investor. The high premium may come from the expectation of a great move in the stock. Such premiums have been seen on stocks which are the subject of takeover rumors, merger stories, lawsuits or other corporate developments. When the premium is too excessive, an alternative, similar to the purchase of the straddle, is the purchase of a **Combination**.

The purchase of a combination has one difference from the purchase of the straddle: the exercise prices. When a combination is purchased, the investor usually purchases an at-the-money or out-of-the-money call and an at-the-money or out-of-the-money put with

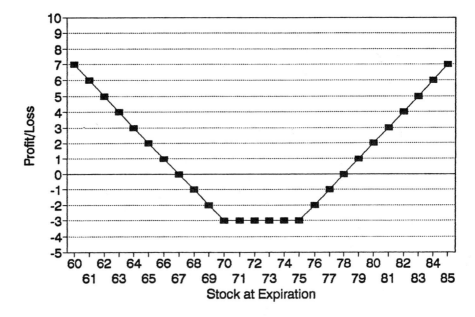

FIGURE 8-2. Purchase of Long Combination.

different exercise prices. The exercise price of the call is usually higher than the exercise price of the put. If the put has an exercise price which is higher than that of the call, at least one of the two option contracts will be in-the-money at all times.

The purchase of a combination will usually require a greater move in the underlying stock than if the straddle was purchased. The break-even levels of using the combination will require a greater move, at least in one direction, in the move in the stock. The greater the move to the break-even, the lower the probability for profit using the strategy.

The maximum risk in purchasing the combination is limited to 100% of the investment in the combination. While the risk is limited in dollar amount, the maximum risk is greater since the loss will be between the two exercise prices instead of just the one exercise price in using the straddle. Therefore, the maximum loss will actually occur in a "zone," shown in Figure 8-2. As can be seen in the figure, the maximum loss at expiration will be realized if the stock is between the lower exercise price (the exercise price of the put) and the upper exercise price (the call). Regardless of where the stock closes in that zone, a 100 percent loss might be realized. In addition, a loss of some type will be realized if the stock closes between the two break-even points. If the stock is between the exercise price and the break-even point, some loss will be realized, but will probably not be a total loss.

The use of the combination should be approached with some additional caution since the distance to break-even from the current stock price will require a greater move. If the investor believes that a very great move will take place, the combination may prove to be as beneficial as purchasing the straddle. It is very unlikely that the combination will prove to be a better investment selection than that of the straddle. This assumes that the investor has *no bias* as to the move of the underlying stock. Should the investor have a bias to the move of the stock, the purchase of a combination with an exercise price at-the-money on the contract which favors that bias should be selected. The combination, in that instance, states that the investor believes that a major move will occur in the underlying stock and that the investor believes the move will probably go in one direction. This conviction, however, is not 100 percent.

The combination, as will be evident soon, can still provide for a great opportunity. Some of these opportunities may involve the use of other option contracts as well as the purchase or sale of the underlying stock. While these investments will not be explored in this chapter, understanding the use of straddles and combinations will provide the ground work for those strategies.

Illustrating the combination is best accomplished when it is compared to the straddle. For that reason, the example of the combination will use the same stock situation that was used in the purchase of the straddle.

Suggested guidelines for purchasing a combination are similar to that of purchasing the straddle. The main difference is the that the option contracts used should have a minimum of 80 days till expiration. This will allow for a greater opportunity than that of using the straddle. Break-even points may be farther away than the 5 percent used in the purchase of the straddle. Caution should be used when selecting the option contracts.

Since the direction of the movement of the underlying stock can only be one way at one time, a gain to only one contract (put or call) can be intrinsically realized. However, if the movement in the underlying stock raises the volatility level sharply, the relative time value of both contracts might rise. This is especially true in companies involved in mergers or takeovers. As the volatility rises, both option contracts, providing there is sufficient time, might realize a small time premium gain. While the price of the contract might drop due to the movement of the stock away from the exercise price, the time value might increase. The greater the volatility of the underlying stock the greater the probability that the stock may reverse direction and retrace a portion if not all of the movement. If the volatility should rise rapidly, the investor who purchased either a straddle or combination might realize an unexpected time premium gain. While this gain might not realize an overall profit, the investor should contemplate selling the contract (opposite to the movement in the stock) and adding the proceeds to the gain realized through the use of the entire strategy when the profitable option is sold.

The investor should consider selling a portion of the winning contract. Just as quickly as profits are made, there is a chance to lose those profits and realize losses. The investor should remove all original capital from the investment and consider the purchase of another contract to replace the contracts sold or to purchase an opposite contract (put versus call) in case the stock has a sudden reversal. Before any purchase is made, the investor should remove all original capital so that a loss can not be realized. By following this methodology, the investor can "ride for free" or use "other peoples money" to

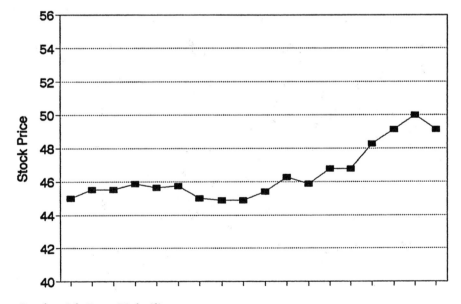

FIGURE 8-3.   Stock with Low Volatility.

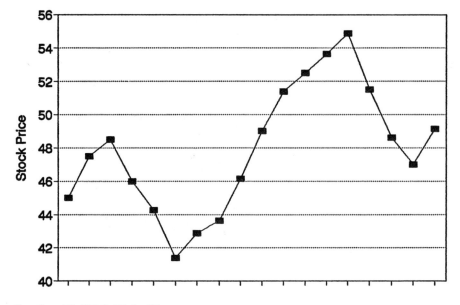

FIGURE 8-4.   Stock with High Volatility.

maintain a position in that stock. Special attention should be paid to Chapter 23, Maintaining Option Positions.

Volatility is not a measure of how much a stock moves up or down but a measure of relative price changes during a period of time. The volatility of a stock can be one level one day and another level for the next day. Most professional investors and traders evaluate the volatility of a stock over a period of time. If the price of stock XYZ moves from 15 to 20 and from 20 to 15, back and forth each day for a week, it would have a higher volatility than stock QRS which rose from 15 to 25 steadily over the period of a week. While QRS might have a larger gain during that period, the volatility of the stock would not be as great since the movement of the stock would not be as violent, for example, see Figures 8-3 and 8-4. As can be seen in the exhibits, during the period from Friday to Friday, the underlying stock of XYZ gained 5 points while the actual movement from day-to-day during that same period showed that the stock moved 25 points during the week. The stock of QRS rose steadily for a seven-point gain with a total seven-point movement. While QRS had a stronger overall showing during the period, XYZ showed a greater volatility.

Writing Straddles

Just as the volatility rises in a stock it also declines. A stock which may have been very active for a period of several weeks may suddenly become tired and have little movement for a period of time. Even the most volatile stocks tend to slow down and rest every once and a while. The reasons for a decline in the volatility of a stock can be from a story dying out on the stock to investors unsure of a direction and unwilling to commit capital. The decline of volatility can also provide the option investor with opportunity for profit.

The movement of a stock rises and falls based on expectations as well as other factors. If investors have few expectations for a stock, its earning potential or any other factor, the movement of the stock will be less frequent and less violent. As the movement for the stock slows down, the time value of the option will also diminish. As the price movement begins to show less activity and the curves on the graph of the stock begin to flatten, the time value of the puts and calls of that stock will also decline. As the time value declines for these options, the opportunity to profit through the writing of straddles and combinations becomes greater.

Before reviewing the next two strategies, it is important to note that writing straddles and combinations is not without its risks. Should the volatility of the underlying stock begin to rise once again, the greater the chance that the investor might lose money. Just as in writing naked calls and naked puts, the potential risk to the writer of these options is unlimited. Caution is strongly suggested.

At the start of this chapter, we reviewed the purchase of a straddle. The purchase of the same amount of puts and calls on the same stock using the same expiration month and the same exercise price for a total debit gave us a straddle. Selling a straddle utilizes the same fundamentals with the exception that instead of purchasing the options for a debit, the writer of a straddle sells or writes the options for a credit. Since the investor is writing naked options, margin will be required of the investor. The margin requirement for a naked option position must be met for only one of the two contracts used. The choice of which contract the margin will be calculated on is based on which contract has a greater margin requirement. Only one margin is required because both the put and call have the same exercise price: only one position can be in-the-money at a time. It is usually the option which is in-the-money on which the margin will be based. Should the position which is in-the-money be exercised against the investor, then the margin would be required on the other option contract, since the position would still be naked.

The goal of the writer of an option straddle is for the stock to remain as close to the exercise price as possible until expiration, without either position being prematurely exercised against it. If the underlying stock were to close right on the exercise price at expiration without a premature assignment, the investor would realize the maximum return of the credit which the straddle was written for. Since both option contracts would expire worthless, the investor would not be forced into repurchasing either contract. The probability of a stock closing exactly on the exercise price, however, is slim and the investor should take special note.

There are two break-even points for the investor writing a straddle. These points are calculated by adding and subtracting the credit received for the straddle to the exercise price. If the straddle were written using an exercise price of 60 for a credit of 10 points, then the break-even points for the straddle would put the stock at 50 or 70. If the stock closes between the two break-even points at expiration, then a profit would be realized by the investor. The closer the stock is to the exercise price, the greater the profit to the straddle writer.

If the stock rises above the upper break-even price or falls below the lower break-even price, the investor would realize a loss. Should the stock violate these levels as expiration nears, the investor should consider the repurchase of the option contract which is in the money. The contract which is out-of-the-money may not be repurchased, if the investor so wishes, but the position should be carefully monitored should the stock take a sudden turn.

The writing of a straddle should be limited to no more than 90 days. Many option professionals choose to limit these positions to a maximum of 60 days until expiration. It is important to remember that the longer the position is to be held, the greater the risk to the investor. It is also important to remember that the greatest decline of the time premium occurs during the final month of the life of the option contract. Should the investor wish to, the strategy may be repeated after the expiration of the current position(s).

Investors who write straddles should carefully monitor the movement of the underlying stock price as well as the value of the puts and calls. During the holding period, an opportunity may arise in which the investor may wish to repurchase one if not both of the written contracts. In addition, if the stock is trading at the exercise price to expiration, the repurchase of the straddle may allow the investor to realize a gain and relieve the account of the margin requirement. By doing so, the investor may elect to commence in another investment with that capital.

The writing of straddles can bring in a substantial amount of additional capital to the investor's account, especially if the option contracts are rich with premium. However, the writing of a straddle may subject the investor to a higher degree of risk than is necessary. As an alternative to writing the straddle, the investor may choose to write an out-of-the-money combination. The use of the combination lowers the capital reward potential but also lowers the potential for a loss.

The writing of an out-of-the-money combination requires that the investor select a call with an exercise price above the current stock price and a put with an exercise price below the current stock price. The margin requirement for writing an out-of-the-money combination is the same as the writing of a straddle. Once again, it is only possible for the call or the put to be in-the-money at one time and therefore, only the margin for one of these positions is required, the higher one. While it is possible for only one of the contracts to be in-the-money, it is possible for both contracts to be out-of-the-money, which is the way that it should be when the strategy is initiated. If the investor is biased to the direction which the stock will move, the strategy should reflect that bias. For example, if the investor feels that the stock might rise in price, a call with a higher exercise price should be used. If the investor feels that the stock may decline in price, the investor should attempt to utilize a put with an exercise price which is further away from the price of the stock than the call is.

Writing Combinations

There are also two break-even points for writing out-of-the-money combinations. The first break-even point (the higher break-even point) is the credit received for writing the combination plus the call exercise price. The lower break-even point is the put exercise price minus the credit received for writing the combination. The maximum profit for writing the out-of-the-money combination is the credit received. The investor will realize the maximum profit if the price of the underlying stock remains between the two exercise prices until expiration.

If the price of the stock rises above the call exercise price or drops below the put exercise price, a profit may still be realized providing that the stock has violated the break-even point.

It is important to realize that just as in writing the straddle, writing of the out-of-the-money combination has the potential for an unlimited loss. While the distance between the break-even points in the two strategies is different, the amount of the potential loss is still unlimited.

The investor who writes the out-of-the-money combination should limit the holding period till expiration to under 90 days. In addition, the distance to the break-even point should be no less than

TABLE 8-1. **Straddle Writing versus Combination Writing**

Stock = 92
Call with 95 Exercise Price = 2½
Call with 90 Exercise Price = 4
Put with 90 Exercise Price = 2½
Put with 85 Exercise Price = ¾

	Straddle	*Combination*
Position	−1 Call with 90 Exercise	−1 Call with 95 Exercise
	−1 Put with 90 Exercise	−1 Put with 85 Exercise
Credit	6½	3¼
Stock at Expiration	*Profits and Losses*	
80	<3½>	<2¾>
85	1½	3¼
90	6½	3¼
95	1½	3¼
100	<3½>	<2¾>
110	<13⅔>	<12¾>
Max Profit	6½	3¼
Max Loss	Unlimited	Unlimited
Down Break-Even Point	82½	81¾
Up Break-Even Point	96½	98¼

10%. If the distance to either break-even point is less than 10%, the writing of the straddle may prove to provide greater opportunity for profit. As with writing any naked option position, the investor should take special care to monitor the price of the stock as well as the price of the option contracts.

The investor should also pay special attention that when writing any naked option position, there is an unlimited dollar risk. The writing of out-of-the-money combinations and/or straddles should not be used on stocks which are the subject of take-over rumors or other stories which might cause a sharp move in the price of the underlying stock and raise the volatility level.

The writing of straddles or combinations can allow the investor to realize a profit when the volatility of the underlying stock declines. While both strategies have advantages as well as risks, choosing between the two can be difficult. Let's take an overall look at the differences between the two and compare them. While this comparison is just a general overview, it should provide a good illustration. Each strategy should be evaluated on its own merits and each should be evaluated against the stock which the investor is interested in using. Table 8-1 compares the use of writing straddles against the writing of combinations. Figures 8-5 and 8-6 graphically depict the use of the short combination and the short straddle.

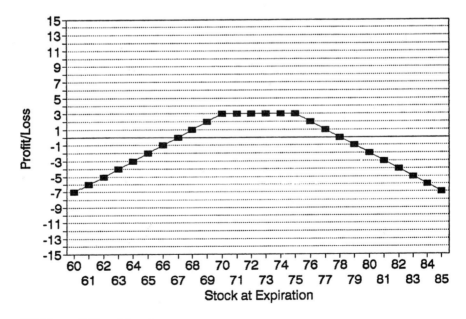

FIGURE 8-5. Writing of Combination.

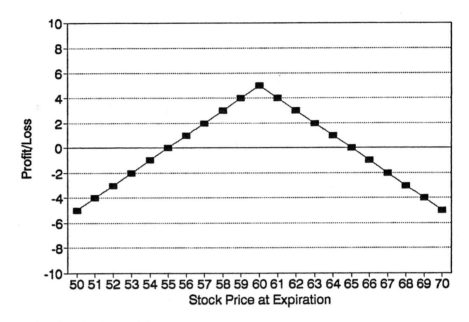

FIGURE 8-6. Sale of Naked Straddle.

Combinations, Straddles and Stocks

Thus far, we have evaluated the writing of straddles and combinations on the basis of profit, loss, and break-even. The investor utilizing these strategies will face a different possibilities. The investor may find that in writing combinations or straddles that the stock may be called or put before or at expiration. While most strategists compute strategies based on where the stock might be at expiration, there the possibility that the short option might be prematurely assigned. Premature assignment can mean that the writer of the option contract would be obligated to fulfill the terms of the contract prior to expiration day. The writer of any option contract should be aware that this risk does exist. It should also be remembered that if the stock is ex-dividend prior to expiration, the probability of a short call being exercised against the writer is higher. The risk of being prematurely called is even greater should the time premium of the option be equal to or less than the amount of the dividend. If the call is exercised on the evening just before the ex-dividend date, the call writer will be required to deliver the stock and might be short the stock on ex-dividend date. If the investor is short the underlying stock, then the amount of the dividend would also be charged against the position, realizing in a capital payment before the stock position is closed.

Evaluating the strategy at expiration, if the stock is called away, then a short stock position would be established at the exercise price. The short price of the position should be adjusted by the credit received for writing the combination or straddle. For example, if a straddle was written with an exercise price of 75 for a credit of 8, then the actual price of selling the stock short at expiration would be 83 (75 + 8). If the stock is below the adjusted price, in this case 83, then the stock may be repurchased for a gain. The writer of the straddle or combination may not be at any financial risk should the stock be called at expiration or even prematurely. If the stock is called prior to expiration, even if a dividend is to be paid, the investor might still realize a gain, should the premium received exceed the dividend and the stock remains below the adjusted sale price.

If the stock drops in price and falls below the put exercise price, then the cost of owning the underlying stock, once it is put to the investor, would be the exercise price of the put less the premium. Using this example, if the stock is purchased at the exercise price of 75, then the cost of owning the stock position would be 67 (75 − 8). If the stock is above the adjusted purchase price of 67, then the investor might realize a gain.

The adjusted stock price(s) should correspond to the break-even points calculated earlier in the chapter. The investor should be cautious not to make the mistake of miscalculating the cost of the stock position. Since the break-even points and the adjusted stock prices are the same, it is easy to misinterpret the cost of the stock position, as this may seem too simple.

If the investor is prematurely assigned on one side of either the combination or straddle, the position(s) and expectation of the underlying stock should be re-evaluated before taking any action on the stock or opposing option position. The investor may still find that the positions being held are favorable to the environment which the stock, market or options might be in. For instance, if the investor who wrote an out-of-the-money combination is prematurely put the stock at the exercise price, then the position which would be held after the purchase of the stock would be a covered write. If the stock moves above the call exercise price, the investor would realize a profit, which might be sizable once all costs are taken into account.

The investor, however, should be willing to own the underlying stock, even if the stock does not rise above the call exercise price. In other words, the investor should have some type of bullish disposition on the underlying stock.

If the stock should be prematurely called away at the higher exercise price, the investor would have a position which would be short the stock and short a put at a lower exercise price. If the stock drops below the put exercise price at expiration, the investor would repurchase the stock at that exercise price. Taking into account all costs, the position might turn out to be extremely profitable. However, the investor should have a bearish opinion on the underlying stock. The investor should also be wary of any upcoming dividend, stock split or distribution which could reduce any profit or cause a sudden movement in the price of the underlying stock.

It is highly recommended that such actions be considered very carefully and with great prudence. In addition, the investor should pay special attention to stocks which are the subject of takeover rumors, stories or other factors which could cause unanticipated movement in the price of the underlying stock and/or raise the level of volatility. Writing combinations or straddles requires a great amount of observation during the holding period and a great amount of restraint and control. In addition, the investor who utilizes such strategies should be able and qualified to handle the risk(s) involved with writing naked option positions.

The purchase and writing of combinations and straddles may be used in conjunction with the underlying stock. Like the covered call write in Chapter 3, the purchase of stock and the writing of a combination or straddle can provide the investor with many unusual and highly profitable situations. It should be noted that any time the stock is purchased by the investor, there is an underlying belief that the price of the stock will rise. Therefore, if the investor believes that the price of the stock is going to decline, those strategies should *not* be used.

Assume that an investor is bullish on the stock of PQR Corporation, a stock which is trading at $42 per share. The investor feels that the stock is going to rise but that the volatility in the stock will decline and therefore does not believe that the upside movement will be very great. The investor decides that instead of purchasing 1000 shares of that stock that only 500 shares will suit his investment needs at this point. The investor would also be willing to purchase more of the underlying stock at a lower price. He decides to purchase

500 share of PQR and write an out-of-the-money combination for three months using a call exercise price of 45 and a put exercise price of 40. For writing this combination, the investor receives a premium of five points.

If the price of PQR rises above 45, the investor effectively sells the stock for 50 (45 exercise price + 5 point premium). This allows the investor to enjoy a profit of 19 percent on a stock movement of only 7 percent, realizing a dollar return of $4000 instead of $1500. The investor, effectively, would not participate in any movement of the stock above 50.

The use of combinations and straddles is not limited to writing. Purchasing combinations or straddles can increase the potential for great profits as well as limit the risk to the investor. The use of puts, calls and the underlying stock can allow the investor to position the investment allowing for several scenarios. Using this methodology can also set the scene for action to be taken further down the line.

As investor who is bullish on ZYX Corp. may decide to purchase 1000 shares of the company for $63 per share. The cost to the investor is $63,000. Should the price of the stock fall dramatically, the entire $63,000 investment would be at risk. In the same thought, should the stock unexpectedly rise, the investor would realize a profit.

Instead of purchasing 1000 shares of ZYX, the investor may select to purchase 500 shares and either a combination or a straddle. For example, let us assume the investor purchases a put with an exercise price of 60 expiring in three months for 2½ and a call with the same expiration date and an exercise price of 65 for 3½ points. The total cost to the investor would be $69 per share or $34,500 for the total position (500 shares, 5 puts and 5 calls).

While the adjusted cost per share might seem high, let us examine the potential. As you are aware, the purchase of the put helps to protect the investor in case of a downturn in the price of the stock. If the stock falls below 60, the investor has the option to sell the underlying stock by exercising the long put. If the investor decides to hold the stock position, the put may be sold and the proceeds of the sale be put toward the value of the overall position. If the stock falls below 55, the maximum loss that the investor could realize, should the put be exercised, would be nine points (adjusted price of 69 − put exercise price of 60). Even if the stock fell to zero, the maximum loss would be nine points.

However, let us assume that the investor has a pleasant surprise and the stock of ZYX climbs to $90 per share. The investor could elect to purchase an additional 500 share of the stock through the exercise of the long call. Additional capital of $32,500 (500 shares × the call exercise price of 65) would be required. The investor may choose to sell the call in the open market realizing a gain. The gain may be applied toward the value of the rest of the position and should the original 500 shares be sold, a profit of $10,500 might be realized on the total position. This pleasant surprise could yield to the investor a return of 30.4 percent (before dividends and commissions are figured). The combination allowed the investor to take advantage of owning an additional 500 shares of stock, if it would be to the advantage of the investor in the future. At the same time, the investor purchased some security in knowing that if the value of the stock eroded quickly, the stock could be sold at a predetermined price.

The examples used here were slightly exaggerated. The investor should try to pay as little as possible for the purchase of the combination or straddle and limit the risk of owning the position to not more than a 10 percent loss in total. If the downside break-even point is more than 10 percent, including the purchase of the calls, then the strategy should be re-examined to assure the needs of the investor. Using a strategy such as this which would expose the investor to a great risk on capital would be self-defeating.

The purchase of a combination or straddle can be used in the same manner for an investor who is selling the underlying stock short. Using the same example as the one above, assume that the investor sold the underlying stock of ZYX short at 63 and purchased the out-of-the-money combination, the investor would have a break-even point of $57 per share (stock price of 63 − the debit of 6 for the combination). In this case the investor would need the stock to drop below 57 before expiration. If the investor is correct, then a profit would be realized in both the short stock position and the put position. If the stock dropped to 50, the investor may select to exercise the put contract and sell an additional 500 shares of ZYX at 60. If so, the average price of the short sale shares would be 68½ (put exercise price of 60 + adjusted short price of 57 divided by 2). The investor could realize a profit of a 8½ per share of $8,500 for the entire position.

Assuming now that the stock rises instead of falls and the shares climb to 80 per share, the investor would be able either to exercise the call option and repurchase the shares at 65 or to sell the long call for a profit to be applied against the loss in the underlying stock. If the investor decided to repurchase the shares sold with the exercise of the call, then the stock position would be flat and the investor would still hold the put option contract. If so, the investor would realize a loss of eight points per share or $4,000 for the 500 shares, assuming that the put contract expires at expiration. If the stock suddenly turns around and drops back below 60, the investor may be able to offset some of the loss by selling the long put contract.

If the investor elects to do so, the long call might be sold allowing the investor to apply the proceeds of the sale toward the loss in the short sale position. As can be seen, there are many different methods for handling such a situation when it comes to taking losses or protecting the investment which one has made.

The investor should keep in mind that all situations which require a choice of exercising a long option or selling the contract in the open market require some analyzing and thought before such action is taken. The investor should consider if the stock is going ex-dividend, the amount of the dividend as well as the value of the option versus the intrinsic value. An option with a high time premium should be sold instead of exercised, allowing the investor to collect the additional premium. In addition, the capital requirement in taking an additional stock position might exceed the capital the investor has.

The use of combinations and straddles requires the investor to carefully evaluate the movement of the stock, the option prices and the relative movement of those prices. In addition, special attention should be paid to the volatility and the expansion or contraction of such volatility. The volatility will play a great part of the value of the option contracts in the future and purchasing option contracts on stocks with decreasing volatility or writing contracts on stocks with expanding volatility might limit or further risk the investment. See Chapter 20 for further information on options pricing and volatility.

This chapter did not include the purchase or writing of in-the-money combinations; Chapter 9 will focus on the use of these strategies, since they open the investor to additional risk and require additional margin for contracts written.

Worksheets 8-1 through 8-4 will enable you to analyze further the strategies discussed in this chapter. The reader should pay special attention to the break-even points when using such strategies and the distance to the break-even points. The use of option strategies should not inhibit the investor or prevent the achievement of profit, but limit risk in the investment. While limiting risk might interfere some what with the goals of the investor, the investor should be able to obtain a median. If the investor is not able to reach a median which is satisfactory, then the use of the strategy may not be appropriate to the needs of the investor or the investment itself. Remember, not all strategies are meant for all investors and not all strategies are meant to work in every investment decision.

Summary

1. The purchase of combinations and straddles allows the investor the opportunity to profit through a large movement in the underlying stock without knowing in which direction the stock will move.

2. Purchasing combinations and straddles also allows the user to take advantage of expanding volatility.

3. Writing straddles and combinations can be very profitable if the stock remains in a narrow trading range.

4. The writing of option combinations is an effective way of taking advantage of declining stock volatility.

5. Combinations and straddles can be combined with the purchase or sale of the underlying stock, creating different and more effective strategies.

WORKSHEET 8-1:

Straddle Purchase

STOCK			SHARES	PRICE	—52 WEEK—		RATING	PIE RATIO	YIELD
					HIGH	LOW			
OPTION CONTRACT			CONTRACTS	PREMIUM +	EXPIRATION DATE		DAYS TILL EXP.		
OPTION CONTRACT			CONTRACTS	PREMIUM +	EXPIRATION DATE		DAYS TILL EXP.		
QUART DIVID	DIVIDS TO EXP	TOTAL DIVID COLLECT		DEBIT	REG. T RATE		MARGIN INT RATE		
INTEREST CHARGES:		INT RATE ×	DAYS ÷365 ×	DEBIT BAL	$ =		TODAY'S DATE		

REQUIRED CAPITAL

Purchase Price of Call		
Purchase Price of Put.	+	
Net Debit.	=	
Equiv. Amount of Shares	×	
Option Cost.	=	
Commission for Call	+	
Commission for Put.	+	
Required Capital.	=	

UPPER BREAK-EVEN POINT

Required Capital.		
Equiv. Amount of Shares	÷	
Exercise Price	+	
Upper Break-Even Point	=	

LOWER BREAK-EVEN POINT

Required Capital.		
Equiv. Amount of Shares	÷	
Exercise Price	−	
Lower Break-Even Point	=	

Notes:
1. Maximum profit is unlimited.
2. Maximum loss is the required capital, which is realized if the stock is at the exercise price at expiration.

131

WORKSHEET 8-2:

Out-of-the-Money Combination Purchase

STOCK			SHARES	PRICE	—52 WEEK—		RATING	PIE RATIO	YIELD
					HIGH	LOW			
OPTION CONTRACT			CONTRACTS	PREMIUM +	EXPIRATION DATE		DAYS TILL EXP.		
OPTION CONTRACT			CONTRACTS	PREMIUM +	EXPIRATION DATE		DAYS TILL EXP.		
QUART DIVID	DIVIDS TO EXP	TOTAL DIVID COLLECT		DEBIT	REG. T RATE		MARGIN INT RATE		
INTEREST CHARGES:		INT RATE ×	DAYS ÷ 365 ×	DEBIT BAL. =	$		TODAY'S DATE		

REQUIRED CAPITAL

Call Purchase Price..............................		
Put Purchase Price	+	
Net Debit.......................................	=	
Equiv. Amount of Shares	×	
Option Cost.....................................	=	
Call Commission	+	
Put Commission	+	
Required Capital................................	=	

UPPER BREAK-EVEN POINT

Required Capital................................		
Equiv. Amount of Shares	÷	
Call Exercise Price	+	
Upper Break-Even Point	=	

LOWER BREAK-EVEN POINT

Required Capital................................		
Equiv. Amount of Shares	÷	
Put Exercise Price..............................	−	
Lower Break-Even Point	=	

Notes:
1. Maximum profit is unlimited.
2. Maximum loss is the required capital and is realized if the stock is between the two exercise prices at expiration.

WORKSHEET 8-3:

Out-of-the-Money Combination Writing

STOCK		SHARES	PRICE	—52 WEEK—		RATING	PIE RATIO	YIELD
				HIGH	LOW			
OPTION CONTRACT		CONTRACTS	PREMIUM +	EXPIRATION DATE		DAYS TILL EXP.		
OPTION CONTRACT		CONTRACTS	PREMIUM +	EXPIRATION DATE		DAYS TILL EXP.		
QUART DIVID	DIVIDS TO EXP	TOTAL DIVID COLLECT	DEBIT	REG. T RATE		MARGIN INT RATE		
INTEREST CHARGES:		INT RATE DAYS × ÷365 ×	DEBIT BAL. =	$		TODAY'S DATE		

REQUIRED CAPITAL—Use Higher Value of Put or Call Option Contract

Stock Price. . . . .

Option Margin Requirement . . . . ×

Per Option Margin Requirement. . . . . =

Equivalent Amount of Shares. . . . . ×

Commission on Call Option . . . . +

Commission on Put Option . . . . +

Required Capital. . . . . =

MAXIMUM PROFIT

Exercise Price . . . .

Call Premium . . . .

Put Premium . . . . +

Equivalent Amount of Shares. . . . . ×

Total Premium . . . . =

Commission Paid for Writing Calls . . . . −

Commission Paid for Writing Puts . . . . −

Maximum Profit. . . . . =

Required Capital. . . . . ÷

Return. . . . . =

*Ann Return (Return × 365 ÷ Days) . . . . =

BREAK-EVEN POINTS

Total Premium . . . .

Commissions Paid for Writing Calls. . . . . −

Commissions Paid for Writing Puts . . . . −

Realized Premiums. . . . . =

Equivalent Amount of Shares. . . . . ÷

Realized Premiums per Share. . . . . =

Exercise Price of Call. . . . .

Realized Premiums per Share. . . . . +

**Upper Break-Even Point. . . . . =

Exercise Price of Put . . . .

Realized Premiums per Share. . . . . −

**Lower Break-Even Point. . . . . =

*Annualized returns may only be used if holding is over 60 days.
**Break-even points do *not* include commissions for close out.
Note: Maximum risk is unlimited.

WORKSHEET 8-4:

Straddle Writing

STOCK			SHARES	PRICE	—52 WEEK—		RATING	PIE RATIO	YIELD
					HIGH	LOW			
OPTION CONTRACT			CONTRACTS	PREMIUM +	EXPIRATION DATE		DAYS TILL EXP.		
OPTION CONTRACT			CONTRACTS	PREMIUM +	EXPIRATION DATE		DAYS TILL EXP.		
QUART DIVID	DIVIDS TO EXP	TOTAL DIVID COLLECT	DEBIT		REG. T RATE		MARGIN INT RATE		
INTEREST CHARGES:		INT RATE ×	DAYS ÷ 365 ×	DEBIT BAL ×	$		TODAY'S DATE		

REQUIRED CAPITAL

Stock Price....................................		
Option Margin Requirement	×	
Per Option Margin Requirement.................	=	
Equivalent Amount of Shares...................	×	
Commission on Call Option	+	
Commission on Put Option	+	
Required Capital.................................	=	

MAXIMUM PROFIT

Exercise Price		
Call Premium		
Put Premium	+	
Equivalent Amount of Shares...................	×	
Total Premium	=	
Commission Paid for Writing Calls	−	
Commission Paid for Writing Puts...............	−	
Maximum Profit..............................	=	
Required Capital.................................	÷	
Return.......................................	=	
*Ann Return (Return × 365 ÷ Days)	=	

BREAK-EVEN POINTS

Total Premium		
Commissions Paid for Writing Calls..............	−	
Commissions Paid for Writing Puts	−	
Realized Premiums.............................	=	
Equivalent Amount of Shares...................	÷	
Realized Premiums per Share...................	=	
Exercise Price		
Realized Premiums per Share...................	+	
**Upper Break-Even Point........................	=	
Exercise Price		
Realized Premiums per Share...................	−	
**Lower Break-Even Point........................	=	

*Annualized returns may only be used if holding is over 60 days.
**Break-even points do *not* include commissions for close out.
Note: Maximum risk is unlimited.

9

Combinations:
In-the-Money

This chapter concentrates on the use of in-the-money combinations. While many traders and investors feel that one combination is not different from another, there is a large difference. Conservative investors will *not* find these strategies of use when initiating a position, but may find similar positions beneficial when the portfolio is adjusted in the future.

Limited Risk for Purchasers

The purchase of an in-the-money combination will provide the investor with a profit, as long as the price of the underlying stock makes a substantial move. Since both the purchase of the put and the call will require a large capital investment, the break-even points might be further in distance from the current stock price than that of purchasing an out-of-the-money combination. Calculating the break-even points is identical to the purchase of the out-of-the-money combination. The upper break-even point is the exercise price of the call plus the total debit. The lower break-even point is the exercise price of the put minus the total debit. The range between the upper and lower break-even points will represent a loss at expiration.

Technically, the potential loss to the investor is the total debit or 100% of the investment. Practically, there should never be a total loss since one of the option contracts should always be in-the-money. This means that the exercise price of the call must be lower than the exercise price of the stock. The exercise price of either the call or the put will be in-the-money. If the price of the stock is between the two exercise prices at expiration, then both the put and call would be in-the-money. Although both the put and call might be in-the-money, the investor can still lose money, but the loss should not be total. The total value of the put and call at expiration should be equivalent to the distance between the two exercise prices. For example, if a call with a exercise price of 30 is purchased and a put with an exercise price of 40 is purchased, then the total value of the put and call at expiration, assuming the stock is between 30 and 40, will be 10 points.

Assume that the stock of EFG is trading at $75 per share. The two-month call with an exercise price of 70 is trading at 7 and the two-month put with an exercise price of 80 is trading at 6½. Assuming that an investor purchased this combination, let us evaluate the potential outcomes for such a strategy.

First, it is important to calculate the break-even points. The upper break-even point puts the stock at $83.50 per share, and the lower break-even point puts the stock at $66.50. This means that the stock must move up or down 8½ points to reach break-even at expiration. This means that the underlying stock must move up or down 11.33% just to break-even. This example makes things easy since the price of the underlying stock is half way between the exercise price of the put and call. In most cases, the arithmetic will not be this easy.

If the stock is at $75 per share at expiration, which is unchanged, then the put and the call would be intrinsically worth five points each or 10 points for the combination. This will result in a loss of 3½ points or $350 per combination almost 26 percent of the investment (excluding commissions). No matter what price the stock is at, as long as it is between 70 (the exercise price of the call) and 80 (the exercise price of the put), the combination would be worth 10 points or a loss or 3½ per combination.

If the investor is fortunate and the price of the underlying stock moves to 90, the value of the combination at expiration would be 20 points (call = 20, put = 0). The investor who purchased this in-the-money combination would realize a gain of 6½ points or $650 per combination or a gain of 48 percent. For this 48 percent gain, the investor required the stock to move 20 percent. Many option professionals would not consider this to be a proper use of leverage, since the strategy requires a substantial move in the stock. Remember, the

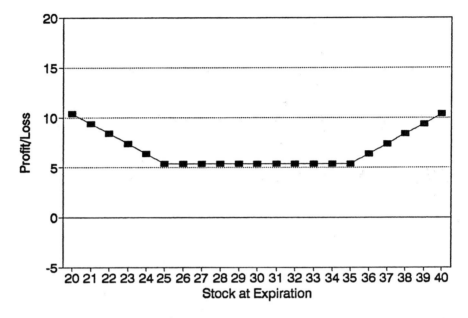

FIGURE 9-1.   Long in-the-Money Combination.

maximum risk to this investor would be 3½ points since the lowest value the combination can be worth is 10 points.

Figure 9-1 depicts the profit and loss potentials at expiration for the purchase of the in-the-money combination. As indicated, a significant movement in the price of the underlying stock will probably be required in order to profit from the use of this strategy. Notice the area in the figure which depicts the potential for loss as compared to the area of the graph which depicts the potential for profit. The area for potential profit is much greater and is actually unlimited, which cannot be accurately shown on a graph. However, evaluate the distance from the price of the stock to the break-even points. The potential for profit is conceivably high as well as the potential dollar amount of that profit. While this is all true, it must be remembered that a fairly large move must be made to reach the break-even point. This move may make the strategy unappealing. Worksheet 9-1 (found at the end of the chapter) has been provided to aid in calculating the benefits of purchasing an in-the-money combination.

Purchasing an in-the-money combination can be very rewarding, if utilized in the correct situation. Assume that an investor purchased an in-the-money combination on a stock which has the subject of a buy out or takeover. If the price of the underlying stock had a dramatic move during the holiday period, the investor could realize a substantial return. It is important to realize that the cost of initiating such a strategy would be high, since premiums on takeover stocks are historically high. However, if the price of the stock rose dramatically, the investor might be able to close out the long call position, realizing a profit over the entire strategy. If the investor chose to do so, the put could be held, especially since the value of the put would have dropped dramatically, and if the deal fell through and the price of the stock dropped back down before expiration, the investor could realize another profit on the put. This situation is rare, but it has happened before, allowing an investor a two-way profit.

Writing in-the-Money Combinations

The writing of in-the-money combination is very different from writing out-of-the-money combinations. The margin requirements for writing in-the-money combinations is much higher than the other strategies examined thus far. The reason for the higher requirements is that the put and the call are treated as two separate positions and the margin requirement is applied to each and then added together. The reason behind this is that both positions may be in-the-money at the same time, requiring the writer to perform both obligations at the same time.

The risk to writing in-the-money combinations is unlimited since the price of the stock could rise to infinity as well as drop to zero. However, regardless of what price the stock moves to, the investor must be prepared to take on the obligation of at least one side of the strategy. The lowest that the combination will be valued at will be the difference between the two exercise prices. Should the stock remain between the two exercise prices, the value of the put and call added together will be the difference. The investor must be ready to repurchase the combination for this value, assuming that the option(s) are not prematurely assigned, requiring the investor to fulfill the obligation of the contract.

The maximum profit in writing an in-the-money combination is the credit received for writing the combination less the difference between the two exercise prices. The maximum profit will be realized if the stock is between the two exercise prices. A profit will be realized as long as the stock remains between the upper break-even point and the lower break-even point. The break-even points are calculated by adding the premium received to the exercise price of the call and subtracting the premium received from the exercise price of the put. As long as the stock remains between the two break-even points, some profit should be realized.

Assume that the stock of QQQ is trading at $115 per share and that a one month call with an exercise price of 110 has a premium of 11½ and that a one-month put with an exercise price of 120 has a premium of 10¼ points. If this combination was written, the investor would receive a credit of 21¾ points. The margin required (according to the industry standard as of the writing of this book) would be the following:

Margin Required for Call = Stock Price × .20 + Call Premium
Margin Required for Put = Stock Price × .20 + Put Premium
Total Margin Required = Margin Required for Call + Margin Required for Put

There is no subtraction done for amount out-of-the-money since both the put and the call are in-the-money. In addition, these requirements are not subject to be checked for a minimum 10% requirement since these requirements will be higher. Therefore, the margin requirement for writing this in-the-money combination will be 67.75 per share or $6775 per combination. The investor would be required to put up $4600 in additional capital since $2175 would be received for writing the combination. The investor should realize that the option positions will be "marked to the market" each day and that the margin requirement will change as the price of the underlying stock and the options change.

The maximum profit in writing this in-the-money combination will be realized if the stock remains between 110 and 120 until expiration. If the stock is between the two exercise prices, the maximum profit would be 11¾ points per combination (21¾ − 10) or $1175 per combination. This would result in a 25.5 percent gain during the holding period (excluding commissions, dividends if prematurely assigned, and other transaction costs). The break-even points in writing this in-the-money combination would be 131¾ and 98¼ or a distance of almost 14% from the current stock price. The maximum loss for writing this combination is unlimited. Worksheet 9-2 (found at the end of the chapter) has been provided to aid in calculating the writing of an in-the-money combination.

As can be seen, the writing of an in-the-money combination can be profitable, if the stock remains in a narrow trading range, especially between the two exercise prices. If the stock has a sudden break-out or downturn, the investor could be subject to a great loss.

The writing of in-the-money combinations should be utilized for stocks on which the investor believes that the volatility will drop or that the stock will remain inside the trading range. Writing combinations requiring a holding period of greater than two months is not advised as it subjects the investor to unforeseen risks in both the stock and the market in general. Usually, the distance from the current price of the stock to the break-even points should be at least 20 percent.

The investor should not expect to earn the maximum profit, even if the stock remains between the two exercise prices. When attempting to repurchase the combination, the investor must be willing to pay a small amount above the intrinsic value. The amount above the intrinsic value should not be more than the cost of the commissions of purchasing and selling the stock upon assignment of the option contracts. However, if the investor intends to allow the assignment of the option contracts, the brokerage firm holding the account may require that the value of the purchase of the underlying security be paid for before the sale of the funds clear, subject to New York Stock Exchange and Securities and Exchange Commission margin and capital requirements.

It cannot be stressed enough that the writing of *any* combinations on stocks which are the subject of takeover rumors, stories or bids contain very high risks. Therefore, it is highly recommended that investors avoid the use of writing both in-the-money and out-of-the-money combinations as well as straddles in such cases.

If the value of the underlying stock approaches one of the break-even levels, the investor should consider the repurchase of the contract which is at risk. Should the stock become extremely volatile, the investor may wish to repurchase both the put and the call options as a means of protecting against a sharp turn around in the stock.

Summary

1. The purchase of in-the-money combinations has less risk to the total capital than the purchase of out-of-the-money combinations.

2. In-the-money combinations require more capital than out-of-the-money combinations, therefore requiring a greater move to reach the break-even point on a dollar basis.

3. Writing an in-the-money combination has limited profit potential and unlimited risk exposure.

4. Writing out-of-the-money combinations and straddles has less risk than in-the-money combinations.

WORKSHEET 9-1:

In-the-Money Combination Purchase

STOCK			SHARES	PRICE	—52 WEEK—		RATING	PIE RATIO	YIELD
					HIGH	LOW			
OPTION CONTRACT			CONTRACTS	PREMIUM +	EXPIRATION DATE		DAYS TILL EXP.		
OPTION CONTRACT			CONTRACTS	PREMIUM +	EXPIRATION DATE		DAYS TILL EXP.		
QUART DIVID	DIVIDS TO EXP	TOTAL DIVID COLLECT		DEBIT	REG. T RATE		MARGIN INT RATE		
INTEREST CHARGES:		INT RATE ×	DAYS ÷ 365 ×	DEBIT BAL. =	$		TODAY'S DATE		

REQUIRED CAPITAL

Call Purchase Price..............................		
Put Purchase Price	+	
Net Debit...	=	
Equiv. Amount of Shares	×	
Option Cost......................................	=	
Call Commission	+	
Put Commission	+	
Required Capital................................	=	

UPPER BREAK-EVEN POINT

Required Capital................................		
Equiv. Amount of Shares	÷	
Call Exercise Price	+	
Upper Break-Even Point	=	

LOWER BREAK-EVEN POINT

Required Capital................................		
Equiv. Amount of Shares	÷	
Put Exercise Price...............................	−	
Lower Break-Even Point.........................	=	

MAXIMUM RISK/LOSS

Required Capital................................		
Diff in Exercise Prices		
Equiv Amount of Shares.........................	×	
Value of In-the-Money Ex	=	
Risks (Req Cap − Value)	=	

Note: Maximum profit is unlimited.

WORKSHEET 9-2:

In-the-Money Combination Writing

STOCK			SHARES	PRICE	—52 WEEK—		RATING	PIE RATIO	YIELD
					HIGH	LOW			
OPTION CONTRACT			CONTRACTS	PREMIUM +	EXPIRATION DATE		DAYS TILL EXP.		
OPTION CONTRACT			CONTRACTS	PREMIUM +	EXPIRATION DATE		DAYS TILL EXP.		
QUART DIVID	DIVIDS TO EXP	TOTAL DIVID COLLECT		CREDIT	REG. T RATE		MARGIN INT RATE		
INTEREST CHARGES:		INT RATE ×	DAYS ÷ 365 ×	DEBIT BAL	$ =		TODAY'S DATE		

REQUIRED CAPITAL—Use Higher Value of Put or Call Option Contract

Stock Price...............................		
Option Margin Requirement	×	
Per Option Margin Requirement................	=	
Equivalent Amount of Shares..................	×	
Commission on Call Option	+	
Commission on Put Option	+	
Required Capital.................................	=	

MAXIMUM PROFIT

Exercise Price		
Call Premium		
Put Premium	+	
Difference Between Exercise Prices	−	
Equivalent Amount of Shares...................	×	
Total Premium	=	
Commission Paid for Writing Calls	−	
Commission Paid for Writing Puts	−	
Maximum Profit..............................	=	
Required Capital..............................	÷	
Return.......................................	=	
*Ann. Return (Return × 365 ÷ Days)............	=	

*Annualized returns may only be used if holding is over 60 days.
Note: Maximum profit is unlimited.

143

10
Ratio Spreads

The use of conventional option spreads can be magnified to greater use. Until this point, the option spreads illustrated in this book have focused on the use of one option contract versus another. Option professionals and investors realize that there are other spread techniques that enable the investor to profit and/or lower risk. The techniques shown in this chapter can be utilized in enhancing the results of different strategies while meeting some of the unique needs based on the expectation of the stock. The spreads covered here utilize the ideal of purchasing one option contract and writing another contract using different qualities.

What Is a Ratio Spread?

The purchasing of one quantity of option contracts and the writing of another quantity is known as **Ratio Spreading**. Ratio spreading is the purchase of one option contract and the sale of a multiple of contracts or vice versa. The ratios used in such spreads can be as simple as 1 to 2 or as complex as 7 to 10. It is important that the investor utilizing ratio spread techniques use caution in calculating the margin requirements as well as the potential profit, loss, and break-even point. When one position has a multiplier which is different from another, mathematical mistakes can easily take place.

Maximum Profit/Loss

The most simple ratio spread which this book will focus on will be the purchase of a 1-for-2 ratio spread. To illustrate this example, we will utilize a bull spread using calls. In such a transaction, the investor will purchase one call option with an exercise price which is lower than the contract to be written, and write two calls with a higher exercise price expiring in the same month. The investor should treat the investment in the following way for *margin reasons only*:

	Bull Spread Using Calls + 1 Lower Exercise − 1 Higher Exercise	+	Naked Call Position − 1 Higher Exercise
Total =	Pay Debit	+	Margin on Naked Call

The maximum profit on the purchase of any call spread when the contracts written have a greater quantity than those purchased will be with the stock at the higher exercise price. Since the calls written will expire worthless and the call(s) purchased will be at their highest value before putting the investor at risk of loss, the investor will always achieve maximum profit at the higher exercise price. Should the stock climb above the higher exercise price, the investor would start giving some of the profit back until all of the written premium is eroded. The point at which the written premium is completely eroded is the upper break-even point. On the 1-for-2 ratio spread, the break-even point is easily calculated by adding the maximum profit to the higher exercise price. Once the stock continues to climb above the upper break-even point, in this example, the investor would start to lose money. The potential loss in this strategy is unlimited, however, it may take a very great movement in the price of the underlying stock to reach that point. The lower break-even point is easily calculated by adding the total debit to the lower exercise price. If the stock remains above the lower break-even point and below the upper break-even point, the investor would realize a profit. If the stock falls below the lower break-even point, the most the investor could lose would be the total debit paid for the spread.

Assume that the stock of SPD is at $72. The calls expiring in three months with an exercise price of 70 are currently trading at 3½ points, and the calls with an exercise price of 75 expiring in the same month are trading at 1¼. The investor purchases one call with the lower exercise price and writes two calls with the higher exercise price for a total debit of one point (3½ − (2 × 1¼)). The maximum downside loss the investor could realize will be 1 point since that is the total debit. The lower break-even point will be at 71 (70 lower exercise price + 1 point total debit paid for spread). The maximum profit on this trade would occur if the stock were at 75 (the higher exercise price) at expiration. That profit would be four points (the difference between the higher exercise price of 75 and the break-even point of 71). The higher break-even point is 79 (the maximum profit potential plus the higher exercise price). Above 79 the investor would begin to realize a loss since the naked call which was written would be greater than the difference than the spread maximum. Therefore, the investor can realize a profit on this strategy as long as the stock remains between 71 (the lower break-even point) and 79 (the higher break-even point). Although more calls were written than purchased, the investor is clearly bullish and believes that the stock will rise to 75 before the calls expire.

The purchase of a similar ratio spread using puts is possible. The difference between two ratio spreads can be measured through the difference in debit/credit value as well as any difference in risk to the user. The investor purchases a put with a *higher* exercise price and writes two puts with a *lower* exercise price. The maximum profit will occur if the stock is at the lower exercise price since the puts which were written will expire worthless. The lower break-even point is the one to watch on this strategy since a break below that level could expose the investor to unlimited risk. The lower break-even point is the lower exercise price minus the maximum profit potential. The higher exercise price is the higher exercise price less the debit paid for the spread. Should the stock remain above this level, the maximum loss to the investor would be the debit paid for the spread.

Figures 10-1 illustrates the use of the 1-for-2 ratio spread. The profit region is the area between the stock at expiration values of 41 and 49. It is suggested that before using either of these strategies that the investor becomes very familiar with these illustrations as well as the worksheets provided at the end of the chapter (Worksheets 10-1 and 10-2).

Note: Should the cost of enacting this strategy be a credit instead of a debit, the credit amount should be treated as a negative debit.

The use of ratio spreads is not limited to the 1-for-2 ratio. Many investors find using a ratio or 1-for-3, 1-for-4, or even higher, allows for greater flexibility and management. The investor should be aware that the greater the ratio, the greater the potential for risk should the stock move more than expected. Such strategies require extreme caution and careful planning.

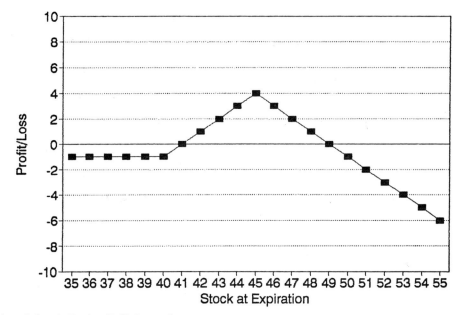

FIGURE 10-1.   1-for-2 Ratio Call Spread.

More Complicated Ratio Spreads

Option ratio spreads can be more complex than the 1-for-2 ratio (see Figure 10-1). Ratio spreads such as 2-for-3 or 4-for-5 are common investment techniques among more sophisticated option traders. The use of such ratio spreads allows the investor to take advantage of changes in stock volatility as well as differences in option premiums. For the most part, the use of such ratio spreads can help the investor in managing portfolios (Chapter 23) and controlling risk.

The purchase of a 2-for-3 ratio spread allows the investor to take advantage of a higher option premium for the option being written, while assuming a lower risk than that assumed in purchasing a 1-for-2 ratio spread Such a technique will have a lower profit range than the 1-for-2 ratio spread, meaning that the break-even points are closer together. While the break-even points may be closer, the dollar amount of the loss incurred once the stock breaks through the out-of-the-money break-even point (higher for calls, lower for puts) will be less since the overall ratio of the spread is less. The initial cost of the 2-for-3 ratio spread is also greater since there are 1½ option contracts being written for each contract purchased as opposed to the 1-for-2 ratio spread.

To illustrate the 2-for-3 ratio spread, this book will use the same example used in the 1-for-2 ratio spread. Assume that SPD is trading at $72 per share and that the three-month call option with an exercise price of 70 is at 3½ points, and the three-month call with an exercise price of 75 is at 1¼. The investor using the 2-for-3 ratio spread would take the following position:

Purchase (+)/ Write (−)	Quantity	Option Contract	Price per Total Value
+	2	SPD 3 month call with 70 exercise at 3½	7
−	3	SPD 3 month call with 75 exercise at 1¼	3¾
		Debit for 2-for-3 ratio spread	3¼

The maximum profit for this spread will occur at the higher exercise price of 75. The profit in this spread is double the difference in the exercise prices minus the debit price or 6¾ points (double the difference in exercise price of 5 = 10, minus debit of 3¼). The lower break-even point will be the lower exercise price plus half the debit or the stock at 71⅝. The higher break-even point will be where the value of two calls with the lower exercise price is equivalent to three calls with the higher exercise price less the total debit. On a 2-for-1 ratio spread, the higher break-even point will be double the difference between the two exercise prices added to the higher exercise price less the debit paid. In this example, the higher break-even price will be as follows:

$$\text{Higher Exercise Price} + (2 \times (\text{Higher Exercise Price} - \text{Lower Exercise Price})) - \text{Debit}$$
$$75 \qquad + (2 \times \qquad (75\text{-}70)) \qquad -3¼$$

Another way of calculating the higher break-even point is adding the maximum profit to the higher exercise price. Therefore, the higher break-even point for this spread would be 81¾. Once the stock rises above the higher break-even point, the loss would be calculated by subtracting the higher break-even point from the current stock price.

The investor should remain aware that the potential loss is still unlimited.

A similar strategy, the purchase of a 4-for-5 ratio spread can also prove to be profitable. The 4-for-5 ratio spread will provide less of a cushion than the 2-for-3 ratio spread, but may appeal to some investors.

The maximum profit for the 4-for-5 ratio spread also occurs with the stock at the higher exercise price. As the stock rises above the higher exercise price, the investor would give back one point for each point the stock rises. Therefore, the higher break-even point would be the higher exercise price plus the maximum profit. The lower break-even point is the lower exercise price plus one quarter of the debit paid.

Using the same example of SPD, let us illustrate the 4-for-5 ratio spread. The investor will take the following position:

Purchase (+)/ Write (−)	Quantity	Option Contract	Price per Total Value
+	4	SPD 3 month call with 70 exercise at 3½	14
−	5	SPD 3 month call with 75 exercise at 1¼	6¼
		Debit for 4-for-5 ratio spread	7¾

The maximum profit for this ratio spread would be 12¼ with the stock at 75. The lower break-even point would place the stock at 71¹⁵⁄₁₆. The higher break-even point would be 87¼.

As can be seen, the use of ratio call spreads can provide the investor with greater flexibility. While there are many combinations of ratio spreads, this chapter will not focus on any other ratio spreads which involve the purchase of one contract and the writing of a greater amount of option contracts. If the investor is interested in pursuing additional ratio spread techniques, caution is suggested as the mathematics involved may become complicated. Tables 10-1, 10-2 and 10-3 compare the uses of spreads and ratio spreads.

Another use of ratio spreads is when the investor purchases more contracts than he writes. The use of such ratio spreads allows the investor to anticipate a greater movement in the underlying stock while only limiting a portion of the contracts purchased. The investor would continue to profit should the price of the underlying stock continue to move favorably after trading through the exercise price

TABLE 10-1. Ratio Bear Spreads Using Puts versus Bear Spread Using Puts

Stock = 25
Put with 25 Exercise Price = ¾
Put with 22½ Exercise Price = ¼

	1-for-2 Put Spread	1-for-3 Put Spread	2-for-3 Put Spread	1-for-1 Put Spread
25 Exercise	+1	+1	+2	+1
22½ Exercise	−2	−3	−3	−1
Debit	¼	-0-	¾	½
Stock at Expiration		*Profits and Losses*		
26	<¼>	-0-	<¾>	<½>
25	<¼>	-0-	<¾>	<½>
24	¾	1	½	½
23	1¾	2	2½	1½
22½	2¼	2½	4½	2
22	1¾	1½	4	2
21	¾	<1½>	3	2
20	<¼>	<3½>	2	2
Dn Break-Even Point	20¼	21¼	20	25½

of the option contract which has been written. At this point, the quantity of contracts in which the investor wrote would theoretically stop gaining value while those contracts which are free and clear would continue to gain value. This is another way which ratio spreads provide flexibility.

Calls

The investor who purchases two calls with a low exercise price and writes one call with a higher exercise price, in the same expiring month, is extremely bullish. Since he has purchased twice as many calls as he has written, the investor might anticipate a break-out in the price of the stock should the stock trade through the exercise price of the written call.

The maximum profit for the investor using this strategy is unlimited, since the value of the calls purchased (with no call written

TABLE 10-2. Ratio Bull Spreads Using Calls versus Bull Spread Using Calls

Stock = 20
Call with 20 Exercise Price = 1
Call with 22½ Exercise Price = ¼

	1-for-2 Call Spread	1-for-3 Call Spread	2-for-3 Call Spread	1-for-1 Call Spread
20 Exercise	+1	+1	+2	+1
22½ Exercise	−2	−3	−3	−1
Debit	½	¼	1¼	¾
Stock at Expiration	*Profits and Losses*			
19	<½>	<¼>	<1¼>	<¾>
20	<½>	<¼>	<1¼>	<¾>
21	½	¾		¼
22	1½	1¾		1¼
22½	2	2¼		1¾
23	1½	1¼		1¾
25	<½>	<3¼>		1¾
Up Break-Even Point	24½	24¾		N/A

against them) can rise as long as the price of the stock continues to rise, until expiration. The maximum loss to the investor is the total debit paid for the position. The break-even point for the stock would be the lower exercise price plus ½ the debit paid, since twice as many calls are owned than written. There is no additional margin when more calls are purchased than are written, since the investor is not subject to a risk which is unlimited.

Using the example of SPD, let us illustrate how such a position would work. Assume that the investor took on the following position:

Purchase (+)/ Write (−)	Quantity	Option Contract	Price per Total Value
+	2	SPD 3-month call with 70 exercise at 3½	7
−	1	SPD 3-month call with 75 exercise at 1¼	1¼
		Debit for 2-for-1 ratio spread	6¼

TABLE 10-3. Ratio Bear Spreads Using Calls versus Bear Spread Using Calls

Stock = 42
Call with 40 Exercise Price = 3½
Call with 45 Exercise Price = ¾

	1-for-2 Call Spread	*1-for-3 Call Spread*	*2-for-3 Call Spread*	*1-for-1 Call Spread*
40 Exercise	−1	−1	−2	−1
45 Exercise	+2	+3	+3	+1
Credit	2	1¼	4¾	2¾
Stock at Expiration		*Profits and Losses*		
46	<2>	<1¾>	4¼	<2¼>
45	<3>	<3¾>	<5¼>	<2¼>
43	<1>	<1¾>	¾	<¼>
41	1	¼	2¾	1¾
40	2	1¼	4¾	2¾
39	2	1¼	4¾	2¾
37	2	1¼	4¾	2¾

The maximum profit for this position is unlimited. The break-even point is 73⅛ (the lower exercise price plus half of the debit). The maximum loss will occur if the stock drops below 70 and will be 100% of the debit paid. If the underlying stock is at the higher exercise price of 75 at expiration, the investment would be worth 10 points for a profit of 3¾ points or a gain of 60 percent (not including commission or other transaction charges).

An investor who is more bullish may consider purchasing three calls and writing one call, also known as the 3-for-1 ratio spread. The 3-for-1 ratio spread provides the investor with a greater potential profit since there are twice as many options which are not covered through the writing of another option contract. The break-even price for using the 3-for-1 spread is higher than the break-even point for the 2-for-1 spread since the investor has additional capital at risk. The break-even point is calculated by adding ⅓ of the debit price to the lower exercise price.

The following example is another illustration using SPD for the 3-for-1 ratio spread:

Purchase (+)/ Write (−)	Quantity	Option Contract	Price per Total Value
+	3	SPD 3-month call with 70 exercise at 3½	10½
−	1	SPD 3-month call with 75 exercise at 1¼	1¼
		Debit for 3-for-1 ratio spread	9¼

The maximum profit is unlimited. The break-even point is 73.08 per share (lower exercise price + (debit / 3)). The maximum loss to the investor occurs if the stock is under the lower exercise price of 70 and is 100% of the debit paid or 9¼ points. If the stock is at the higher exercise price of 75 at expiration, the value of the position will be 15 points or a profit of 5¾ points, resulting in a gain of 62 percent (not including commission and other transaction charges).

Thus far, the purchase of a greater amount of option contracts than those written can provide the investor with great opportunity and potential. Another ratio spread using the same methodology allows the investor to purchase three contracts and write two contracts. Once again, a great amount of flexibility might be realized in using such a strategy.

The investor who purchases three contracts of a call with a lower exercise price and writes two with a higher exercise price has the opportunity for unlimited profit since one of the calls purchased is not covered by a written call. As long as the value of the stock appreciates (until expiration) the value of this option will continue to rise. The break-even point for this 3-for-2 ratio spread is the lower exercise price plus ⅓ of the total debit paid. The maximum loss to the investor will occur if the stock is below the lower exercise price and will be 100 percent of the total debit paid. Once again, no additional margin is necessary since the risk is limited to the total debit.

Using the SPD example, the use of the 3-for-2 ratio spread can be illustrated as:

Purchase (+)/ Write (−)	Quantity	Option Contract	Price per Total Value
+	3	SPD 3-month call with 70 exercise at 3½	10½
−	2	SPD 3-month call with 75 exercise at 1¼	2½
		Debit for 3-for-2 ratio spread	8

The maximum profit for this position is unlimited. The break-even point is located with the stock at 72.67 per share (the lower exercise price plus ⅓ of the total debit). The maximum loss occurs if the stock is under 70 and the debit is 8 (100 percent of the debit). If the stock is at the higher exercise price, the value of the investment would be 15 points for a profit of seven or a gain of almost 47 percent (excluding commissions and other transaction charges). The maximum profit is unlimited.

The 5-for-3 ratio spread provides the investor with greater potential but additional capital risk. The investor has unlimited profit potential, as long as the stock rises before expiration.

To illustrate the 5-for-3 ratio spread:

Purchase (+)/ Write (−)	Quantity	Option Contract	Price per Total Value
+	5	SPD 3-month call with 70 exercise at 3½	17½
−	3	SPD 3-month call with 75 exercise at 1¼	3¾
		Debit for 5-for-3 ratio spread	13¾

As can be seen, the total debit is 13¾ which can be lost if the stock drops below the lower exercise price (70). The break-even point puts the value of the stock at 72¾ (lower exercise price plus (the debit divided by 5)). The value of this strategy with the stock at the higher exercise price of 75 is 25 which realizes a profit of 11¼ points or almost 82 percent (excluding commissions and other transaction charges). The use of the 5-for-3 ratio spread can provide a great deal of profit with just a small movement in the underlying stock (in this case only 4.2 percent).

The use of ratio spreads in which more calls are purchased than written can provide a great amount of flexibility and profit while lowering the risk involved in just purchasing the calls outright (assuming that the same amount of calls is purchased). In addition, the use of such ratio spreads allows the investor to take advantage of a high option premium on the calls being written. These spreads allow investors greater opportunity and selection for investments. As with all investment decisions, the use of these spreads should be evaluated carefully.

Puts

The use of puts in the strategies described provides greater opportunity for an investor who is bearish on a stock and believes that the stock will have a greater downward movement after writing the put which has a lower exercise price. Since these put spreads are similar to the Bear Spread Using Puts, the investor is taking an even greater negative view of the value of the stock since a portion of the puts purchased are not held back through the writing of other puts against them.

As with the calls, the risk in using these ratio spreads is the total debit paid should the stock rise above the higher exercise price. If this should happen, the investor might lose 100 percent of the debit paid. This debit, however, would be less than if the same amount of puts were purchased with nothing written against them. The break-even point for such strategies is the debit divided by the amount of contracts purchased subtracted from the higher exercise price. The value of the ratio spread will be greater than if the puts were purchased outright, with the stock at the lower exercise price.

Summary

1. The use of ratio spreads can provide for many different scenarios, with respect to the expectations of the underlying stock.

2. Ratio spreads allow the investor or trader to take advantage of high option premiums.

3. Unlike one-for-one spreads, there is a possibility of loss which is greater than the debit on ratio spreads.

Ratio Bull Spread Using Calls

STOCK			SHARES	PRICE	—52 WEEK—		RATING	P/E RATIO	YIELD
					HIGH	LOW			
OPTION CONTRACT			CONTRACTS	PREMIUM	EXPIRATION DATE		DAYS TILL EXP.		
OPTION CONTRACT			CONTRACTS	PREMIUM	EXPIRATION DATE		DAYS TILL EXP.		
QUART DIVID	DIVIDS TO EXP	TOTAL DIVID COLLECT	DEBIT/ CREDIT		REG. T RATE		MARGIN INT RATE		
INTEREST CHARGES:		INT RATE	DAYS	DEBIT BAL	$		TODAY'S DATE		
			÷ 365 ×						

REQUIRED CAPITAL

Amount of Calls Purchased		
Premium of Calls Purchased....................	×	
Option Multiplier..............................	×	
Commission on Calls Purchased	+	
Cost of Calls Purchased	=	
Premium on Calls Written		
Option Mutiplier	×	
Amount of Calls Purchased	×	
Commission on Calls Written	−	
Credit to Calls Purchased......................	=	
Cost of Calls Purchased	−	
Spread Purchase Cost	=	
Current Stock Price		
Margin Requirement	×	
Out-of-Money Amount	−	
Margin Result.................................	=	
Current Stock Price		
Option Margin Requirement Minimum...........	×	
Minimum Margin Required.....................	=	
Greater of Two Requirements		
Amount of Naked Contracts Written.............	×	
Option Multiplier.............................	×	
Required Margin	=	
Spread Purchase Cost	−	
Capital Required..................................	=	

MAXIMUM PROFIT

Exercise Price of Calls Written		
Difference Between Exercise Prices		
Amount of Calls Purchased	×	
Option Multiplier.............................	×	
Maximum Value of Spread	=	
Capital Required..............................	−	
Commission on Long Calls at Max Spread Value..	−	
Maximum Profit...............................	=	
Capital Required..............................	+	
Return..	=	
*Ann Return (Return × 365 ÷ Days)		

UPPER BREAK-EVEN POINT

Maximum Profit...............................		
Amount of Calls Written Naked.................	÷	
Option Multiplier.............................	÷	
Higher Exercise Price..........................	+	
Upper Break-Even Point	=	

*Annualized returns may only be used if holding is over 60 days.

157

WORKSHEET 10-2:

Ratio Bear Spread Using Calls Worksheet

STOCK			SHARES	PRICE	—52 WEEK— HIGH LOW		RATING	PIE RATIO	YIELD
OPTION CONTRACT			CONTRACTS	PREMIUM	EXPIRATION DATE		DAYS TILL EXP.		
OPTION CONTRACT			CONTRACTS	PREMIUM	EXPIRATION DATE		DAYS TILL EXP.		
QUART DIVID	DIVIDS TO EXP	TOTAL DIVID COLLECT		DEBIT/ CREDIT	REG. T RATE		MARGIN INT RATE		
INTEREST CHARGES:		INT RATE DAYS × ÷365×	DEBIT BAL	$ =			TODAY'S DATE		

REQUIRED CAPITAL

Amount of Puts Purchased......................		
Premium of Puts Purchased	×	
Option Multiplier...............................	×	
Commission on Puts Purchased..................	+	
Cost of Puts Purchased	=	
Premium on Puts Written......................		
Option Mutiplier	×	
Amount of Puts Purchased......................	×	
Commission on Puts Written....................	−	
Credit to Puts Purchased.......................	=	
Cost of Puts Purchased	−	
Spread Purchase Cost	=	
Current Stock Price		
Margin Requirement	×	
Out-of-Money Amount	−	
Margin Result..................................	=	
Current Stock Price		
Option Margin Requirement Minimum...........	×	
Minimum Margin Required......................	=	
Greater of Two Requirements		
Amount of Naked Contracts Written.............	×	
Option Multiplier...............................	×	
Required Margin	=	
Spread Purchase Cost	−	
Capital Required.................................	=	

MAXIMUM PROFIT

Exercise Price of Puts Written		
Difference Between Exercise Prices		
Amount of Puts Purchased......................	×	
Option Multiplier..............................	×	
Maximum Value of Spread	=	
Capital Required...............................	−	
Commission on Long Calls at Max Spread Value..	−	
Maximum Profit................................	=	
Capital Required...............................	÷	
Return..	=	
*Ann Return (Return × 365 ÷ Days)		

LOW BREAK-EVEN POINT

Maximum Profit................................		
Amount of Puts Written Naked	÷	
Option Multiplier..............................	÷	
Lower Exercise Price	−	
Low Break-Even Point...........................	=	

*Annualized returns may only be used if holding is over 60 days.

11
Butterfly Spreads

Ratio spreads can provide great profitability, but in certain situations they put the investor in a situation of unlimited risk. A three-sided ratio spread allows the user to take advantage of high option premiums while limiting risk. This type of spread, known as a **butterfly spread,** is a very popular strategy among investor and market-makers alike.

The butterfly spread is actually a combination of two different spreads. The use of the butterfly gives the investor additional flexibility while limiting the risk to a fixed amount. The two separate spreads that make up the butterfly spread do not have to be enacted at the same time. An investor may enact a ratio spread and then at a later date initiate another spread, thus creating the butterfly spread. This is known as "legging" into a spread. An investor may "leg" into a butterfly spread from a ratio spread, if the stock has moved too quickly or the investor's opinion of the stock has changed.

The ratio bull spread using calls, as illustrated in Chapter 10, is a strategy in which the investor purchases one call with a lower exercise price and writes two calls with a higher exercise price, in the same expiration month. The expectation of the investor is for the stock to reach and not climb above the higher exercise price. If the stock remains at the higher exercise price until expiration, the investor would realize the maximum profit which is the difference between the exercise prices less the total debit paid for the spread. If the stock climbs above the higher exercise price, the investor will give back ⅛ of a point for each ⅛ of a point the stock moves above the higher exercise price. Once the profit is eaten away, the investor will begin to realize a loss, which can be unlimited.

An alternative to using the ratio bull spread using calls is for the investor to purchase the bull butterfly spread using calls. The cost for initiating such a spread will be slightly higher than the ratio spread, but the risk is also limited. The butterfly spread adds one position onto the ratio spread, the purchase of an out-of-the-money call, with an exercise price higher than the calls which were written. The amount of contracts purchased is equal to the amount of the lower exercise call options which were purchased. Since these calls are so far out-of-the-money, the additional investment to the investor will be low. The exercise price of the additional call purchased should be just as far away from the exercise price of the calls written as the distance from the lower calls which were purchased. Table 11-1 illustrates the purchase of a butterfly spread using calls. Most broker-

TABLE 11-1. Purchase of a Butterfly Spread Using Calls

Stock = 42
3-Month Call with 40 Exercise Price = 4
3-Month Call with 45 Exercise Price = 1½
3-Month Call with 50 Exercise Price = ¾

Butterfly Spread

B/S	QTY	Option Contract	Price	$Value
B	1	40 Exercise Price	4	400.00
S	2	45 Exercise Price	1½	300.00
B	1	50 Exercise Price	¾	75.00
	-0-		1¾	175.00

Two Different Spread Positions

Bull Spread Using Calls:	Bear Spread Using Calls:
+1 40 Exercise Price	−1 45 Exercise Price
−1 45 Exercise Price	+1 50 Exercise Price
Required Margin	*Required Margin*
Debit Spread 2½	Difference between Exercise Prices (5 points)

age firms treat the butterfly spread as two separate positions for margin reasons. This spread would be treated as a bull spread using calls and a bear spread using calls. Therefore, the butterfly spread requires that the investor have a neutral opinion, and in this case a slightly bullish bias.

The purchase of the butterfly spread will achieve maximum profit at the middle exercise price. If the stock is at the middle exercise price at expiration, the lower exercise price will be worth five points, the middle and higher exercise prices will have no value, so the total value of the butterfly spread would be five points. There are two break-even points for the butterfly spread, calculated by adding the debit to the lower exercise price and subtracting the debit from the higher exercise price. If the stock is between the two break-even points, the investor will realize a profit. If the stock is below the lower break-even point or above the higher break-even point, then the investor will lose ⅛ of a point for each ⅛ of a point that the stock moves, till the stock hits the lower or higher exercise price. The difference between the break-even point and the exercise price will be the maximum loss, which is also the debit paid for the butterfly spread. Therefore, no matter how low the stock drops or how high the stock rises, the investor has a maximum risk of the total debit paid for the spread. Figure 11-1 illustrates the profit & loss of the purchase of the call butterfly spread at expiration, with the stock at different levels.

The purchase of a butterfly spread may also be used with put options. Purchasing a put butterfly spread requires that the investor have a slightly bearish opinion on the value of the underlying stock, but he does not foresee the value of the stock dropping drastically. The use of the put butterfly spread is usually slightly harder to execute for two reasons: (1) put premiums are usually lower in value than the call premiums, making the debit to be paid slightly higher; and (2) since calls are more popular than puts, the liquidity may not be as great, making the execution of a three-way spread more difficult.

Just as with the calls, the value of the put butterfly spread will be at its maximum if the stock as at the middle exercise price (the puts which were written). In addition, break-even points are calculated just as they were with the calls, and as long as the stock remains between the two break-even points, the investor will realize some profit.

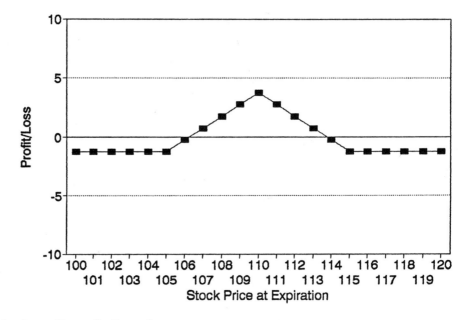

FIGURE 11-1. Long Butterfly Spread.

As discussed, the maximum profit is realized when the stock is at the middle exercise price and once the stock rises above that level (calls) or drops below that level (puts), the investor will begin giving back profit until a loss is realized. Since there are two possibilities for loss as opposed to one in a regular type of spread, the investor should limit the debit paid for such a spread to approximately ⅕ or 20 percent of the maximum value of the spread. In addition, the purchaser of a butterfly spread should have a minimum of 30 days till expiration as a general guideline, allowing the investor time to be correct, if the stock is not close to the middle exercise price. If the stock is close to the middle exercise price (the options which were written) the investor may wish a shorter-term holding period, as the longer the holding period the greater the risk that the stock moves away from the middle exercise price.

Butterfly spreads may also be written or sold. Butterfly spreads are commonly sold by market-makers, specialists, and traders who believe that the price of the underlying stock will drop below the lower exercise price or rise above the higher exercise price. This strategy usually requires an opinion which is not bullish or bearish, but one in which the person executing the trade feels that the volatility of the stock will increase, causing the stock to violate one of those exercise prices.

To illustrate, assume that JXZ's stock is trading at 44½, and that a one-month call with an exercise price of 40 is worth 5½, the call with the an exercise price of 45 is at two and the call with an exercise price of 50 is at ¼. The trader takes on the following position:

B/S	Qty	Option Contract	Price/Opt	Dollar Val
S	1	Exercise price 40	5½	$550.00
B	2	Exercise price 45	2	400.00
S	1	Exercise price 50	¼	25.00
		Credit	1¾	175.00

In taking on this position, the trader takes on two strategies, if broken down simply: a bull spread using calls (+45/-50), and a bear spread using calls (−40/+45). The following diagramatically represents the two strategies:

Bear Spread   **Bull Spread**

−40 Exercise
Price Call

+45 Exercise
Price Call

+45 Exercise
Price Call

−50 Exercise
Price Call

If the stock drops below the 40 exercise price, then the value of the 40 call is zero, the 45 call is zero and the 50 call is zero. Therefore, the value of the butterfly spread is zero and the trader keeps the 1¾ point credit. If the stock is at the higher exercise price or above, then the 40 call is worth 10, the 45 call is worth 10 (5 points × 2 contracts) and the 50 call is worth zero. Therefore the spread is worth nothing and the trader can keep the credit received. It is important to note that in-the-money options may have to be liquidated or the options may be exercised and assigned, leaving the trader with less of a gain after commissions and other transaction fees, which might inhibit the trader from doing this butterfly spread.

If the stock is at the middle exercise price (the calls purchased), then the 40 calls would be worth 5 points, the 45 calls would be worth zero and the 50 calls would be worth zero. After calculating all three positions, the trader would have a maximum loss of the maximum value of the spread (which is the difference between exercise prices) less the credit received, or in this case 3¼ points (difference of exercise prices of 5 points less 1¾ point credits).

There are two break-even points, just as in the purchase of a butterfly spread. The lower break-even point is the lower exercise price plus the credit received and the higher break-even point is the higher exercise price less the credit received. In between these two break-even points, the trader will lose money. If the stock is below the lower break-even point or higher than the higher break-even point, the trader will make a profit.

The trader should note that the margin requirement for this spread is the same as writing a bear spread using calls, which is the difference between exercise prices (or five points in this example), according to industry margin requirements.

The writing of butterfly spreads is not limited to calls. Writing put butterfly spreads requires a little more patience as put premiums are usually lower than those of the calls and the level of liquidity is lower than that of the calls. These two problems are the same problems as those in purchasing the put butterfly spread.

Using the JXZ example, let us examine the sale of a put butterfly spread.

B/S	Qty	Option Contract	Price/Opt	Dollar Val
S	1	Exercise price 40	⅛	$125.00
B	2	Exercise price 45	2½	500.00
S	1	Exercise price 50	6¾	675.00
		Credit	1⅞	187.50

If the stock drops to 40, the value of the 40 put would be zero, the 45 put would be worth 10 points (5 points × 2), and the 50 put would have a value of 10 points. Therefore, the value of the spread would

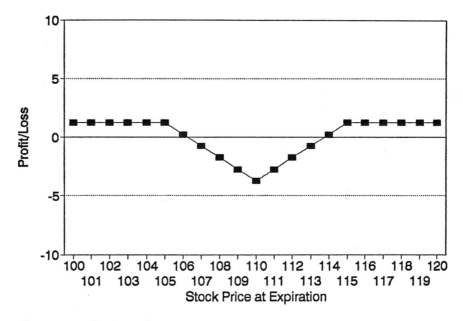

FIGURE 11-2. Short Butterfly Spread.

be zero, and the trader would collect the 1⅞ point credit or realize a profit of $187.50. If the stock rose above 50, the 40 put would have a value of zero as well as the 45 put and the 50 put. Therefore, once again the value of the spread would have no worth and the trader would collect the entire credit as profit. If the stock is at 45 at expiration, the 40 put would be worth zero, the 45 put would be worth zero, but the 50 put would be worth 5 points. At this level, the trader would realize a loss of 3⅛ points (the difference in exercise prices less the credit received). Figure 11-2 shows the profit and loss for both the calls and the puts in writing butterfly spreads.

Once again, it is important for the trader to realize that if the stock drops below the lower exercise price, the trader may be subject to closing the spread for a premium or subject to higher transaction charges and other fees associated with exercising and assigning option positions.

It is generally suggested that traders writing butterfly spreads have less than 45 days till expiration and that a credit of approximately 20 percent the difference between the exercise prices. While this value might seem on the low end, there is a double opportunity for realizing a profit, since no matter which direction the stock moves in, as long as it drops below the lower exercise price or rises above the higher exercise price the trader will profit.

Summary

1. Butterfly spreads allow the investor to achieve maximum profit if the stock reaches a midpoint. The maximum profit is small but the cost of the spread is also low.

2. The writing of a butterfly spread permits the writer to achieve profit of the credit if the stock remains in a certain range.

3. The butterfly spread is a neutral type strategy while the writing of the butterfly spread expects the stock to move one direction or another, but without the need for a significant move.

4. Butterfly spreads are moderately aggressive strategies.

12
Creating Different Positions

The use of option contracts can provide a great deal of versatility as well as flexibility. One of the great benefits of the use of option contracts is the ability to create different positions and duplicate the actions of other instruments. Synthetic option strategies provide the investor with the ability to duplicate different stock and option strategies or positions.

Synthetic strategies can be understood by analogy. A synthetic material, such as polyester, is a man-made material which is used in place of another natural material, such as cotton. The use of such a material allows the manufacturer to make a garment, such as a shirt, with a man-made fiber for a lower cost. Both a cotton shirt and a polyester shirt can be worn and washed, but the cotton shirt may need to be dryed in an electric dryer while the polyester shirt may need to be hung dryed. While both shirts can be worn in the same manner, the maintenance is not the same on both.

Similar to the shirt example, option contracts can be used in lieu of stock. Simulating a stock position using puts and calls can duplicate the movement of the underlying stock but has two draw backs. First, since the actual stock is not owned, the investor utilizing such a strategy would *not* be permitted to collect any dividends paid during the holding period. Second, a stock can be held forever, while the option position can only be held till expiration, which may be very short term.

Purchasing Stock Using Options

Simulating the purchase of a stock through options is accomplished through the purchase of a call option and the writing of a put option, both having the same expiration date and exercise price. This position is known as a **Synthetic Long Stock Purchase**. The purchase of the call must be paid in full, while the writing of the put contract is subject to the required margin for writing naked options. As the price of the stock rises, a rise in the call contract and a decline in the value of the put should be equivalent (or close) to the movement in the price of the stock. If the value of the underlying stock declines, the value of the call will drop and the price of the put should gain. The combination of the change in the two option contracts should be equivalent to the drop in the price of the stock. If the price of the underlying stock rises one point, then a combination of the long call and short put position should add up to an unrealized gain of one point. However, if the price of the stock declines by one point, then the deterioration of the call and the appreciation of the put value will

TABLE 12-1. Long Stock Purchase versus Synthetic Long Stock

	Long Stock			*Synthetic Stock*		
Position	Buy Stock at 51			Buy Call 50 Exercise at 1¾ Sell Put 50 Exercise at ⅞		
Cost/Debt	51			⅞		
B.E. Pt.	51			50⅞		
Stock Pr	*Stk Val*	*P/L/Share*		*Call Val*	*Put Val*	*P/L/Sh*
45	45	(6.00)		-0-	5	(5.88)
47½	47½	(3.50)		-0-	2½	(3.38)
50	50	(1.00)		-0-	-0-	(0.88)
50⅞	50⅞	(0.13)		⅞	-0-	-0-
51	51	-0-		1	-0-	0.13
52½	52½	1.50		2½	-0-	1.38
55	55	4.00		5	-0-	4.13
57½	57½	6.50		7½	-0-	6.38
60	60	9.00		10	-0-	9.13

result in an unrealized loss of one point. The change in value between the stock price, the call value and the put value is illustrated in Table 12-1. Figure 12-1 shows the value of the synthetic long stock strategy at expiration.

There are several advantages in using the synthetic long stock strategy. The first advantage is that the cost in purchasing the position can be substanially less (in capital). Second, the purchaser usually has greater freedom in closing out the position since a lower capital outlay was initially required. In addition, an expiration draws near, the buyer will be forced to close the position in the synthetics or to purchase the stock. A third advantage to the investor is that if the underlying stock does appreciate, the investor could close the entire synthetic position or may wish to repurchase the puts and hold the long call position. An alternative to repurchasing the put is to roll the entire synthetic to a higher exercise price and possibly into a longer expiration period. Worksheet 12-1, the synthetic long stock worksheet, has been provided to assist you in contemplating the use of this strategy.

A note of caution to the investor using the synthetic long stock position: If the put contract is in-the-money (call would be out-of-

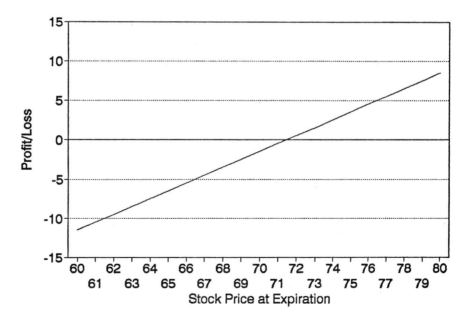

FIGURE 12-1. Synthetic Long Stock.

the-money), the investor might be put the stock versus the short put, leaving the investor with a position similar to a covered write.

Going Short Using Options

Creating a short stock position can be accomplished in a similar manner to the long synthetic stock. To create a short stock position using options, the investor would purchase a put and write a call with the same expiration date and the same exercise price. This position is called a **Synthetic Short Stock Position**. The synthetic short stock position will result in a gain equivalent to a gain in a short stock position. While this equivalent gain may not be exact, it should be very close. If the stock declines one point, the combination of the gain in the put and the decrease in the call should equal the one point drop in the price of the underlying stock. However, if the stock appreciates in value by one point, then the rise in price on the call and the deterioration in value of the put should equal the one point rise in the stock. Table 12-2 illustrates the change in values for the synthetic

TABLE 12-2. **Short Stock Sale versus Synthetic Short Stock**

	Long Stock			Synthetic Short Stock		
Position	Sell Stock at 51			Sell Call 50 Exercise at 1¾ Buy Put 50 Exercise at ⅞		
Credit	51			⅞		
B.E. Pt.	51			50⅞		
Stock Pr	*Stk Val*	*P/L/Share*		*Call Val*	*Put Val*	*P/L/Sh*
45	45	6.00		-0-	5	5.88
47½	47½	3.50		-0-	2½	3.38
50	50	1.00		-0-	-0-	0.88
50⅞	50⅞	0.13		⅞	-0-	-0-
51	51	-0-		1	-0-	(0.13)
52½	52½	(1.50)		2½	-0-	(1.38)
55	55	(4.00)		5	-0-	(4.13)
57½	57½	(6.50)		7½	-0-	(6.38)
60	60	(9.00)		10	-0-	(9.13)

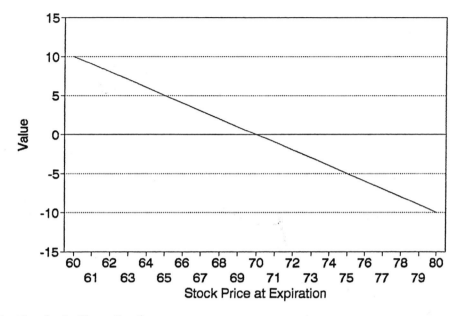

FIGURE 12-2. Synthetic Short Stock.

short stock position. The synthetic short stock strategy is graphically represented in Figure 12-2.

In addition to the advantages mentioned for the use of the synthetic long stock position, there are three more advantages particular to using the synthetic short stock position. The investor who utilizes the synthetic position is not subject to the "uptick" rule which short stock sellers are required to follow. Since the synthetic position does not require stock, the investor does not have to borrow stock for selling short. Along with that advantage is that the synthetic short position is not subject to being bought in (stock is repurchased before the investor is ready, since the lender wishes to sell the securities). Probably the greatest advantage of all is that the investor using the synthetic position is not subject to paying out of dividends which are paid during the holiday period.

A word of caution to the investor who utilizes the synthetic short stock position. If the call option is in-the-money (the put option would be out-of-the-money), the investor might be subject to having the stock called away at the exercise price, leaving the investor with a short-stock position plus a long put, which is an extremely bearish position. Worksheet 12-2 at the end of the chapter will help you calculate the benefits of the synthetic short stock position.

Creating a Synthetic Long Call

Synthetic stock positions are innovative means for duplicating stock positions. In addition to creating stock positions through the use of option contracts, it is also possible to create option positions through the use of the underlying stock and another options contract. Options can provide a great deal of flexibility, and synthetic option positions provide further versatility and flexibility of option contracts. It is possible for an investor or trader to create a long call, long put, short call, and short put.

The creation of a synthetic long call encompasses the purchase of the underlying stock and the purchase of a put with the exercise price and expiration month which would be the same as if the call were purchased. Like the purchase of the call option, this strategy would provide the investor with unlimited profit potential (as the stock moves higher) and a limited dollar loss. The actual position taken is the same as the married put strategy discussed in Chapter 5. An additional benefit of the synthetic long call position is that the investor is entitled to collect any dividend paid during the holding

TABLE 12-3. Long Call Purchase versus Synthetic Long Call

	Long Call		*Synthetic Long Call*		
Position	Buy Call at 1¾ (with 50 exercise)		Buy stock at 51 Buy Put 50 Exercise at ⅞		
Debit	1¾		51⅞		
B.E. Pt.	51¾		51⅞		

Stock Pr	*Call Val*	*P/L/Share*	*Stock Val*	*Put Val*	*P/L/Sh*
45	-0-	(1.75)	45	5	(1.88)
47½	-0-	(1.75)	47½	2½	(1.88)
50	-0-	(1.75)	50	-0-	(1.88)
50⅞	⅞	(0.88)	50⅞	-0-	(1.00)
51	1	(0.75)	51	-0-	(0.88)
52½	2½	0.75	52½	-0-	0.63
55	5	3.25	55	-0-	3.13
57½	7½	5.75	57½	-0-	5.63
60	10	8.25	60	-0-	8.13

period of the position. If the stock appreciates in price, the investor will profit. If the stock declines in price, the investor will realize a loss of the debit paid for the stock and the put minus the dividend collected and the exercise price of the put. If the stock remains unchanged to expiration of the put and the stock is sold at that point (assuming the put is out-of-the-money), the loss would be the option premium paid for the put less any dividend collected (not including commissions and other transaction charges). Table 12-3 illustrates the parallel of the long call and the synthetic long call.

The break-even point for the synthetic long call position is higher than if the stock were purchased outright. The break-even point is the stock price plus the put premium less any dividends collected till expiration (not including commissions or other transaction charges). Investors wishing to calculate the maximum risk and break-even points can use the Married Put Buyers Worksheet (Worksheet 5-1).

Synthetic Long Puts

The synthetic long put is more involved than the synthetic long call position. To implement the synthetic long put the investor must sell the underlying stock short (see Chapter 2 on the purchase of long puts versus short stock sale) and purchase a long call with an exercise price and expiration date which are the same as the call that would have been purchased. The risk of the synthetic long put is similar to that of the long put. If the stock drops in price, the value of the synthetic long put will appreciate, similar to that of the long put, but it is subject to payment of any dividend paid during the holding period. If the stock appreciates in price, the risk to the investor will be limited by the call position (less any dividend). Therefore, the maximum risk is calculated by subtracting the short sale price less the premium paid for the call from the exericse price plus any dividend paid (not including commissions and other transaction charges). This strategy is the same as the protective call on a short stock position, illustrated in Chapter 2. If the stock remains unchanged until expiration, and the call is out-of-the-money, the investor will realize a loss of the call premium plus any dividend paid during the holding period (not including commissions and other transaction fees). Table 12-4 illustrates the parallel of the long put versus the synthetic long put.

The break-even point for the synthetic long put position can be calculated by subtracting the call premium plus any dividends paid

TABLE 12-4. Long Put Purchase versus Synthetic Long Put

	Long Put			Synthetic Long Put		
Position	Buy Put at ⅞ (with 50 exercise)			Sell Stock at 51 Buy Call 50 Exercise at 1¾		
Debit	⅞			50¼ Credit		
B.E. Pt.	49⅛			50¼		
Stock Pr	*Put Val*	*P/L*		*Stock Val*	*Call Val*	*P/L*
45	5	4.13		45	-0-	5.25
47½	2½	1.88		47½	-0-	2.75
50	-0-	(0.88)		50	-0-	0.25
50⅞	-0-	(0.88)		50⅞	⅞	0.25
51	-0-	(0.88)		51	1	0.25
52½	-0-	(0.88)		52½	2½	0.25
55	-0-	(0.88)		55	5	0.25
57½	-0-	(0.88)		57½	7½	0.25
60	-0-	(0.88)		60	10	0.25

from the short sale price of the stock (not including commissions). If the stock drops below the break-even point, the synthetic long put position would become profitable.

Synthetic Short Calls

The **synthetic short call** position, like the short call position, contains the possibility of unlimited loss, should the assumption of the direction in stock price be incorrect. The synthetic short call position also involves the risks associated with selling stock short, as mentioned in the synthetic long put position. To initiate the synthetic short call strategy, the investor must sell the underlying stock short and write a put contract with the same expiration month and exercise price as in the call which would have been written. If the value of the stock depreciates in value, then the investor could realize a potential profit of the short sale price plus the put premium less the exercise price and any dividends paid during the holding period. The potential maximum profit would be realized if the stock drops to or below the exercise price. Should the stock drop below the exercise price, the

TABLE 12-5. Short Call Writing versus Synthetic Short Call

	Short Call			Synthetic Short Call		
Position	Sell Call at 1¾ (with 50 exercise)			Sell Stock at 51 Sell Put 50 Exercise at ⅞		
Credit	1¾			51⅞		
B.E. Pt.	51¾			51⅞		
Stock Pr	Call Val	P/L	Stock Val	Put Val	P/L	
45	-0-	1.75	45	5	1.88	
47½	-0-	1.75	47½	2½	1.88	
50	-0-	1.75	50	-0-	1.88	
50⅞	⅞	0.88	50⅞	-0-	1.00	
51	1	0.75	51	-0-	0.88	
52½	2½	(0.75)	52½	-0-	(0.63)	
55	5	(3.25)	55	-0-	(3.13)	
57½	7½	(5.75)	57½	-0-	(5.63)	
60	10	(8.25)	60	-0-	(8.13)	

investor would be put the stock by expiration of the option position, which would close the position out. If the stock rises, the potential loss to the investor utilizing this strategy is unlimited, as there is no protection against the short stock position, plus the risk associated with the dividend. If the stock is unchanged till expiration, the investor would realize a profit (if the stock is above the exercise price) of the option premium less any dividend paid. The major difference between the short call and the synthetic short call is the risk of the dividend. The writer of the call option is subject to being called and in turn short the underlying stock at a future date, where the use of the synthetic short call puts the investor in a situation of being short the underlying stock immediately. Table 12-5 illustrates the short call versus the synthetic short call.

The break-even point for the synthetic short call can be calculated by adding the short stock price and the put premium and subtracting any dividend paid during the holding period (excluding transaction charges). If the stock remains below the break-even point, a profit may be realized. Investors wishing to evaluate the use of the synthetic short call can use the synthetic short call worksheet (Worksheet 12-2).

The Synthetic Short Put

The synthetic short put position, like the short put, is subject to a limited profit and an unlimited (limited only to the fact that zero is the lowest the stock can go) loss. The synthetic short put requires the investor to purchase the underlying stock and to write a call with the same exercise price and expiration date as in the put which would have been written. This is the same strategy outlined in Chapter 3, the covered call write. If the stock appreciates, the investor would earn the maximum profit, once the stock breaks above the exercise price. This profit would be the exercise price plus any dividends paid during the holding period plus the option premium less the amount paid for the underlying stock. If the stock drops in value, the investor could realize a loss of the stock price less the call premium and the dividend. If the stock remains unchanged to expiration, assuming that the stock is below the exercise price, the investor would realize a profit of the option premium plus the dividend. Table 12-6 illustrates the use of the short put versus the synthetic short put.

The break-even point for the synthetic short put can be calculated

TABLE 12-6.   Short Put Writing versus Synthetic Short Put

	Short Put		Synthetic Short Put		
Position	Sell Put at ⅞ (with 50 exercise)		Buy Stock at 51 Sell Call 50 Exercise at 1¾		
Credit	⅞		49¼ Debit		
B.E. Pt.	50⅞		49¼		
Stock Pr	*Put Val*	*P/L*	*Stock Val*	*Call Val*	*P/L*
45	5	(5.88)	45	-0-	(4.75)
47½	2½	(1.38)	47½	-0-	(1.75)
50	-0-	0.88	50	-0-	0.75
50⅞	-0-	0.88	50⅞	⅞	0.75
51	-0-	0.88	51	1	0.75
52½	-0-	0.88	52½	2½	0.75
55	-0-	0.88	55	5	0.75
57½	-0-	0.88	57½	7½	0.75
60	-0-	0.88	60	10	0.75

by subtracting the call premium and the dividend from the purchase price of the underlying stock (excluding transaction charges). If the stock is above the break-even point, the investor should realize a profit. Maximum profit and the break-even point can be easily calculated using the Covered Call Writers Worksheet (Worksheet 3-2).

The use of synthetic positions has other advantages. For example, the synthetic stock position could reduce capital required over purchasing the stock in a cash or margin account. The use of the synthetic short stock position can reduce all of the headaches associated with selling a stock short. The use of the synthetic long call and synthetic long put positions may reduce time premium if the option were purchased outright. If the investor chose to, the use of the synthetic short call or synthetic short put might realize additional time value over the writing of the call or put options contract. In addition, the use of synthetic positions may be used to offset the opposite position an investor might be holding, similar to a stock position known as "short against the box," which requires selling a stock short against the position being held.

Synthetic option strategies can provide the investor with many diverse methods for accomplishing certain goals. Synthetic option positions can be used to offset other, already established, positions. Simulation of different stock and option positions can also be valuable when used with index option contracts (see Chapter 15) or other positions where the underlying instrument cannot be purchased or sold.

Summary

1. Synthetic stock positions provide the investor with an artificial method of either purchasing the underlying stock or selling it short.

2. Synthetic positions have a very close correlation to the created strategy and the positions which they attempt to duplicate.

3. The use of a synthetic position can provide a means of hedging an opposing position.

4. Creating a synthetic short stock position can help the investor

to avoid many of the disadvantages of selling the underlying stock short.

5. Table 12-7 summarizes the different synthetic strategies outlined in this chapter.

TABLE 12-7.   Synthetic Option Strategies

Synthetic Strategy	Stock	Call	Put	Risk	Reward	B.E.
Long Stock		Buy	Write	Limited	Unlimited	Call − Put
Short Stock		Write	Buy	Unlimited	Limited	Put − Call
Long Call	Buy		Buy	Limited	Unlimited	Stock + Put + Div − Exercise Price
Long Put	Sell	Buy		Limited	Unlimited	Exercise Price + Call − Stock − Div
Short Call	Sell		Write	Unlimited	Limited	Stock + Put − Div
Short Put	Buy	Write		Unlimited	Limited	Stock + Div − Call

WORKSHEET 12-1:

Synthetic Long Stock

STOCK			SHARES	PRICE	—52 WEEK—		RATING	PIE RATIO	YIELD
					HIGH	LOW			
OPTION CONTRACT			CONTRACTS	PREMIUM	EXPIRATION DATE		DAYS TILL EXP.		
OPTION CONTRACT			CONTRACTS	PREMIUM	EXPIRATION DATE		DAYS TILL EXP.		
QUART DIVID	DIVIDS TO EXP	TOTAL DIVID COLLECT		DEBIT	REG. T RATE		MARGIN INT RATE		
INTEREST CHARGES:		INT RATE | DAYS | | DEBIT BAL | $					TODAY'S DATE		
		× ÷ 365 × =							

REQUIRED CAPITAL

Call Purchase Price.............................

Equiv. Amount of Shares .... ×

Call Commission Charges....................... +

      Call Cost .... =

Stock Price.....................................

Option Margin Requirement .... ×

Put Out-of-Money Amount .... −

Put Margin Requirement........................ =

Stock Price.....................................

Minimum Option Margin Requirement........... ×

Minimum Margin Charge........................ =

Greater of Margin Requirement/
     Minimum Margin Requirement..............

Put Commission Charges .... +

     Put Requirement............................ =

REQUIRED CAPITAL (Call Cost +
     Put Requirement) ....

COST OF OWNING STOCK—CALL EXERCISED / PUT ASSIGNED

Exercise Price ....

Equiv. Amount of Shares .... ×

Principal....................................... =

Commission @ Exercise Price .... +

Call Cost .... =

Put Premium ....

Equiv. Amount of Shares .... ×

Put Commission Charges .... −

COST OF OWNING SHARES .... =

Equiv. Amount of Shares .... ÷

Cost of Owning Stock per Share/
     Break-Even Point .... =

WORKSHEET 12-2:

Synthetic Short Stock

STOCK			SHARES	PRICE	—52 WEEK—		RATING	PIE RATIO	YIELD
					HIGH	LOW			
OPTION CONTRACT			CONTRACTS	PREMIUM	EXPIRATION DATE		DAYS TILL EXP.		
OPTION CONTRACT			CONTRACTS	PREMIUM	EXPIRATION DATE		DAYS TILL EXP.		
QUART DIVID	DIVIDS TO EXP	TOTAL DIVID COLLECT		DEBIT/ CREDIT	REG. T RATE		MARGIN INT RATE		
INTEREST CHARGES:		INT RATE	DAYS	DEBIT BAL	$		TODAY'S DATE		
		×	÷ 365 ×		=				

REQUIRED CAPITAL

Put Purchase Price . . . .

Equiv. Amount of Shares . . . .   ×

Put Commission Charges . . . .   +

       Put Cost . . . .   =

Stock Price . . . .

Option Margin Requirement . . . .   ×

Call Out-of-Money Amount . . . .   −

Call Margin Requirement . . . .   =

Stock Price . . . .

Minimum Option Margin Requirement . . . .   ×

Minimum Margin Charge . . . .   =

Greater of Margin Requirement/
    Minimum Margin Requirement . . . .

Call Commission Charges . . . .   +

    Call Requirement . . . .   =

REQUIRED CAPITAL (Put Cost +
    Call Requirement) . . . .

COST OF SHORTING STOCK—PUT EXERCISED / CALL ASSIGNED

Exercise Price . . . .

Equiv. Amount of Shares . . . .   ×

Principal . . . .   =

Commission @ Exercise Price . . . .   +

Put Cost . . . .   =

Call Premium . . . .

Equiv. Amount of Shares . . . .   ×

Call Commission Charges . . . .   −

COST OF SHORTING SHARES . . . .   =

Equiv. Amount of Shares . . . .   ÷

Cost of Shorting Stock Per Share/
    Break-Even Point . . . .   =

WORKSHEET 12-3:

Synthetic Put/Protective Call Worksheet

STOCK			SHARES	PRICE	—52 WEEK—		RATING	PIE RATIO	YIELD
					HIGH	LOW			
OPTION CONTRACT			CONTRACTS	PREMIUM	EXPIRATION DATE		DAYS TILL EXP.		
QUART DIVID	DIVIDS TO EXP	TOTAL DIVID PAID		CREDIT	REG. T RATE		MARGIN INT RATE		
INTEREST CHARGES:		INT RATE	DAYS	DEBIT BAL	$		TODAY'S DATE		
		x	÷ 365 x		=				

REQUIRED CAPITAL

Stock Price...............................		
Amount of Shares...........................	×	
Margin Requirement	×	
Commission on Stock	+	
Total Stock Margin	=	
Option Premium............................		
Amount of Shares...........................	×	
Commission on Option.......................	+	
Option Cost...............................	=	
Required Capital (Total Stock Margin + Option Cost)......................		
Stock Price...............................		
Amount of Shares...........................	×	
Commission on Stock	−	
Option Cost...............................	−	
Proceeds.................................	=	

MAXIMUM RISK

Exercise Price of Option......................		
Amount of Shares...........................	×	
Stock Commission at Exercise Price.............	+	
Proceeds.................................	−	
Dividends Paid	+	
Maximum Loss.............................	=	
Required Capital...........................	÷	
Maximum Loss (%).........................	=	

BREAK-EVEN POINT

Proceeds.................................		
Dividends Paid	−	
Amount of Shares...........................	÷	
Break-Even Price...........................		

13
Options Arbitrage

The trading of puts and calls is not limited to investors and traders, it is also a means for professionals (market makers, specialists, arbitrageurs) to make profits or fulfill a customer's order. Option professionals also help to keep the premiums on puts and calls in line by taking advantage of price discrepancies between the quoted prices of puts, calls and the underlying security. This technique is known as **Options Arbitrage.**

Arbitrage is a method of taking advantage of price differences Before the age of high technology trading, market professionals and traders would purchase a security on one exchange and sell that same security on another exchange for a higher price. The difference between the two prices would be a profit to the trader. If the discrepancy in the two prices continued, the trader would continue to purchase the stock on the first exchange and sell the stock on the other exchange, until such action was no longer profitable. Eventually, either the exchange where the stock was being purchased would raise the quoted price or the exchange where the stock was being sold would lower the quoted value. This basically riskless strategy has been almost eliminated through the use of high technology computer programs which flag both traders and stock specialists when price differences do occur, greatly reducing the availability of such opportunities.

The use of arbitrage is alive and well in the options markets. Through a combination of several positions, option arbitrage allows traders to take advantage of differences in the pricing of option contracts and the value of the underlying stock. In addition to taking advantage of these price differences, the use of options arbitrage helps to keep the options market efficient. Should the market become out-of-line, the price difference will be picked up by market makers or traders via sophisticated computer programs.

The Forward Conversion

There are two major strategies used in conjunction with options arbitrage:

(1) **the forward conversion,** also known as the **conversion.**

(2) **the reverse conversion,** also known as the **reversal.**

Both the conversion and the reversal involve the use of three positions, the calculation of a dividend and interest calculations. Calculation of the conversion or reversal should be made with great care, because if the mathematics are incorrect or one variable in the formula changes, the opportunity for profit may wind up being a locked in loss.

In order to keep things from getting complicated, we shall first explore the use of the forward conversion, followed by the reversal and then compare the use of both strategies.

The forward conversion requires that the trader purchase the underlying stock, write a call and purchase a put. The put and call utilize the same expiration month and the same exercise price. Once the strategy is initiated, the trader can assume that the stock will be sold on expiration day at the exercise price of the option contracts. If the stock is above the exercise price, the stock will be called from the trader. If the stock is below the exercise price, the put will be exercised and the stock will be sold at the exercise price. Thus, regardless of the value of the underlying stock at expiration, the trader should be able to sell the stock at the exercise price.

While the ideal of the conversion seems simple, there is a little more that goes into using this strategy. The first point is the dividend. The trader assumes that if the stock pays a dividend, the amount of the dividend and the date at which it is paid will remain consistent. If the date of the dividend paid is moved and will not be paid during the holding period, the trader may risk what was supposed to be a gain and may actually realize a loss. The same scenario is possible should the dividend amount be reduced or eliminated. If the dividend to be paid is increased, the trader may realize an additional profit. It should also be noted that if a special dividend, stock split or stock dividend arises, even if it is positive, it might have a negative impact on the holding of the conversion if the stock or option contracts are adjusted.

The second point which should be noted is any type of transaction charges. If an investor implements the forward conversion strategy, the following factors should be factored into the equation:

Stock Purchase Commission

Commission for Call Option Written

Commission for Put Option Purchased

Commission on Sale of Stock (at exercise price)

Margin Interest (if stock is purchased in margin account)

Professional traders may not be subject to the commission charges that investors are subject to, but they are subject to the following transaction charges:

Floor brokerage and clearing charges for stock purchase

Floor brokerage and clearing charges for call writing

Floor brokerage and clearing charges for put purchase

Capital interest charges

If the charges outlined above are not factored into the calculation, the strategy might result in a loss from the beginning.

Calculating Interest

Calculating interest charges, known as the cost-of-carry, (both margin and capital) requires the following formula:

Cost-of-carry for Long Stock = Stock Price × (Interest Rate × (Days Held/365))

The stock price for traders may be substituted at some firms by the exercise price of the options, since this will be the price at which the stock is sold. The amount of days held is the time from which the stock is purchased until expiration day (some firms may use settlement date instead of trade date on both purchase and sale).

Calculating the Conversion

Once the cost-of-carry (COC) is calculated, the following formula will return the value of the profit or loss (if result is a negative number) on a per share basis:

$$\text{Profit of conversion per share} = \text{Exercise Price} - (\text{Stock} - \text{Call} + \text{Put}) - (\text{COC} - \text{Div})$$

In most situations, if the calculations are done correctly and the variables in the calculation are correct, the potential profit should be a number which is relatively low. If the value of the profit is high, it either means that the calculation is incorrect or some factor is being overlooked, such as a possible take over or a wrong quote on one of the option contracts.

For the total profit for the investment, the trader should multiply the profit by the amount of *shares* and not the option contract.

To illustrate, let us evaluate the following information about SHF Corp. and it's option contracts with respect to a forward conversion. SHF is currently trading at 41½ and the three-month call with an exercise price of 40 is at 3⅞, while the put is at 2⅜. The current interest rate is 9 percent (.09) and there are 40 days left until expiration. During the holding period, the stock will pay a dividend of 75 cents per share. Using the formulas above, let us evaluate the conversion:

$$
\begin{aligned}
\text{Cost of Carry (COC)} &= 41\tfrac{1}{2} \times (.09 \times (40/2 = 365)) \\
&= 41\tfrac{1}{2} \times (.09 \times .109) \\
&= 41\tfrac{1}{2} \times .00981 \\
&= .409 \text{ or } .41
\end{aligned}
$$

Profit of conversion per share $= 40 - (41\frac{1}{2} - 3\frac{7}{8} + 2) - (.41 - .75)$
$$= 40 - (39.625) - (-.34)$$
$$= .715$$

Profit of conversion on 100 shares $= \$71.50.$

The profit on the above conversion does *not* include commission charges, brokerage charges or clearing fees, and is merely a simple calculation for computing profitability of a forward conversion. The charges mentioned should be considered when evaluating whether or not the strategy would return a profit. Should the strategy not include those charges, a loss might be realized. Worksheet 13-1, the forward conversion worksheet, can be found at the end of the chapter to assist in the computation of this strategy.

The Reverse Conversion

The reverse conversion or reversal also utilizes the use of the stock, put and call, but in the opposite positions. To initiate the reversal, the trader must sell the underlying stock short, purchase a call and write a put with the same exercise price and expiration date as the call purchased. The purchase of the call and the writing of the put ensures that the trader will repurchase the stock sold short at the exercise price by expiration.

The trader must keep in mind that any dividend paid during the holding period must also be paid by the short seller. In addition, should a special dividend, new dividend or an increase in the dividend be declared by the company, the trader would be liable for any such payments during the holding period.

Traders who are trading for a firm or market-maker account (market professionals) are usually permitted to collect interest on the sale of short stock. Interest collected for the holding period will benefit the trader by adding additional credit to any profit at that point. Some traders will only trade positions to collect interest income and actually use the interest income to offset any loss from the trade positions itself.

The interest income is calculated in the same manner as the cost-of-carry is calculated in the conversion example. For the sake of simplicity, we will continue to call this figure cost-of-carry (COC).

The calculation used to determine the profit per share on a reversal is:

Profit of Reversal per share = (Stock + Put - Call) +
(COC - Div) - Exercise Price

The above formula omits the following variables from the calculation:

Commission and floor brokerage on the short sale of stock

Commission and floor brokerage on the purchase of the call

Commission and floor brokerage on the writing of the put

Interest and other fees relating to short sale of stock

The total profit for the reversal can be calculated by multiplying the profit per share by the quantity of shares sold short and *not* by the options quantity.

Calculating the Reverse Conversion

Let us evaluate the use of the reverse conversion through an illustration. Assume that PZZ Corp.'s stock is trading at 71½ per share. The PZZ call with an exercise price of 70 is trading at 2¼ points and the put with the same exercise price is at ⅞ of a point. There are 50 days until expiration and the interest rate for a short sale credit is 7 percent (.07). During the holding period, the stock pays a dividend of 20 cents per share. First, we must evaluate the cost-of-carry.

Cost-of-Carry (COC) = 71½ × (.07 × (50/365)
= 71½ × (.07 × .14)
= 71½ × .0098
= .70

Next, we can view the profit (loss if the number returned is negative) by replacing the variables in the formula with the values we have for the reversal.

$$\text{Profit of Reversal per share} = (71\tfrac{1}{2} + \tfrac{7}{8} - 2\tfrac{1}{4}) + (.70 - .20) - 70$$
$$= 70.125 + .50 - 70$$
$$= .625$$

To calculate the profit on the total amount of shares, simply multiply the profit by the amount of shares. In this example, we shall use 100 shares, so the total profit on the above reversal would be $62.50.

Like the conversion, the profit on the reversal should be relatively low. If the profit seems high, then one of more of the following might be wrong: the value of one of the variables, the computation, or the quotes on one of the option contracts. The trader should take special care to note this as incorrect information or computation could lead to a loss. Worksheet 13-2, the Reverse Conversion Worksheet, should help to compute the use of the reversal.

The use of the reversal has some possible disadvantages which the trader should carefully note. The first is that selling the stock short might be a problem. As in other option strategies which use short stock positions, the reversal is also subject to these problems (see disadvantages of selling short stock in Chapter 2). In addition, should the stock declare a special dividend or other distribution, the trader might be held liable for an additional unforeseen risk.

There are some special cautionary notes which the trader of the conversion and reversal should be made aware of. As interest rates change and/or fluctuate, the trader might gain or lose. If the firm has interest computed daily based on the changes in interest rates, a gain might result in a loss. In addition to the flucuations of interest rates, most firms have two different interest rates for long stock and short stock. The interest rate for interest earned (short stock) is usually considerably lower than for interest paid on stock borrowed.

One fact of life exists in the stock and options markets, "Nobody gives away something for nothing." If the conversion or reversal looks too appetizing, it is usually because there is something wrong with it. For example, if it looks as if a profit of two points is just waiting to be eaten up on a reversal, then why has nobody else picked up on that fact? The reason for such a discrepancy might be that there is no stock around to be borrowed for a short sale, or if the stock is a foreign company, the dividend might be paid in a foreign currency which when converted might be very different from the last dividend paid.

Professional traders have some tools to provide grater availability of information. One of these tools is the computer, which can evaluate the strategies on all option stocks in a matter of seconds. A second tool is the use of interest rate sheets. These sheets, which can be used by almost any investor and/or trader will show the amount of interest per share till expiration based on either the stock price or strike price of the option contract being used. These sheets are usually generated by a computer on a daily basis, so they are up-to-the-minute accurate. Table 13-1 is a sample of an interest sheet on long stock and Table 13-2 is a sample of an interest sheet on short stock.

Option arbitrageurs or firm option traders do not limit themselves to the use of conversions and reversals. Many professionals use other hedged strategies to make money while maintaining a limited risk. One very popular strategy among option professionals is the use of the synthetic put, since the firm account can earn interest on the short sale of the stock, while maintaining a hedge using the long call to protect against any upward movement in the underlying security. If the stock rises, the trader is not affected since the call will allow for the repurchase of the underlying stock at the exercise price, regardless of how high the stock climbs. The trader still has two risks: (1) an increase or declaration of a special dividend and (2) the reduction of interest paid during the holding period. If the stock should go ex-dividend during the holding period, the trader would be required to pay the dividend on the borrowed shares. Since the interest earned might only be pennies per share, a reduction in the interest rate on the cost-of-carry can have a severe impact on the gain the synthetic put might have been thought to realize.

Option arbitrageurs also use different strategies on stocks which are the subject of takeovers, special dividends, distributions or other unusual activity. The options professional will attempt to calculate present value of the underlying stock, option contracts and any other instruments (bonds, rights, warrants, and so on) and attempt to calculate what they should be worth at both the present time and in the future (expiration date or expiration of another instrument such

TABLE 13-1. Long Interest Rate Sheet

Options Evaluation System   Date: 01-14-1992

Rate: 7.500%

Strike	01–17	02–21	03–21	04–18	05–16	06–19	07–17	08–21	09–19	10–17	11–20	12–20
	4	39	67	95	123	157	185	220	249	277	311	341
5.0	0.00	0.04	0.07	0.10	0.13	0.16	0.19	0.23	0.26	0.28	0.32	0.35
7.5	0.01	0.06	0.10	0.15	0.19	0.24	0.29	0.34	0.38	0.43	0.48	0.53
10.0	0.01	0.08	0.14	0.20	0.25	0.32	0.38	0.45	0.51	0.57	0.64	0.70
12.5	0.01	0.10	0.17	0.24	0.32	0.40	0.48	0.57	0.64	0.71	0.80	0.88
15.0	0.01	0.12	0.21	0.29	0.38	0.48	0.57	0.68	0.77	0.85	0.96	1.05
17.5	0.01	0.14	0.24	0.34	0.44	0.56	0.67	0.79	0.90	1.00	1.12	1.23
20.0	0.02	0.16	0.28	0.39	0.51	0.65	0.76	0.90	1.02	1.14	1.28	1.40
22.5	0.02	0.18	0.31	0.44	0.57	0.73	0.86	1.02	1.15	1.28	1.44	1.58
25.0	0.02	0.20	0.34	0.49	0.63	0.81	0.95	1.13	1.28	1.42	1.60	1.75
30.0	0.02	0.24	0.41	0.59	0.76	0.97	1.14	1.36	1.53	1.71	1.92	2.10
35.0	0.03	0.28	0.48	0.68	0.88	1.13	1.33	1.58	1.79	1.99	2.24	2.45
40.0	0.03	0.32	0.55	0.78	1.01	1.29	1.52	1.81	2.05	2.28	2.56	2.80
45.0	0.04	0.36	0.62	0.88	1.14	1.45	1.71	2.03	2.30	2.56	2.88	3.15
50.0	0.04	0.40	0.69	0.98	1.26	1.61	1.90	2.26	2.56	2.85	3.20	3.50
55.0	0.05	0.44	0.76	1.07	1.39	1.77	2.09	2.49	2.81	3.13	3.51	3.85
60.0	0.05	0.48	0.83	1.17	1.52	1.94	2.28	2.71	3.07	3.42	3.83	4.20
65.0	0.05	0.52	0.89	1.27	1.64	2.10	2.47	2.94	3.33	3.70	4.15	4.55
70.0	0.06	0.56	0.96	1.37	1.77	2.26	2.66	3.16	3.58	3.98	4.47	4.90
75.0	0.06	0.60	1.03	1.46	1.90	2.42	2.85	3.39	3.84	4.27	4.79	5.26
80.0	0.07	0.64	1.10	1.56	2.02	2.58	3.04	3.62	4.09	4.55	5.11	5.61

<F1> Change Rate   <+> Higher Strikes   <–> Lower Strikes   <ESC> Quit

TABLE 13-2. **Short Interest Rate Sheet**

Rate: 6.500%
Date: 01-14-1992

Options Evaluation System

Strike	01-17 (4)	02-21 (39)	03-21 (67)	04-18 (95)	05-16 (123)	06-19 (157)	07-17 (185)	08-21 (220)	09-19 (249)	10-17 (277)	11-20 (311)	12-20 (341)
5.0	0.00	0.03	0.06	0.08	0.11	0.14	0.16	0.20	0.22	0.25	0.28	0.30
7.5	0.01	0.05	0.09	0.13	0.16	0.21	0.25	0.29	0.33	0.37	0.42	0.46
10.0	0.01	0.07	0.12	0.17	0.22	0.28	0.33	0.39	0.44	0.49	0.55	0.61
12.5	0.01	0.09	0.15	0.21	0.27	0.35	0.41	0.49	0.55	0.62	0.69	0.76
15.0	0.01	0.10	0.18	0.25	0.33	0.42	0.49	0.59	0.67	0.74	0.83	0.91
17.5	0.01	0.12	0.21	0.30	0.38	0.49	0.58	0.69	0.78	0.86	0.97	1.06
20.0	0.01	0.14	0.24	0.34	0.44	0.56	0.66	0.78	0.89	0.99	1.11	1.21
22.5	0.02	0.16	0.27	0.38	0.49	0.63	0.74	0.88	1.00	1.11	1.25	1.37
25.0	0.02	0.17	0.30	0.42	0.55	0.70	0.82	0.98	1.11	1.23	1.38	1.52
30.0	0.02	0.21	0.36	0.51	0.66	0.84	0.99	1.18	1.33	1.48	1.66	1.82
35.0	0.02	0.24	0.42	0.59	0.77	0.98	1.15	1.37	1.55	1.73	1.94	2.13
40.0	0.03	0.28	0.48	0.68	0.88	1.12	1.32	1.57	1.77	1.97	2.22	2.43
45.0	0.03	0.31	0.54	0.76	0.99	1.26	1.48	1.76	2.00	2.22	2.49	2.73
50.0	0.04	0.35	0.60	0.85	1.10	1.40	1.65	1.96	2.22	2.47	2.77	3.04
55.0	0.04	0.38	0.66	0.93	1.20	1.54	1.81	2.15	2.44	2.71	3.05	3.34
60.0	0.04	0.42	0.72	1.02	1.31	1.68	1.98	2.35	2.66	2.96	3.32	3.64
65.0	0.05	0.45	0.78	1.10	1.42	1.82	2.14	2.55	2.88	3.21	3.60	3.95
70.0	0.05	0.49	0.84	1.18	1.53	1.96	2.31	2.74	3.10	3.45	3.88	4.25
75.0	0.05	0.52	0.89	1.27	1.64	2.10	2.47	2.94	3.33	3.70	4.15	4.55
80.0	0.06	0.56	0.95	1.35	1.75	2.24	2.64	3.13	3.55	3.95	4.43	4.86

<F1> Change Rate   <+> Higher Strikes   <-> Lower Strikes   <ESC> Quit

as rights). If a price discrepancy does exist, the options trader would attempt to take advantage of that difference and lock in a profit. It is not in the scope of this book to address the individual cases. Since each case is difference, it is important for the investor and trader alike to have a basic understanding of options arbitrage in conjunction with special situations.

Making the Options Market Efficient

Option professionals realize that waiting for conversions and reversals to come into line can be very unprofitable, since very few opportunities do arise. In order to make for more profitable trading, option arbitrageurs will "leg into" a position. The technique of "legging" has the trader taking risk by establishing only part of the position, while attempting to get a better price if the stock or option moves favorably. In most cases, traders like to complete the transaction as soon as possible or as soon as practical, lowering exposure to risk.

The activity of option professionals usually aids the individual investor. Through the activity of options arbitrage, the investor will notice that option prices tend to be more efficient and of fair value. In addition, the trading of options by professionals lends to their liquidity and allows for greater volume executions. Another benefit for the investor is the execution of two- or three-sided orders, such as spreads, covered writes, married puts, and so on, since the professional might be willing to execute the entire trade. Most of the option exchanges also have rules which provide the individual customer with the ability of placing an order in the official order book, allowing for priority over the professionals who are not provided with that opportunity. Option professionals, trading for the accounts of their firms, must designate orders entered for the firm as such, and since they are not allowed to place orders on the book, they are not eligible to enter good-till-canceled (GTC) orders, another advantage for the individual investor.

The trading of puts and calls by option professionals provides several benefits for the firms in which they trade. The most important is a benefit for the investor is that the firm executing an order for the customer might attempt to get the customer a better execution price by taking the other side of the trade, especially if the firm is already taking a position in that stock or options contract. In addition, many firms that trade option positions will spread the cost of executing such business among the firm accounts and the customer accounts, allowing the firm to reduce overhead costs per account and to reduce commission charges for the customer accounts.

In summary, the trading of option contracts by professional traders provides the individual investor with many advantages. Greater liquidity in trading, efficient option markets and valuation of contracts are just some of the benefits which the investor receives from the trading of puts and calls by option arbitrageurs and firm traders. The comprehension of options arbitrage and firm trading benefits the investor who utilizes option contracts and some of the reasoning of option pricing. More explanation of options pricing can be found in Chapter 20.

Forward Conversion—Arbitrage

STOCK			SHARES	PRICE	—52 WEEK—		RATING	PIE RATIO	YIELD
					HIGH	LOW			
OPTION CONTRACT			CONTRACTS	PREMIUM	EXPIRATION DATE		DAYS TILL EXP.		
OPTION CONTRACT			CONTRACTS	PREMIUM	EXPIRATION DATE		DAYS TILL EXP.		
QUART DIVID	DIVIDS TO EXP	TOTAL DIVID COLLECT	DEBIT		REG. T RATE		MARGIN INT RATE		
INTEREST CHARGES:		INT RATE ⎮ DAYS ⎮ ⎮ DEBIT BAL ⎮ $ × ÷365× =					TODAY'S DATE		

REQUIRED CAPITAL

		CASH	MARGIN
Stock Price.....................................			
Amount of Shares..............................	×		
Stock Commission	+		
Stock Cost.................................	=		
Reg T Rate	×		
Equity Required	=		
Call Option Premium			
Amount of Shares..............................	×		
Call Option Commissions.......................	−		
Call Option Proceeds.......................	=		
Put Option Premium			
Amount of Shares..............................	×		
Put Option Commissions	+		
Put Option Proceeds	=		
REQUIRED CAPITAL (Equity Required − Call Proceeds + Put Proceeds)			

PROFIT ÷ LOSS AT EXERCISE PRICE AT EXPIRATION

Exercise Price			
Stock Quantity	×		
Commissions at Exercise Price....................	−		
Dividends Expected	+		
Interest Charges	−		
Debit Balance	−		
Required Capital...............................	−		
Profit..	=		
Return (Profit ÷ Required Capital)..............			
*Annualized Return (Return × 365 ÷ Days)......			

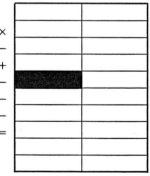

*Annualized returns may only be used if holding is over 60 days.

WORKSHEET 13-2:

Reverse Conversion—Arbitrage

STOCK		SHARES	PRICE	—52 WEEK—		RATING	PIE RATIO	YIELD
				HIGH	LOW			
OPTION CONTRACT		CONTRACTS	PREMIUM	EXPIRATION DATE		DAYS TILL EXP.		
OPTION CONTRACT		CONTRACTS	PREMIUM	EXPIRATION DATE		DAYS TILL EXP.		
QUART DIVID	DIVIDS TO EXP	TOTAL DIVID PAID		CREDIT	REG. T RATE		MARGIN INT RATE	
INTEREST CHARGES:		INT RATE ×	DAYS ÷ 365 ×	DEBIT BAL	$ =		TODAY'S DATE	

REQUIRED CAPITAL

		CASH	MARGIN
Stock Price.....................................			
Amount of Shares.............................	×		
Stock Commission	+		
Short Stock Proceeds........................	=		
Reg T Rate	×		
Equity Required	=		
Call Option Premium			
Amount of Shares.............................	×		
Call Option Commissions......................	−		
Call Option Proceeds........................	=		
Put Option Premium			
Amount of Shares.............................	×		
Put Option Commissions	+		
Put Option Proceeds	=		
REQUIRED CAPITAL (Equity Required − Call Proceeds + Put Proceeds)			

PROFIT ÷ LOSS AT EXERCISE PRICE AT EXPIRATION

Exercise Price			
Stock Quantity	×		
Commissions at Exercise Price..................	−		
Dividends Expected	+		
Interest Charges	−		
Debit Balance	−		
Required Capital...............................	−		
Profit..	=		
Return (Profit ÷ Required Capital)			
*Annualized Return (Return × 365 ÷ Days)			

*Annualized returns may only be used if holding is over 60 days.

14
Combining Strategies

Option professionals have developed new strategies by combining one strategy with another or by taking pieces of one strategy and pieces of another and putting them together. This chapter links the use of both combinations and straddles with stock positions. By adding a stock position to these strategies, the outlook of the stock as well as the attitude of the investor is changed.

In Chapter 8, we discussed the use of purchasing and selling out-of-the-money combinations. The buyer of such a combination has the expectation that the price of the underlying stock will have a substantial move, either up or down. If the investor is correct, the maximum potential profit is unlimited while the potential loss may be 100% of the total investment. If the stock remains between the two exercise prices until expiration, the investor is almost sure to lose most if not all of the investment.

Covered Combinations

The writer of the out-of-the-money combination would welcome the stock remaining between the two exercise prices, as this is the range in which the maximum profit of the credit received will be realized. If the stock has a major break-out in one direction or the other, the potential loss is unlimited. In such an instance, the writer could lose point for point once the break-even point has been violated. The last thing that a combination writer wants is the stock to rise above the call exercise price or drop below the exercise price of the put.

The purchaser of a covered combination takes a different position and has a different opinion of the stock. The covered combination is the purchase of the underlying stock and the writing of an out-of-the-money combination. The ultimate goal of the covered combination is to have the stock rise above the exercise price of the call at expiration, and have the position closed. If the stock remains unchanged to expiration, or between the two exercise prices, the put and call expire worthless, if both are out-of-the-money, and the premiums are kept. The investor may then write another combination or just a call. If the stock drops below the exercise price of the put, the investor would purchase an additional amount of shares equal to the original purchase. The cost of the additional shares is equivalent to the exercise price of the put less the premiums for the options written. The average price of the total position, if put, would be calculated using the following formula:

$$\text{Avg. Cost if Put} = ((\text{Qty} * \text{Orig Stock}) + ((\text{Qty} * \text{Put Exercise}) - (\text{Call} + \text{Put Prem})) / 2$$

The break-even point for this strategy is the debit cost of the position less the dividends collected during the holding period.

While it is the ultimate goal of the covered combination buyer for the stock to rise above the exercise price of the call, the investor would not mind owning a second lot of shares at the lower put exercise price. It is suggested that the quantity of stock purchased be half of the position that the investor would ultimately wish to own. If the stock is called away, the annualized return should be greater than twice the riskless rate, and closer to three times that level. [The cost of purchasing the additional shares if put and the current stock price should be difference of 15 percent.] If the premiums are excessive, the covered combination should be accompanied by the purchase of an even further out of the money put for a quantity of stock which may be owned if the stock is put. This is merely a preventive measure. The covered combination profit/loss analysis can be seen in Figure 14-1.

The purchase of the stock and the writing of a combination is a position which has more bullish implications than a covered write strategy. It commits the investor to possibly purchase a quantity double that of the original stock position. The Covered Combination/ Straddle Worksheet (Worksheet 14-1 at end of chapter) provides a format for computing the use of these strategies. The use of the combination also requires that the put position be subject to the naked margin requirement.

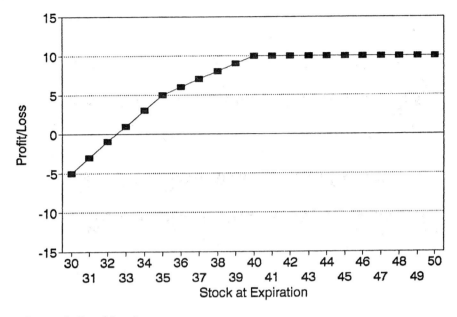

FIGURE 14–1. Covered Combination.

Short Stock and Combinations

The writing of combinations may also be used in conjunction with selling stock short. Use of such a strategy implies a very bearish attitude on the underlying stock, since the investor is taking the obligation of possibly selling an additional stake of stock at the exercise price of the call, should the stock rise. If the stock declines below the exercise price of the put, the stock will be repurchased for an effective price of the put exercise price less the premium received for writing the combination.

The goal when using this strategy is for the stock to drop below the exercise price of the put, and for the stock to be repurchased. If the stock rises above the exercise price of the call, the investor will be short double the amount of the original shares. The effective sale price of the second lot will be the exercise price of the call plus the premiums received for writing the options. If the stock remains between the two exercise prices until expiration, both options will expire worthless, allowing the investor to write another combination or a put by itself.

It is suggested that the investor who is selling stock short and

TABLE 14-1. Short Stock/Short Put versus Short Stock

Stock = 86
Put with 80 Exercise price = 2¼

	Short Stock/Short Put	Short Stock
Position	− 100 Shares	− 100 Shares
	− 1 Put	
Credit	88¼	86

Stock at Expiration	Profits and Losses	
95	<6¾>	<9>
90	<1¾>	<4>
86	2¼	-0-
84	3¾	2
80	8¼	6
75	8¼	11
Max Profit	8¼	86
Max Loss	Unlimited	Unlimited
Break-Even Point	88¼	86

writing a combination ensure that the effective price of selling additional shares short, if called, be more than 15 percent higher than the original price for which the shares were sold. It is also suggested that the effective price of repurchasing the stock, at the exercise price of the put, be at least three times the riskless rate, allowing for ample profit.

Selling a stock short while writing a combination is a similar strategy to selling the stock short and writing a put. While these strategies are similar, the use of the combination is a more agressive strategy since a quantity which is double the original short position may ultimately be short. Table 14-1 compares the short stock/short put strategy against the short stock/short combination strategy, while Table 14-2 illustrates the short stock/short combination versus the short stock position. It should be noted that the call on the short combination is subject to the naked margin requirement.

Another short stock combination position involves the purchase of a combination and the short sale of stock. The purchase of the

TABLE 14-2.   Short Stock/Short Combination versus Short Stock

Stock = 86
Put with 80 Exercise price = 2¼
Call with 90 Exercise Price = 2½

	Short Stock/Short Combination	Short Stock
Position	− 100 Shares − 1 Put − 1 Call	− 100 Shares
Credit	90¾	86

Stock at Expiration	Profits and Losses	
95	<9¼>	<9>
90	¾	<4>
86	4¾	-0-
84	6¼	2
80	10¾	6
75	10¾	11
Max Profit	10¾	86
Max Loss	Unlimited	Unlimited
Break-Even Point	90¾	86

combination protects the investor against a sudden rise in the price of the stock, allowing for the stock to be repurchased at the exercise price of the put. The effective repurchase price of the stock is the call exercise price plus the premium paid for the combination. If the stock declines, as the investor expects, then an election of selling an additional amount of shares short by exercise of the put or selling the put for a profit.

The ultimate goal for the investor is for the stock to decline below the exercise price of the put. Once the stock drops below the put's exercise price, the investor's profits will almost double. If the price of the stock rises, in the worst case scenario the investor will repurchase the stock at the exercise price of the call. If the stock remains between the two exercise prices until expiration, the options will expire worthless. In such a case, the strategy failed since neither the goal of the stock declining or the protection of the call was employable.

TABLE 14-3.   Short Stock/Long Call versus Short Stock/Long Combination

Stock = 64
Call with 65 Exercise Price = 3
Put with 60 Exercise Price = 1

	Short Stock/Long Call	Short Stock/Long Combination
Position	− 100 Shares	− 100 Shares
	+ 1 Call with 65 Exercise	+ 1 Call with 65 Exercise
		+ 1 Put with 60 Exercise
Credit	61	60
Stock at Expiration	*Profits and Losses*	
55	6	10
59	2	2
60	1	-0-
65	<4>	<5>
70	<4>	-0-
75	<4>	5
Max Profit	61	Unlimited
Max Loss	4	5
Down Break-Even Point	61	60
Up Break-Even Point	61	70

The use of the short stock/long combination strategy is similar to the short stock/protective call strategy. The use of the long combination is a more aggressive strategy than the protective call. Table 14-3 compares the protective call against the short stock/long combination strategy and Table 14-4 compares the short stock/long combination versus the sale of short stock.

Long Stock/Long Combination

The purchase of a stock signifies that the investor is bullish. Combining that with the purchase of a long combination reinforces the bullishness of the investor. The goal of the investor is for the stock to rise above the exercise price of the call, allowing the investor to

TABLE 14-4. Short Stock/Long Combination versus Short Stock

Stock = 64
Call with 65 Exercise Price = 3
Put with 60 Exercise Price = 1

	Short Stock	*Short Stock/ Long Combination*
Position	− 100 Shares	− 100 Shares
		+ 1 Call with 65 Exercise
		+ 1 Put with 60 Exercise
Credit	64	60
Stock at Expiration	*Profits and Losses*	
55	9	10
59	5	2
60	4	-0-
65	<1>	<5>
70	<6>	-0-
75	<9>	5
Max Profit	64	Unlimited
Max Loss	Unlimited	5
Down Break-Even Point	64	60
Up Break-Even Point	64	70

increase the potential return, which is unlimited. The investor has a choice of action if the stock climbs above the exercise price of the call, of either exercising the call and purchasing additional stock or selling the call for a profit. If the stock declines below the exercise price of the put, the investor is protected. In such a situation the stock can be sold through the exercise of the put. If the price of the stock remains between the two exercise prices, then the purchase of the combination was unsuccessful since both the put and call will expire worthless.

It is suggested that the maximum loss be limited to less than 10 percent. This should include the purchase of the option contracts and take the dividend into account. In addition, it is suggested that a 10 percent appreciation in the stock will result in the call doubling in value, allowing for full impact of purchasing the combination. The period until expiration of the combination should be at least 60 days, allowing for ample stock movement without rolling the positions due to time.

Like some of the other strategies explored in this chapter, the purchase of a stock and a long combination is more aggressive than the purchase of a stock and a protective put or the stock by itself.

Stock and Straddles

Combinations and straddles are very similar but there are some differences. The use of the straddle, in either purchase or writing, is more aggressive than the combination. The purchase and sale of a straddle require that the investor have great conviction as to the anticipated move in the stock price, as well as the amount of the movement. Let us evaluate the stock position combined with a straddle on a case by case basis.

The purchase of the underlying stock combined with the purchase of a straddle is an extremely bullish strategy. If the stock rises, the value of the call will also rise, while the value of the put declines. The profit of the call will add to the profit on the stock position, once the stock rises above the break-even point. The break-even point is the stock price plus the cost of both put and call, less any dividends collected. If the stock rises above this price, the call and the stock will increase the profit of the combined positions as the stock continues to rise. If the stock drops below the exercise price the put can be exercised, allowing the investor the opportunity to sell the long stock position and limit the loss.

It is suggested that the maximum loss be limited to less than 10 percent. It is also suggested that a 10 percent rise in the stock price return a profit of 100 percent. While this may not be totally reasonable for the call versus the loss in the put, the added value of the stock should supplement the loss of the put.

The comparison of the long stock/long straddle and the long stock/long combination will help to show the aggressive use of the straddle. Table 14-5 illustrates the comparison of these strategies. While all situations are different, careful analysis of each strategy in each case is both prudent and warranted.

Another bullish strategy is the purchase of the underlying stock and the sale of the straddle. The writing of the straddle commits the investor to selling the stock at the exercise price, should the stock be

TABLE 14-5.   Long Stock/Long Straddle versus Long Stock/Long Combination

Stock = 82
Call with 80 Exercise Price = 3½
Put with 80 Exercise Price = ⅝
Call with 85 Exercise Price = 1

	Short Stock/Long Straddle	*Long Stock/ Long Combination*
Position	+ 100 Shares	+ 100 Shares
	+ 1 Call with 80 Exercise	+ 1 Call with 85 Exercise
	+ 1 Put with 80 Exercise	+ 1 Put with 80 Exercise
Debit	86⅛	83⅝

Stock *at Expiration*	*Profits and Losses*	
70	<6⅛>	<3⅝>
75	<6⅛>	<3⅝>
80	<6⅛>	<3⅝>
82	<2⅛>	<1⅝>
85	3⅞	1⅜
90	13⅞	11⅜

above the exercise price. The effective sale price of the stock is the exercise price plus the premium received for writing the straddle. If the stock is below the exercise price, the investor is committed to purchasing an additional amount of stock, at the exercise price. The effective cost of purchasing the additional stock is the exercise price less the credit received for writing the straddle.

It is suggested that the effective sale price of the stock, if called, have a return of at least three times the riskless interest rate. In addition, it is suggested that the effective purchase of the stock be at least 10 percent below the current stock price. Furthermore, the average cost of the original stock and the cost of stock if put should be five percent below the exercise price of the straddle.

The use of the straddle is more aggressive than the use of the combination. Table 14-6 compares the two strategies, showing the differences between the cost if put and the effective return if called. Once again, it is suggested that the investor carefully evaluate the difference between the use of each strategy.

TABLE 14-6.   Straddle versus Combination

Stock = 134
Put with 130 Exercise Price = 2¼
Call with 135 Exercise Price = 4
Put with 135 Exercise Price = 4½
Call with 140 Exercise Price = 2

	Straddle	*Combination*
Position	+ 1 Call with 135 Exercise	+ 1 Call with 140 Exercise
	+ 1 Put with 135 Exercise	+ 1 Put with 130 Exercise
Debit Cost	8½	4¼
Stock at Expiration	*Profits and Losses*	
125	1½	¾
128	<1½>	<2¼>
130	<3½>	<4¼>
135	<8½>	<4¼>
140	<3½>	<4¼>
142	<1½>	<2¼>
145	1½	¾
Max Profit	Unlimited	Unlimited
Max Loss	8½	4¼
Up Break-Even Point	143½	144¼
Down Break-Even Point	126½	125¾

The use of straddles can also be applied to positions which utilize short stock. As with the purchase of stock, the use of a straddle is more aggressive than that of the combination. The straddle can limit both profits as well as losses. These limitations can help the investor, but careful evaluation is warranted.

The short sale of the stock and the purchase of a straddle can help to limit potential loss while allowing the investor to sell additional stock through the exercise of the put contract. If the stock rises above the exercise price, the investor can repurchase the stock through the exercise of the call. If the stock drops below the exercise price, the investor can either sell additional stock, for an effective price of the exercise price plus the premium received for writing the straddle, or sell the put for a profit.

The maximum loss to the investor should be limited to less than 15 percent, while the maximum profit is unlimited, providing that the stock declines sharply. The purchase of the straddle should have at least 60 days until expiration.

The sale of the stock and the sale of the straddle can obligate the investor to sell additional stock at the exercise price or repurchase the stock at the exercise price. If the call is exercised against the investor, an additional lot of stock will be sold at an effective price of the exercise price plus the premium received for the straddle. In such a situation, the average price of the new short position would be calculated by averaging the original short sale with the effective sale price of the stock upon being called. If the stock declines, then the effective price of repurchasing the stock would be the exercise price less the premium received for the writing of the straddle.

The difference between using the long straddle and the short straddle is the difference of choice. When purchasing a combination, straddle, or an option contract, the buyer is the person who decides if a position should be exercised, and is under no obligation to exercise any position. The writer, however, is obligated to performing the action if the position is exercised.

Combining Covered Writes and Married Puts

Covered writes and married puts are very popular strategies among conservative investors. The return of a covered write along with its low risk factor makes the strategy appealing to investors looking for a slightly higher return with ease of use. The married put provides protection for the long stock position, assuring the investor that the maximum loss until expiration of the put contract. This strategy also provides for ease of use while limiting risk. Combining the two strategies together provides the investor with a window of possibilities while limiting the risk of owning the stock.

The combination of the covered write and the married put strategy involves the purchase of the underlying stock, the writing of an out-of-the-money call and the purchase of an out-of-the-money put. This strategy, known as the **Hedge Wrapper**, defines a range where the stock will be sold at expiration, regardless of the stock movement. If the stock rises above the exercise price of the call, the stock will be sold through assignment of the call at the exercise price. If the stock drops below the exercise price of the put, the stock may be sold by the investor exercising the put contract at the exercise price. The range between the two exercise prices is an area in which the stock may be sold, or held and another set of strategies implemented upon the expiration of the option contracts.

The maximum profit for the hedge wrapper occurs if the stock is called at expiration. This allows the investor to sell the stock at the exercise price of the call, and collect any dividends paid during the period which the stock is held. The worst case scenario, the maximum loss, occurs if the stock is sold by exercise of the put contract. The maximum loss is the cost of the hedge wrapper less the exercise price of the put contract plus any dividends collected during the holding period. The break-even price is the cost of the hedge wrapper less any dividends collected during the holding period. If the break-even price is higher than the exercise price of the call option contract, the strategy should be *avoided* since any sale between the two exercise prices will result in a loss. Worksheet 14-2, the Hedge Wrapper Worksheet, found at the end of the chapter, provides a tool for computing this strategy.

Let us look at an example of the hedge wrapper. Assume that an investor purchased 100 shares of a stock for $78 per share. At the same time, the investor wrote a three-month call with an exercise price of 80 for three points and purchased a three-month put with an exercise price of 75 for 1½ points. The debit for this hedge wrapper would be 76½ points. During that three month period, a dividend of .25 per share would be collected. If the stock rose above the exercise price of 80, the stock would be sold for a profit of 3¾ points (80 + .25 − 76½) or 4.9 percent. If the stock dropped below the exercise price of the put, the stock could be sold for a loss of 1¼ points (76½ − 75 + .25) or 1.6 percent. The break-even price for this hedge wrapper would be 76¼ (76½ − .25) or a decline of 2.2 percent for the stock. Table 14-7 compares the hedge wrapper to the covered write and the married put.

It is suggested that an annualized return, if called, be at least twice the level of the return on T-bonds. It is also suggested that the risk level or maximum loss be limited to 4 percent of the cost of the hedge wrapper and that the break-even point be less than half of the distance between the two exercise prices. The days till expiration should be at least 60 with a top of 180 days.

Like most of the other option strategies, the hedge wrapper can be turned around. The **Reverse Hedge Wrapper** involves the short sale of the underlying stock, the purchase of an out-of-the-money call

TABLE 14-7. Hedge Wrappers versus Covered Call Writing

Stock = 74
Put with 70 Exercise Price = 1
Call with 75 Exercise Price = 3½

	Hedge Wrapper	*Covered Call Writing*
Position	+ 100 Shares	+ 100 Shares
	− 1 Call with 75 Exercise	− 1 Call with 75 Exercise
	+ 1 Put with 70 Exercise	
Debit Cost	71½	70½

Stock at Expiration	*Profits and Losses*	
65	<1½>	<5½>
68	<1½>	<2½>
70	<1½>	<½>
72	½	1½
75	3½	4½
80	3½	4½
Max Profit	3½	4½
Max Loss	1½	70½
Break-Even Point	71½	70½

and the writing of an out-of-the-money put. Do not confuse this strategy with the combinations discussed earlier in this chapter. The goal of the reverse hedge wrapper is for the stock to drop below the exercise price of the put. This would require the investor to re-purchase the stock, at a lower price. The maximum profit would be the credit for the reverse hedge wrapper less the exercise price of the put plus any dividends which had to be paid on the short stock during the holding period. The maximum loss occurs if the stock rises above the exercise price of the call. The maximum loss is the exercise price of the call plus any dividends paid during the holding period less the credit for the reverse hedge wrapper. The break-even point for the reverse hedge wrapper is the credit received less any dividends paid.

The reverse hedge wrapper is not as popular as the hedge wrapper strategy for several reasons. First, the short sale of the stock presents some obstacles, as outlined in Chapter 2. Second, the risk of repurchasing the stock usually are higher than the potential maximum profit. It is to the advantage of the investor to have the odds in favor of a profit. Finally, for all of the effort which is involved in setting up the reverse hedge wrapper, the return is slim, making the strategy a disappointment.

Other Strategies

The combining of strategies can lead to very profitable experiences, while also locking the investor or trader into the possibility of a loss. It is beyond the reasonable expectation for any one book to go into the hundreds of different possible strategy combinations. The combining of different strategies can be very complex, and the user of those strategies should take special care to evaluate all of the positions at different possible prices and to pay attention to the dividends paid during the holding period. It is also suggested that extreme caution be taken if the strategy is used. This caution note means that the user should start with a small quantity and monitor the stock and all of the option positions very carefully.

The purchase of a stock and a bull spread can be very rewarding if the stock rises, but it can also present additional loss if the stock does not rise as desired. In the same thought, the short sale of stock and the purchase of a bear spread can be rewarding if the stock declines but can be an added headache if the stock rises. Some adventurous investors have explored the use of a long stock/bear spread strategy, allowing the investor to hedge the long stock position with little extra cost. These possibilities can protect an investment but can also add costs, including commissions and other transaction charges.

Summary

1. The combining of different option strategies with stock positions can prove to be profitable while lowering possible risks.
2. It is also possible that by combining a stock and option strategy that potential return is reduced while the risk of the position is raised.

3. Strategies, such as the hedge wrapper, can lock the investment into a window of profitability and loss, limiting profit potential while limiting loss liability.

4. Conservative strategies, such as the covered combination and hedge wrapper, can provide increased return while allowing the investor the opportunity of selling the existing shares or purchasing additional shares at the exercise price of the put.

WORKSHEET 14-1:

Covered Combination / Straddle

STOCK			SHARES	PRICE	—52 WEEK—		RATING	PIE RATIO	YIELD
					HIGH	LOW			
OPTION CONTRACT			CONTRACTS	PREMIUM	EXPIRATION DATE		DAYS TILL EXP.		
OPTION CONTRACT			CONTRACTS	PREMIUM	EXPIRATION DATE		DAYS TILL EXP.		
QUART DIVID	DIVIDS TO EXP	TOTAL DIVID COLLECT	DEBIT	REG. T RATE			MARGIN INT RATE		
INTEREST CHARGES:	INT RATE DAYS DEBIT BAL. $						TODAY'S DATE		
	× +365× =								

REQUIRED CAPITAL

		CASH	MARGIN
Stock Price..................................			
Amount of Shares...........................	×		
Stock Commission	+		
Stock Cost..............................	=		
Reg T Rate	×		
Equity Required	=		
Call Premium			
Put Premium	+		
Option Net	=		
Amount of Shares.........................	×		
Call Commission	−		
Put Commission	−		
Option Proceeds............................	=		
REQUIRED CAPITAL (Equity Required − Option Proceeds)			

RETURN IF CALLED

Call Exercise Price			
Amount of Shares...........................	×		
Commissons @ Call Exercise.................,........	−		
Dividends Expected	+		
Interest Charges	−		
Debit Balance	−		
Required Capital.............................	−		
Profit ÷ Loss if Called........................	=		
Return if Called (Profit ÷ Req. Cap)			
*Annualized Return (Return × 365 ÷ Days)......			

COST OF ADDITIONAL SHARES IF PUT

Put Exercise Price............................			
Amount of Shares...........................	×		
Commission @ Put Exercise	+		
Cost of Additional Shares..................	=		
Dividends Expected	−		
Interest Charges	+		
Required Capital.............................	+		
Debit Balance	+		
Cost of Additional Shares.....................	+		
Cost of Total Position.......................	=		
Total Amount of Shares	÷		
Average Cost of Position	=		

*Annualized returns may only be used if holding is over 60 days.

212

WORKSHEET 14-2:

Hedge Wrapper Worksheet

STOCK			SHARES	PRICE	—52 WEEK—		RATING	P/E RATIO	YIELD
					HIGH	LOW			
OPTION CONTRACT		PUT	CONTRACTS	PREMIUM +	EXPIRATION DATE		DAYS TILL EXP.		
OPTION CONTRACT		CALL	CONTRACTS	PREMIUM -	EXPIRATION DATE		DAYS TILL EXP.		
QUART DIVID	DIVIDS TO EXP	TOTAL DIVID COLLECT		DEBIT	REG. T RATE		MARGIN INT RATE		
INTEREST CHARGES:		INT RATE ×	DAYS ÷ 365 ×	DEBIT BAL =	$		TODAY'S DATE		

REQUIRED CAPITAL

		CASH	MARGIN
Stock Price..................................			
Amount of Shares............................	×		
Stock Commission	+		
Stock Cost................................	=		
Reg T Rate	×		
Equity Required	=		
Call Premium			
Put Premium	−		
Option Net	=		
Amount of Shares............................	×		
Call Commission	−		
Put Commission	−		
Option Proceeds	=		
REQUIRED CAPITAL (Equity Required − Option Proceeds)			

RETURN IF CALLED

Call Exercise Price			
Amount of Shares............................	×		
Commission @ Call Exercise...................	−		
Dividends Expected	+		
Interest Charges	−		
Debit Balance	−		
Required Capital.............................	−		
Profit ÷ Loss if Called........................	=		
Return if Called (Profit ÷ Req. Cap.)............			
*Annualized Return (Return × 365 ÷ Days)......			

LOSS IF PUT IS EXERCISED

Exercise Price of Put			
Amount of Shares............................	×		
Commission @ Put Exercise	−		
Dividends Expected	+		
Interest Charges	−		
Debit Balance	−		
Required Capital.............................	−		
Loss if Exercised.............................	=		
Loss % (Loss ÷ Req. Capital)			
*Annualized Loss (Max % × 365 ÷ Days)			

BREAK-EVEN POINT

Capital Required.............................			
Debit Balance	+		
Interest Charges	+		
Dividends Expected	−		
Subtotal	=		
Amount of Shares............................	÷		
Break-Even Point			

*Annualized returns may only be used if holding is over 60 days.

213

15

Index Options:
Investing on the Market

Equity options can provide the investor with a variety of opportunities as well as versatility. Until now, this book has focused on the uses of puts and calls in creating many different strategies which can provide diverse methods to achieve the same goals. The choice of strategy is dependent on the investor's view of risk, reward, and stock opinion.

The use of puts and calls is not limited merely to equity options, but may also be used by the investor to make investment selections on a specific market industry or on the market as a whole. Index options can provide the investor with the ability of choosing market direction without limiting that decision to one or two stocks. For many, the use of index options removes the risk of choosing what they believe to be the correct stock, which may prove to be the one stock that does not perform as desired. Index options permit the investor to make market investment calls similar to the investments made on individual stocks.

A New Method of Investing: Buy or Sell the Market

In 1983, the Chicago Board Options Exchange (CBOE) answered the needs of both individual investors as well as market-makers and institutions and developed the first index options which were known as the CBOE 100 or by its ticker symbol "OEX." The CBOE 100 was comprised of 100 of the largest stocks and was weighted by the value of the corporation. Shortly after its inception, the CBOE and Standard & Poor's Corporation merged the CBOE 100 and renamed the index the Standard & Poor's 100 Stock Index. Since 1983, the OEX (as it is commonly known) has become the biggest success in the option business since the introduction of listed options trading. Just as the listing of options by the CBOE changed the options business and the listing of option contracts on other exchanges, the listing of the OEX changed the business once again, providing the other option exchanges with the opportunity to list more option/index option products. In fact, the listing of index options launched the New York Stock Exchange (NYSE) into the listed options trading business with the listing of options on its New York Stock Exchange Composite Index (NYA).

Two Categories of Index Options

Index options can be classified in two categories, which show the type of index represented. The first category is known as the Broad-Based Index. This index option is an index which is based upon a wide range of stocks which represent a variety of corporations. While the amount of stocks in an index has been as low as 20, the fact that the stocks comprising that index are so broad in scope permits the index to be considered a broad-based index.

The second type of index is known as a Narrow-Based Industry Index. This index is a group of stocks in the same industry. A move in this group may or may not be in conjunction with the overall market (broad-based). For example, an investor who is bullish on the computer industry may wish to purchase a call on the American Stock Exchange's Computer Technology Index (XCI).

Before proceeding further, it is important to realize that there are certain differences beween the two index categories. (1) The broad-based indexes are usually more volatile than the narrow-based indexes. (2) The broad-based index options usually have a greater open interest and volume than those of the narrow-based indexes. (3) The margin requirements in the broad-based index are higher (by industry standards) than the narrow-based indexes due to higher volatility. The industry margin requirements are outlined in Table 15-1.

Like stock options, most index options trade with a 100 multiplier (100 × Index Value) or represent 100 shares of the underlying

TABLE 15-1.   Margin Requirements for Naked Index Options

Broad Based Index

Margin Required = 15% of the Underlying Index Value
— the amount the contract is out-of-the-money
subject to a minimum of 10% of the Underlying
Index Value

Narrow Based Index

Margin Required = 20% of the Underlying Index Value
— the amount the contract is out-of-the-money
subject to a minimum of 10% of the Underlying
Index Value

index. Index options are settled for cash upon exercise with the difference between the index value and the exercise price multiplied by the multiplier being returned to the investor (if the index is in-the-money). Some index options are known to have a special property known as European settlement. If an index has European settlement, the option can *only* be exercised on the *last trading day*. If the investor wishes to take a profit before the last trading day, the option must be sold and *cannot* be exercised. Those indexes which can be exercised at any time are known to have American settlement. The merits of using indexes with European settlement will be discussed later in this chapter. Table 15-2 outlines some of the different index options along with the category and settlement types.

Investors are fortunate to have the opportunity to make investment decisions on the market via index options. While investors are able to use many of the same strategies on indexes as they do on stock options, there are some limitations. Such strategies as covered call writing and married put purchases are not possible when using index options since no stock is involved. Even though index option strategies may be limited in this respect, the creation of synthetic positions duplicating the index is possible. For example to duplicte the purchase of the index, the purchase of a call and the writing of a put on an at-the-money exercise price would simulate the movement of the index until expiration of the options. For more information on the use of synthetic positions, see Chapter 12.

TABLE 15-2.   Table of Index Option Contracts

Name of Index	Symbol	Exch	Narrow/ Broad	Settlement
Amex Computer Index	XCI	AMEX	Narrow	American
*Amex Institutional Index	XII	AMEX	Broad	European
Amex Oil & Gas	XOI	AMEX	Narrow	American
CBOE Long-Term Interest Rate	LTX	CBOE	Narrow	American
CBOE Short-Term Interest Rate	IRX	CBOE	Narrow	American
Financial News Network	FNC	PSE	Broad	European
Japan Index, The	JPN	AMEX	Broad	European
Major Market Index	XMI	AMEX	Broad	European
Natl O.T.C.	XOC	PHLX	Broad	American
NYSE Composite Index	NYA	NYSE	Broad	American
Phil. Gold/Silver	XAU	PHLX	Narrow	American
Phil. Utility Index	UTY	PHLX	Narrow	European
*S&P 100 Index	OEX	CBOE	Broad	American
*S&P 500 Index	SPX	CBOE	Broad	European
S&P Midcap Index	MID	AMEX	Broad	European
Value-Line Index	XVL	PHLX	Broad	European

*Longer term options are also available.

Index Option Values

Option premiums on indexes are usually higher compared to those of options on individual stocks. First, the higher value of the underlying instrument results in lower percentage movements on an index with a comparable point movement between an index and an underlying stock. For example, if a $30 stock rises five points, there is a rise of almost 17 percent as compared to a five point rise in a 300-point index which realizes a gain of almost 1.7 percent. Therefore, if the entire market rose 10 percent, the $30 stock would rise three points while the 300 point index would rise 30 points. The stock may not trade through one higher exercise price while the index might rise through six exercise prices. In addition, a greater volatility is present on an index than on an individual stock (in most cases), raising option premiums higher. Option strategists have observed that many index options hold time value almost to the last minute of trading on expiration. The decline of time premium is very sharp during the final days of the expiration month, however, it is not uncommon for five point out-of-the-money options to be trading with up to one point of time premium the day before trading ceases in that contract. Many traders believe that high premiums are the result of program trading and wild price fluctuations as a result of the expiration of stock options, index options and futures contracts, especially during the quarterly "triple witching" expiration which occurs at the end of each quarter.

American Style Versus European Style

American style index option contracts usually have a higher premium than those index contracts with the European settlement feature, since the American style option contracts can be exercised at any time until expiration while the European style options can only be exercised on the final day. Traders and market-makers have witnessed that many of the in-the-money contracts on European style index options trade at a "discount" to their intrinsic value, due to the cost the market-makers and other option professionals have in holding the position to expiration (interest cost, also known as cost of carry). Due to the cost of maintaining such an option position, option professionals are unable to pay premiums on these positions as they would lock in a loss on the position, should the market fail to move.

The use of European style index options can provide the investor with certain advantages when trading positions which involve writing option contracts. Such strategies as spreads and combinations can limit unforeseen market risk if the option positions cannot be exercised or assigned until expiration. For example, an investor who purchases a bull spread using calls on an American style index option may believe that the only risk in holding such a position is the debit paid for the spread. Unlike options on equity issues, there is the potential for an unlimited loss. Assume that an investor purchased one call with an exercise price of 360 and writes a call with an exercise price of 365. If the index rises above 365, the investor may be called at 365 and would have to deliver the cash value of the index minus the exercise price. When the investor finds out about the assignment the next morning, a choice of selling the long call or exercising (that night) would have to be made. Should the market gap open lower and the value of the index drop below the 360 level, the investor would not be able to exercise the long call and would realize a further loss. If such a situation occurred on a stock position, the investor could merely purchase the stock in the open market with no further risk. While the situation illustrated above does not happen frequently, it is a real possibility and has occurred to investors in the past, therefore, the investor should pay special attention to the possibility that such risk is real.

Index Correlations

Broad-based index options usually have a trading ratio between the index and the Dow Jones Industrial Average. The ratio may vary when a component of one index is not a component of the other index. In addition, slight variations do change the ratios between the two indexes from time to time. To calculate the ratio between an

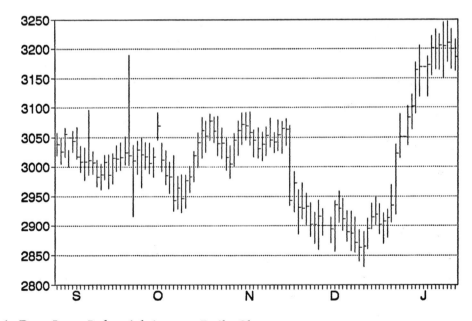

FIGURE 15–1. Dow Jones Industrial Average Daily Chart.

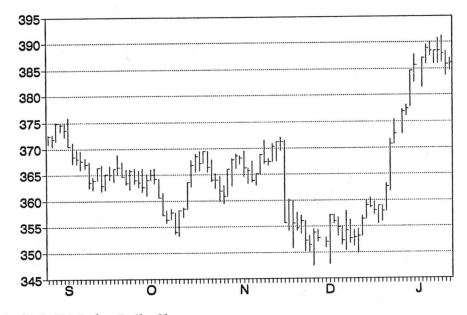

FIGURE 15–2. S&P 100 Index Daily Chart.

index and the Dow Jones Industrial Average (DJIA), simply divide the value of the DJIA by the index which you wish to compare. For example, if the DJIA is at 3011.85 and the OEX is at 370.07, the ratio between the two indexes would be 8.14 (3011.95/370.07). The same method may be used to compare one index versus another, such as the Major Market Index versus the S&P 100 Index. It is suggested that this method not be used on narrow-based industry indexes since these indexes do not adequately represent the market and are too narrow in focus. A graphic comparison of the Dow Jones Industrial Average and the S&P 100 Index is illustrated in Figures 15-1 and 15-2.

When evaluating the purchase or sale of a new index option position, the investor may wish to compare the trading ratios of several indexes as a means of deciding which investment selection would be profitable.

Options as Market Indicators

Index options are not just limited to use as investment tools. Many strategists, technicians, and other market professionals will use index options as a means for evaluating the market on a technical basis.

While it is not the intention of this book to explain or elaborate on technical analysis, a quick look at using index options as a market indicator could prove to be helpful. For those interested, further reading is suggested, as there are many publications on the use of technical analysis which focus on the use of options as a technical indicator.

Many technicians will utilize an indicator known as the **put/call ratio** to help evaluate market sentiment. The put/call ratio measures the amount of put contracts traded to the amount of call contracts traded. It is believed that the greater the amount of puts traded, the greater the bearish sentiment and the more positive for the market. The put/call ratio is known as a contrary indicator, meaning the more individuals who are bearish, the greater the chance of them being wrong, leading to a bullish conclusion. The put/call ratio is usually evaluated on a day-to-day basis as well as on a moving average basis. Some technicians tend to use a ten day moving average while others use only a four day moving average. The shorter the moving average, the more the indicator is used for speculative trading. In addition, some professionals will plot two different moving averages and watch for those moving averages to cross, indicating a market turn or change in market sentiment. The put/call ratio is calculated by dividing the amount of puts traded on an index by the calls traded on that index. The volume figures for the index options are easily obtained in *The Wall Street Journal, The New York Times*, and in *Investors Daily*.

Option premiums are another means of attempting to evaluate the movement or the prediction of movement in the market. Before going further, it is important to remember that call premiums are usually slightly higher than put premiums. Comparing option premiums, especially as expiration nears, can provide some insight into market direction. For example, assume that an index is at the 400 level and a put with one week till expiration and an exercise price of 395 is set at four points and a call with an exercise price of 405 is at eight points. In this case, it is believed that the market is going to move higher since investors and professionals are willing to pay much more for a call five points away from the current market value than the put which is the same distance from the market.

Using options as technical tools can provide great insight into the alternative techniques used by small and medium sized investors. It is understood that the greater the amount of oddlot short sales (oddlots are trades on stock with less than 100 shares), the greater the probability that the market will go higher, since small investors are usually wrong. Therefore, examining different technical tools, including put/call ratios and option premiums can assist in the formation of an opinion with respect to market direction. While these tools help in providing market direction, the use of these tools should be utilized in conjunction with other market indicators and should not be used soley on their own merit. In addition, one of the reasons technicians and other professionals use moving averages for the put/call ratios is to provide a smoothing effect as aberrations, such as expiration, may provide incorrect, slanted or biased results.

Industry Indexes

Just as there are index options which focus on the broad market, narrow-based index options usually focus on a particular industry. Industry-based options can provide the investor with a vehicle for purchasing a package of stocks on a particular industry such as computers or oil and gas. Therefore, an investor with an opinion on a particular group of stocks can make an investment decision using one vehicle instead of a making a trade on each stock in that particular stock in that industry.

Interest Rates

The CBOE, after its success with the S&P 100 Index, has introduced two interest rate index options which trade similarly to the S&P 100 Index: the long-term interest rate index (LTX) and the short-term interest rate index (IRX). These two indexes trade with a 100 multiplier and are also settled for cash, just like the OEX. Both of these two indexes are American-style options which may be exercised at any time until expiration, by the holder.

The two interest rate indexes are based on the value of "longer-term" bonds and notes and short-term notes and bills, respectively. As the rate of interest rises (bond prices decline), the value of the interest rate index will rise. If the rate of interest declines (bonds rise in price), the interest rate index will decline. Call prices rise and put prices decline when interest rates rise, and vice versa.

The values of the indexes and their option exercise prices are valued with the 10 multiplier, to make the index tradable. Therefore, if the interest rate is at 7½ percent, the value of the index will read as 75.00 and the exercise price would be 75. Exercise prices gapped at 2½ point intervals which would be equivalent to ¼ percent.

Interest rate index options provide the investor with the unusual ability and opportunity to hedge such personal obligations as adjustable rate mortgages. If the investor fears a rise in interest rates, the purchase of a call option may hedge against an adjusted rise in interest charged when the mortgage is adjusted by the bank. A person or bank may hedge against a drop in interest rates by either purchasing a put or writing a call on an interest rate index, if a loan is going to be made in the future. These are just some of the additional uses of interest rate index options.

The use of interest rate indexes, narrow-based industry indexes and broad-based indexes and their respective options can provide the investor or trader with the opportunity of trading a non equity instrument just like and equity instrument. The power of such tools should not be overlooked or under-utilized.

Using index options as technical tools is an additional benefit of using indexes. Another benefit which is illustrated in Chapter 16 allows the investor to hedge the value of an entire portfolio using index options.

Summary

1. Index options allow the investor to participate in market movements without being limited to one stock.

2. The use of industry index options allows for the investment on a particular industry.

3. Index options can be used as a tool in forecasting market movement.

16

Index Options:
Protecting Your Portfolio

Index options have many of the same properties as equity options. While the use of index options may have a broader focus than equity options, many of the strategies which can be used for equities can be used for indexes, in a broader sense. One of the major advantages of using index options allows the investor to protect or hedge a portfolio. In some cases the portfolio which may be hedged may have a narrow focus, such as a specific industry, while in many cases the portfolio might be broad-based (diverse) or even a group of blue-chip stocks.

Protecting a Portfolio of Stocks

Chapter 15 described the various index options available. The investor should first determine which index would best describe the portfolio which the investor is trying to hedge. If the portfolio is made up of mostly companies which mine gold and silver, the Gold and Silver Index would be the most appropriate for the hedge. Utilizing an index which has little common value with the portfolio will only defeat the use of the hedging strategy since the value of the stocks comprising that index may move in one direction while the value of the portfolio moves in the opposite direction. There are many instances when the broad market moves in one direction and a particular index or industry group moves in another direction. For example, if the price of oil rises dramatically, the oil and gas stocks will move higher while the broad market will move lower due to higher costs and inflation directly related to the rise in the price of oil.

The second factor which the investor must determine lies in the scenario which the investor is trying to protect against. Many investors choose a "worst case scenario" which they believe would have the hardest impact on their portfolio. The scenario which the investor has painted may be accurate, worse or not as bad as what actually

TABLE 16-1. Portfolio Protection: An Example

Portfolio Value = $500,000
Dow Jones Industrial Average (DJIA) = 3255.00
S&P 100 (OEX) = 389.80; Value = 38,980.00
OEX Put with 390 Exercise Price = 7

	Portfolio with Protection	Portfolio without Protection
Additional Position	+ 13 OEX with 390 Exercise	-None-
Additional Capital	$9100	-0-
Total Capital	$509,100	$500,000

Market at Expiration	Approximate Portfolio Value	
DJIA: 2929.50 OEX: 350.82 Down 10%	$491,834	$450,000
DJIA: 3092.25 OEX: 370.31 Down 5%	491,497	475,000
DJIA: 3255.00 OEX: 389.90 Unchanged	490,900	500,000
DJIA: 3417.75 OEX: 409.40 Up 5%	515,900	525,000
DJIA: 3580.50 OEX: 428.78 Up 10%	540,900	550,000

happens, or might be entirely wrong. Therefore, the cost of such protection should be kept to a minimum while the quality of such protection should be kept as high as possible. From the scenario the investor should determine two factors: (1) how bad can the situation be (how much of a correction is anticipated), and (2) in what time frame might this correction take place. If the correction is not expected for several months, the investor may wish to hold off on taking a position. If the market moves higher, the investor will probably wish to use an exercise price which is higher in value. In addition, it is not practical to purchase an option too early, since time premium would be too high to allow the investor to effectively hedge the position. Table 16-1 compares the use of the portfolio hedge against an unprotected portfolio. The Portfolio Hedge Worksheet (Worksheet 16-1 at the end of the Chapter) will aid in the decision of using such a strategy.

How Many Contracts Are Needed?

Before deciding on the appropriate option to purchase for the hedge, the investor should determine how many contracts should be purchased to efficiently protect the portfolio. Calculating the amount of contracts involves equating the value of the portfolio to the value of the index on which an option might be purchased or written. To evaluate this equation, use the following formula:

$$\text{Contracts for Hedge} = \frac{\text{Portfolio Value}}{(\text{Index Value} \times \text{Index Multiplier})}$$

Note that adjustment to the amount of contracts held during the period may be necessary due to fluctuations between the value of the investor's portfolio and the value of the underlying index.

The value of the underlying index can be compared to any other index in a similar manner to calculating the amount of contracts needed for the hedge. The formula for the ratio between two indexes is:

$$\text{Index Comparison} = \frac{\text{Index to Be Compared Against}}{\text{Index Being Compared}}$$

If you wanted to compare the S&P 100 Index (OEX) to the Dow Jones Industrial Average, simply divide the OEX Index into the DJIA. For example if the DJIA is at 3017.67 and the OEX is at 370.40 then the ratio of Dow Jones points to one OEX point would be 8.15 (3017.64 / 370.40) DJIA points. This ratio is a general ratio since a component of one index may make a large move and not be a component of the other index, temporarily making the ratio for the index incorrect. Therefore, if the investor expects the market to decline by 100 DJIA points, an expectation of a 12¼ points (100 / 8.15) decline in the OEX Index would be a reasonable assumption. The assumption of a decline in the index which is being used as a hedge is very important, as will be seen shortly.

Which Option Should Be Purchased?

Selecting the correct put option is essential if the strategy is going to work correctly. If the investor believes that a correction to the market will occur during the next two months, a put contract with at least 60 days till expiration should be utilized. Purchase of a put with only 30 days till expiration may only protect against half of the move, a subsequent purchase of another put will result in the investor paying additional premium and commission charges.

Selection of the correct exercise price is as important as the time till expiration. The use of a put with an exercise price at-the-money or just out-of-the-money is usually desired. The selection of an exercise price which is close to the value of the index will provide the greatest amount of leverage if the investor is correct about a decline. Those investors with sophisticated option models (see Chapter 21 on computers and options) should use a put contract with a high hedge ratio (also known as delta). Chapter 20 explores the use of option models and pricing and explains the use of the hedge ratio.

Next, if the premium seems to be too high, move on to the next strategy of hedging your portfolio by writing calls. If the premium seems to be of fair value, evaluate the put contract, the value of the portfolio and the value of the package combined, as is done in Figure 16-4. Through this evaluation, it is possible to see exactly how effective the hedge technique will be if there is a correction. Note, in most cases only a percentage of the value lost in the portfolio will be recovered through the put. The investor should attempt to recover the greatest loss of the portfolio, on a percentage basis, through the use of the put.

In order to fully understand the use of this strategy, let us examine an investor's portfolio versus a possible 10 percent correction in the market. Our investor has a portfolio with a current value of $100,000. The Dow Jones Industrial Average is at 3013 and the OEX Index is at 368.55. Our investor is nervous and believes that there is a possibility for a 10 percent correction, which could deteriorate the DJIA to approximately 2700 (300 points). To reduce the risk of this correction, our investor decides to hedge the portfolio using OEX put options since the portfolio is broad-based.

First, our investor determines that three puts will be purchased to hedge the portfolio. Next, our investor decides to purchase a put with at least 60 days till expiration. With the OEX at 368.55, our investor decides to evaluate the use of a put with an exercise price of 365 and an exercise price of 360. The 365 put is currently trading at 5⅞ and the 360 put is at 4⅝. If the market declines 300 DJIA points, OEX will drop approximately 37 points to a level of 331.55 and the value of the portfolio will decrease by approximately $10,000 to a new value of $90,000.

Evaluating the Value of the Contract

Evaluating both puts with OEX at 331.55 at expiration, we find that the put with the 365 exercise price is worth 33.45 points (on an intrinsic basis) and the put with the 360 exercise price is worth 28.45 points. Therefore, the offsetting profit if the 365 put were purchased would be $8,272.50, while the purchase of the 360 put would return a profit of $7,147.50. If the investor purchased the 365 put, a net loss to the portfolio would be $1,727.50. If the investor purchased the 360 put, a net loss to the portfolio of $2,852.50 would be realized. In this case, the use of the 365 put would provide the greater amount of protection/leverage in case the market did suffer a correction of 10 percent. In this case, the investor's loss would be reduced by 71 percent, some of which might be further offset through the collection of dividends. Note: This example did not take into account commissions or other transaction charges which should be included when calculating the use of this strategy.

As the market fluctuates, and the volatility of the market increases and decreases, the value of the index options will change. In times of expanding volatility, option premiums tend to rise, while when the volatility in the market decreases, so do the option premiums. When the option premiums are high and the volatility is rising, some investors feel that this is the time to purchase protection for their portfolio.

When option premiums are very high, the investor may seek an alternative by writing out-of-the-money calls on the index. Before exploring this strategy, it is important to note that writing index calls might exceed the risk that the investor wishes to take in protecting the portfolio, since if the market rises, the calls might become in-the-money, which would subject the investor to the liability associated with writing index options.

Some Suggested Guidelines

The writing of the index calls should be limited to as short a term as possible. Reasons for the use of the shorter-term call include: (1) The call can be rewritten for the next month, allowing the investor to take full advantage of the decay in time premium. (2) It forces the investor to re-evaluate his opinion of the market and the risk involved in writing the call. If the market has moved higher, the investor would have the opportunity of writing a call into the next month with a higher exercise price, known as a diagonal roll-up (see Chapter 23 on following up option strategies). The possibilities for future opportunities are limitless if the investor's assumptions about the market are correct; however, caution is strongly suggested.

If the investor writes out-of-the-money calls, and the market declines, the investor should repurchase these calls. Once the call is repurchased, the investor may wish to write another out-of-the-money call or purchase a put, if the premiums have deteriorated. If the market remains virtually static, the option premium should deteriorate and the put premiums should deteriorate, allowing the investor to repurchase the call option for a profit, and purchase a put option with a longer term till expiration for less capital than when the strategy was initially contemplated.

Another Method

Writing out-of-the-money calls should utilize an exercise price which is at least 10 percent away from the current value of the index. This will allow the investor some market price movement before an adjustment would need to be made. Adjusting the exercise price should be done once the market has gained between 5 and 6 percent from the original value of the index. The premium which the call should be carrying should be at least 1 point. When option premiums are low, the writing of calls against a stock portfolio should be abandoned and the use of the purchase of puts should be favored.

If the premiums on the put contracts seem excessive, a second alternative may be sought by the investor. The purchase of a bear spread using puts will allow the put which is written to offset a great amount of the extra premium. The put which should be purchased should use the same criteria as for the purchase of the put against the stock portfolio.

Summary

1. One advantage to using index options is to hedge the value of a portfolio against a sudden decline in market value.

2. A major decline in the market can be offset through the purchase of the right put or the writing of the right call.

3. While 100 percent of a loss in the portfolio may not be recovered, the gain in the options should recover a good part of that loss.

4. The cost of protecting a portfolio is usually low compared to the value of the portfolio.

WORKSHEET 16-1:

Portfolio Hedge Worksheet

REQUIRED CAPITAL

Value of Portfolio............................		
Index Value.................................	÷	
Index Multiplier............................	×	
Contracts Required	=	
Option Premium.............................	×	
Index Multiplier............................	×	
Commission on Puts	+	
Capital Required for Hedge....................	=	

HEDGE EVALUATION

Current Value of Portfolio.....................		
Percentage of Market Decline		
Projected Value of Portfolio...................	−	
Projected Portfolio Loss	=	
Current Index Value		
Percentage of Market Decline	×	
Projected Value of Index......................	=	
Exercise Price of Put	−	
Amount Put Is In-The-Money	=	
Amount of Puts Purchased.....................	×	
Value of Puts Held...........................	=	
Capital Required for Hedge....................	−	
Profit on Put Hedge..........................	=	
Projected Portfolio Loss		
Profit on Put Hedge..........................	−	
Projected Loss Reduced To	=	
Projected Portfolio Loss	÷	
Effect of Put Hedge..........................	=	

17

Understanding Futures on Indices

The use of index options and the value of the underlying indexes is not limited to trading puts and calls. Some of the indexes on which options are traded also trade futures contracts. While the focus of this book is on the use of different option strategies, certain techniques using futures contracts allow the investor to create spreads or arbitrage positions using futures, options, and a basket of securities. The use of such strategies may not be appropriate for small or medium size investors, but the knowledge of how these strategies work will not only help to improve your knowledge of options trading, but may also help you to form an opinion on the direction of the market on a very short-term basis.

A futures contract is different from an options contract in that it is either purchased or sold and will be settled on the last trading day. Upon settlement, the purchaser of a futures contract will exchange that contract plus the current value of the contract for the commodity which the contract represents. In the case of an index, the commodity might either be the stocks which make up that index, or the cash value of the index. The seller of futures would sell the commodity in exchange for the current value of the future. The gain or loss is dependent on what the initial value of the commodity or future was when the position was initiated.

Futures are similar to options in that they both expire. On most instruments, the expiration is not the third Friday of the month, but another date set by the Exchange on which it trades. Because of the nature of futures on indexes, those contracts expire either on the same day or the trading day before the expiration of the options contract.

Unlike options contracts, the purchaser and seller of a futures contract can only trade the commodity in a margin account. The margin account is "marked-to-the-market" daily, with the investor subject to additional capital requirements or credits on a daily basis. As the value of the commodity rises, so does the required margin. If the value of the commodity or future declines, the required margin declines. The margin required is usually only a small percentage of the value of the contract, but during times of volatile trading, the requirement may be raised with less than a day's notice. It is therefore important that anyone trading futures have excess capital in an account to cover any additional and unforeseen requirements. The initial requirement for trading a futures contract may be as little as 5 percent of the value of the future. Brokerage firm margin requirements may be higher than the requirements of the commodities exchange.

Futures contracts are standarized and may be purchased and sold with a fair amount of ease. Unlike option contracts, futures contracts are not set with a predetermined standarized multiplier. Each future has its own multiplier and contracts which may trade on the same commodity but may have different properties such as the quantity which the future represents. Publications such as *The Wall Street Journal*, *The New York Times*, *Barrons*, and *Investors Daily* list the futures contracts in a table which also includes the quantity which each contract represents. The value of each contract is the quoted price multiplied by the quantity which the contract represents.

Let's look at an example of a gold futures contract and examine the properties and price changes on that contract. Table 17–1 shows how this contract might be listed in the newspaper.

TABLE 17-1. Listing of Gold Futures Contract

	Open	High	Low	Settle	Change	High	Low	Interest
	GOLD (CMX)-100 troy oz.; $ per troy oz.							
Oct.	351.5	353.3	351.4	352.1	+1.90	476.0	346.5	8,608
Dec.	354.3	357.0	354.3	355.2	+1.80	483.0	350.1	65,412
Feb.	356.5	359.5	357.5	358.3	+1.90	456.5	353.5	10,173
Apr.	360.8	361.3	360.6	361.2	+1.90	446.0	355.0	6,442

This is just a partial listing of gold futures. In examining the headings, the terms **open, high,** and **low** are self explanatory. **Settle** is the closing price of the day, followed by the **change** in price for the day. The **lifetime high** and **low** is the high and low for *that* contract, since its creation. The **open interest** is the amount of outstanding contracts (like options). The second line gives the definition for the contract. **CMX** is the Commodity Exchange in New York. **− 100 troy oz.** is the quantity value for each futures contract, and in this case this contract represents 100 troy ounces. The **$per troy oz.** is the term for which each contract is quoted. In this case, although the contract represents 100 troy ounces, the price for which it is quoted is based on 1 troy ounce. Therefore, the October contract, which settled for 352.1 is actually worth $35,210,00 per contract (352.1 × 100). The margin requirement for this contract is $1,330 for traders and speculators and $1,000 for people who are using the contract as a legitimate hedge, as defined by the Exchange. In the case of most readers and investors, the larger margin account would be appropriate.

The current value of the October gold contract is 352.1. If the price of gold rises, the purchaser of the contract could sell the contract for a profit in the open market or wait until the contract ceases trading and exchange the contract, at current value, for 100 troy ounces of gold. Therefore, if the price of gold rises to $370 per troy ounces, the investor may take one of two actions:

1. Sell the contract for $370 and make a profit of $17.90 per troy ounces or $1790 per future contract.

2. Exchange the contract for 100 troy ounces of gold. The actual cost of gold, after the exchange will be $352.10 per ounces of gold. The investor will actually have to purchase the 100 troy ounces at 370 per ounce and sell the future back for 370 per ounce which adjusts the price for the gold to the original value of the futures contract.

Let us look at a decline in the value of the commodity. Assume that you purchased the October gold contract at $352.10 per troy ounce and the price of gold drops to $330 per ounce. Again, the investor has two decisions which can be made:

1. The future may be sold for $330 per troy ounce, realizing a loss of $22.10 per troy ounce or $2,210 per contract, which is a 6.3 percent loss.

2. The contract may be exchanged to receive the package of 100 troy ounces of gold. Once the prices are adjusted for the original purchase price, the cost of owning the gold will be $352.10 per troy ounce. At the time the future is exchanged, the holder of the contract sells the contract to the person who is selling the gold for the current price of $330 per troy ounce. The investor will have an unrealized 6.3 percent loss.

The value of futures contracts is not the same as option contracts. It is not necessarily true that a future with a longer term till expiration will trade with a higher value. For example, assuming that it is November, a crude oil future with January delivery will trade at a higher value than the same contract with a July delivery, since there is a higher demand for oil during the winter heating season than there is during the summer. In this case, the value of time can work *against* the purchaser of a longer contract.

Futures contracts are available on many commodities, including silver, platinum, crude oil, wheat, pork bellies, insurance, treasury issues, and so on. Contracts are also available on currencies and other financial futures.

Investors who follow the price of futures may benefit from price moves, trend changes, and such. Those investors who do not trade commodities may also benefit from following the prices of commodities and their relationships to certain stocks or industry groups. For example, when gold and silver rise, stocks such as ASA Mining and Homestake Mining may also rise, reflecting the appreciation in assets. Those investors who trade the stocks of oil corporations would do well to follow the price of changes of crude oil futures, while investors who trade paper and furniture companies would benefit to follow the price changes in lumber contracts. Table 17–2 provides some suggested guidelines for the trading of financial futures contracts, while Table 17–3 lists some of the reasons for using futures instead of option contracts.

Just as an investor would follow the specific commodities, following financial future can aid in short-term market timing and quick trend changes. Options traders and arbitrage specialists monitor the price changes and trends of futures on indexes, and attempt to take advantage of price discrepancies, much in the same manner as options arbitrageurs. There are various ways to take advantage of price differences, such as spreading between the financial future and an options contract or even the difference between the index of

TABLE 17-2. Suggested Guidelines for Trading Financial Futures

Monitor prices of futures, basket, and options.

Monitor fair value and break-even levels of futures.

Check dividends for adjustments.

Watch for opportunities for pre-mature close-out of position or roll to another contract.

Remember to monitor margin levels of futures, options and for the basket of stocks.

Stock positions may require adjustments to reflect the price movements of individual issues.

Short basket portfolio should be monitored to ensure against "buy-in" situation.

---

stocks and the futures contract, through the use of basket trading which results in program trading. We shall examine the differences in the use of index futures and options as well as basket trading shortly.

Market-makers on the exchanges as well as other option professionals will adjust both option markets and their own limits based on movement in the futures contracts. As the value of the financial future rises, the values of calls will rise and puts will decline. If the futures decline, the calls will also decline while the puts rise. These price changes will actually take place before the values of the stocks which make up the underlying index change. For example, if the futures contract on the S&P 500 rises, traders and market-makers in the OEX pit will raise call prices and lower put quotes immediately. This can be frustrating to investors who enter limit orders and miss trades since the quoted market on computer terminals has not adjusted to the new quotes. This can lead to missed trades as well as missed opportunities for the investor.

Option professionals will attempt to create different strategies using a combination of puts, calls, and futures to take advantage of price differences. One popular technique among traders is to purchase a futures contract which is trading at a level near the actual value of the index and write a call against that future, creating a position which is *similar* to a covered write, although the position is not actually covered. If the value of the index rises, the future will also rise, and if the index falls, the value of the future will fall. This position is beneficial if the index rises or remains relatively unchanged until expiration. As expiration nears, the call's time premi-

TABLE 17-3.   Reasons for Using Financial Futures Over Options

Option time premiums fluctuate greater than the movement of the futures contracts.

Options must be purchased for cash, futures require a small margin providing for greater leverage.

Commissions on futures are generally less than on options.

---

um will decay and the position can be reversed for a profit. If the index declines by more than the *time-premium* of the call written, the strategy may be closed.

It is important to realize that *all* of the examples shown assume a multiplier of 100, which may not be correct in all cases but helps to illustrate the strategy. Users of this strategy should use *extra-caution* when evaluating such strategies.

To illustrate, assume that the Major Market Index (XMI) is at 632.50 and the one-month future contract is at 633. The XMI one-month call with an exercise price of 635 is trading at six points. The market-maker may purchase one futures contract and write the 635 call for six. If the index rises to 640 at expiration, the value of the futures contract would yield a seven-point profit. The call would have to be repurchased for five points, realizing a one-point profit on the option or a total gain of seven points. If the index remains at 632.50, then the future would realize a ½ point loss and the call would expire worthless, for a gain of six points, realizing a net gain of 5½ points. If the index fell to 625, then the position on the future contract would realize a seven-point loss and the call would expire worthless, for a net loss of two points (7 − 5). The break-even point for this strategy would put the index at 637. The maximum profit can be figured at the exercise price and would be computed using the following formula:

$$\text{Max Profit of Future/Call Write} = (\text{Exercise Price} - \text{Future Cost}) + \text{Option Premium}$$

The maximum loss of this strategy is the cost of the future less the option premium, should the index decline to zero. Figure 17–1 shows

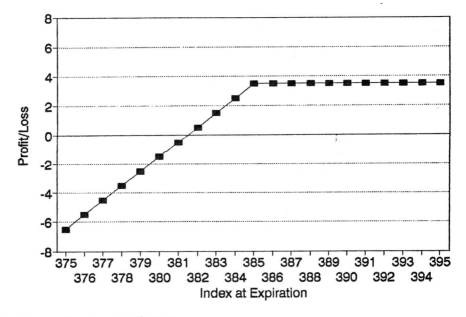

FIGURE 17–1. Future Purchase/Call Write.

the use of such a strategy in pictoral form. As it can be seen, this is a bullish strategy.

A second strategy, a put which is married to a future contract, is *similar* to that of the married put. In this strategy, the trader would purchase the future, and purchase a put to protect against the future declining. The maximum profit for such a strategy is unlimited, although the profit will be reduced by the premium paid for the put option. The loss for such a strategy would be limited to the cost of the future plus the option premium less the exercise price of the put contract. The break-even point for this strategy is the debit price of the put option and the futures contract. This strategy is even more bullish than the purchase future/call write.

Writing puts and selling futures is just another way of taking advantage of a high premium in the puts. The trader will sell both the futures contract and a put which is out-of-the-money. This bearish technique has an unlimited risk should the value of the index rise. If the index falls, a maximum profit should be achieved when the put contract and the future is repurchased below the exercise price of the put option. The break-even price for this strategy is the price the future is sold for plus the premium received for writing the put option. Let us examine the use of this strategy. Assume that the XMI one-month future at 633 is sold and a one-month put with an exercise price of 625 is written for three points. If the index declines to 625, the maximum profit will be realized. The put will expire worthless and the future will be repurchased for a gain of eight points or a net profit of 11 points. If the index drops below the exercise price, any gain in the put will be offset by a corresponding loss on the put. If the index remains unchanged at 633, then the put expires worthless and the future is repurchased for the same price at which it was sold, netting a gain of three points (the put premium).

Still, another method of taking advantage of price differences between the options and the futures is through the use of synthetic option strategies. The creation of a synthetic long index position and the sale of an inflated future value, allows the trader to take advantage of low call premiums and high future prices. The trader will sell the future contract, purchase a call and write a put using the same exercise price and expiration month. If the value of the index rises, the combination of the long call and short put should rise almost point for point with the index, offsetting any loss which might be realized on the rise of the future. If the index falls, the fall of the future will be partially offset through the decline in the value of the long call short put combination. The profit is made since the future contract will come into line with the value of the index at expiration. Therefore, any premium will be eroded from the future and that premium should wind up being the rough profit.

If, however, the value of the future is at a discount to the actual value of the index, a synthetic short using the options may be employed against the futures contract. To create such a strategy, the trader would purchase the future, write a call and purchase a put with the same exercise price expiring in the same month. If the index declines, the combination of the long put and short call would rise approximately one point for each point that the index declines. If the index rises, the rise in the futures price would be partially offset by the decline in the long put short call combination. The maximum profit should be the discount of the futures contract less any time-premium paid for the options combination.

For example, assume that XMI is at 632.50 and the future contract is at 630.50, a two-point discount. The trader purchases the future and sells the one-month call with the exercise price of 635 for four and purchases the 635 put for five. The overall difference in the prices is 1½ points. If the index rises to 640, then the future will gain

8½ points, the call will have a loss of one-point and the put will have a loss of five points. The total net gain with the index at 640 would be 2½ points (8½ − 1 − 5). If the index declines to 625 then the future would realize a loss of 5½ points, the call would be worthless for a gain of four and the put would rise to 10 for a total gain of ½ point. While this gain may not be that great, it is almost guaranteed.

Attempting to take advantage of such differences in market prices should be left to professionals, who have high technology as a means to look for these discrepancies, as well as the ability to execute such strategies via computer, which lowers the execution risk substantially. In addition, by the time that most investors notice the difference in prices, the professionals have already been in the market and brought the prices back into line. This is not to say that investors should refrain from using any of these strategies; however, using these strategies to take advantage of price differences is not recommended. Many investors may wish to use the aforementioned strategies after executing one or two of the positions and later executing the third side, to lock in profits or take advantage of a price difference at that time.

Fair Value

Like stocks, bonds, and even option contracts, the value of a financial futures contract can mathematically be determined. Computation of the fair value of the financial future must take into account several factors. First and most important, the value of the future should reflect the value of the basket of stocks which the contract represents. It would be very unfair to purchase a contract which is worth only half of the value of the basket of stocks to have it worth the full value of the basket at expiration. If this were the case, investors and professionals alike would forego the use of other investment vehicles to purchase the financial future. In addition, arbitrageurs would take advantage of such opportunity to do program trading, which will be outlined shortly.

Next, the value of the financial futures contract should take into the account of what it would cost to carry the basket of stocks until expiration. This charge is a real charge for many professionals who must purchase the basket for different strategies and is part of the fair value. For example, assume that you purchased a basket of stocks with a value of $63,000 and had to pay interest at 10 percent for a period of 60 days. The interest charge would be calculated as follows:

$$
\begin{aligned}
\text{Cost-of-Carry} &= \text{Principal} \times (\text{Rate} \times \text{Time}) \\
&= 63{,}000 \times (.10 \times (60\,/\,365)) \\
&= 63{,}000 \times (.10 \times .1644) \\
&= 63{,}000 \times .016 \\
&= 1{,}035
\end{aligned}
$$

To carry the above position, a real cost of $1,035 in interest should be calculated. By adding in the real interest charge, the break-even point for purchasing such a position would be raised to $64,035 or 1.6 percent higher than the current value of the basket. Offsetting this interest charge is the value of any dividends collected by holding the basket until expiration. If during this holding period, the basket collected $350 in dividends, the value of the future should reflect it. Therefore, the cost of holding the position could be reduced by $350, lowering the interest expense to $685 for the period. The new break-even point for the basket would be $63,685 or 1.1 percent higher than the current value of the basket.

The following is the formula for simple calculation of fair value for a financial futures contract:

$$
\text{Fair Value of Financial Future Contract} = \text{Basket Value} + (\text{Interest} - \text{Div Collected})
$$

The fair value of the futures contract can be calculated by any investor, therefore giving the investor the ability to simply figure the value where program traders would break-even for buy programs. Program trading, as outlined in the next section, takes advantage of any price discrepancies between the value of the futures contract and the value of the underlying basket of stocks.

Program Trading

Taking advantage of price differences is not limited to the use of option contracts. Traders can take advantage of a difference between the price of the future contract and the actual value of the basket of stocks which make up that basket. This is known as **Program Trading**. If the price of the future is "overvalued" then the future would be sold and the basket of stocks would be purchased. If the price of the future is at a sizable discount, then the future would be purchased and the basket of stocks would be sold, probably short, to take advantage of the difference in the prices.

The basic concept for program trading is that as the futures contract rises to a premium value, the trader will sell the future and purchase the basket of stocks. However, if the future declines to a discount, the trader will purchase the future and sell the basket of stocks. Most traders use the spot month contract for such use. As the contract comes closer to expiration, the trader can roll out to the next month's contract or unwind the position. It can be to the advantage of the trader to sell the basket and repurchase the future when the future is at a discount or to buy the basket and sell the future if the future has risen to a premium. This can provide an extra added bonus for the trader.

Compared to trading options, computing levels for basket arbitrage involves a few extra steps. Please note: The following examples are geared for firm trading and do *not* include commission or other transaction charges.

As with the conversion and reversal strategies in Chapter 13, we must compute the cost-of-carry (COC) for the stock position. As with the conversions and reversals, there is usually a higher interest for the purchase of the stock position and a lower rate for the credit on the short-stock position. The rate is multiplied by the time till expiration and then the cash value of the index. For example, assuming the long interest rate is 10 percent and the short interest rate is 9 percent, with the Major Market Index at 632.50 and 20 days till expiration, the following interest charges (COC) are computed:

$$
\begin{aligned}
\text{Long Cost-of-Carry} &= (632.50 \times 100) \times (.10 \times (20 / 365) \\
&= 63250 \times (.10 \times .0547) \\
&= 63250 \times .0054 \\
&= 341.55 \\
\text{Short Cost-of-Carry} &= (632.50 \times 100) \times (.09 \times (20 / 365) \\
&= 63250 \times (.09 \times .0547) \\
&= 63250 \times .0049 \\
&= 309.93
\end{aligned}
$$

In these calculations, the purchase of the basket would require the trader to pay interest charges of 341.55 per 100 shares. The interest earned on the short sale of the basket of 100 shares would be 309.93.

The next step in program trading involves calculating the dividends paid by the stocks in the basket until expiration. A total of .23 in dividends, per share, will be paid on this example. Many traders can easily calculate the dividends to expiration via computer programs. The dividends are subtracted from the cost of carry on the buy programs and subtracted from the credit earned on the sell program. Now, with all of this information, the break-even point of both of these arbitrage situations can be calculated using the following formulas:

B.E. for Buy Program = (Basket Val − Future) − (COC − DIV)
B.E. for Sell Program = (Future − Basket Val) + (COC − DIV)

Using the information outlined, let us evaluate these strategies using the break-even formulas, as follows:

B.E. for Buy Program = (632.50 − 630.50) − (3.42 − .23)
= 2.00 − 3.19
= −1.19

Since the future is at a lower value than the actual basket, the resulting break-even point is a negative value. The break-even point according to this formula states that the future must be sold for an additional 1.19 more than the basket, in order for the strategy to break-even. This means, with the basket at this value, the future must be sold for 633.69. Should the dividends till expiration decrease or the interest rate rise during this period, the break-even point would rise. Now, let us examine the break-even point for a sell program using the formula above:

B.E. for Sell Program = (630.50 − 632.50) + (.31 − .23)
= −2 + .08
= −1.92

Since the value of the future is lower than the actual basket, the resulting value is a negative number. Based on the formula above, the sale of the basket of stocks must be 1.92 higher than the value that the future is purchased for, to break-even. Should the level of dividends paid till expiration rise or the interest rate fall, the break-even would require a lower purchases on the future contract or a higher value for the basket to be sold to break-even.

Since the individual investor is not able to pay the rates which brokers or institutions pay, the ability for the individual investor to utilize the buy program strategy is limited. Most investors who utilize such a strategy, usually wind up purchasing the basket of stocks and await the rise of the futures contract, legging into the strategy. In addition, the use of such a strategy is inhibited through the payment of commissions and other transaction charges, which put the break-even point out of the reach of most investors. The payment of commissions also inhibits the use of the sell programs. In addition, almost all investors are unable to collect interest on the sale of short stock positions. While it may be difficult to enact such a strategy, knowing the levels of where such program trades take place can be of great advantage to the investor purchasing or selling both stocks and/ or option contracts.

The purchase or sale of futures contracts are based on the payment of margin requirements. In some cases, it is possible that the margin required for the purchase or sale of a futures contract could be as low as 5 percent of the value of the futures contract. This requirement is "marked-to-the-market," meaning that the requirement is adjusted on a daily basis. The low margin requirements allow for great leverage.

The use of program trades by professionals has stirred many debates by investors, institutions and professional organizations. Due to the dramatic price fluctuations which can take place from several program trades hitting the floor of the exchange at one time, the New York Stock Exchange as well as other regulatory agencies, has enacted rules and circuit breakers to help eleviate the effects of program trading during periods of high volatility and activity. It is beyond the scope of this book to discuss the different circuit breakers, especially since they are subject to change as market conditions warrant. In addition, futures exchanges may raise margin requirements during periods of high volatility, which also lowers the amount of leverage which the contract may provide. This allows the exchanges to regain control of market fluctuations during periods of high market activity.

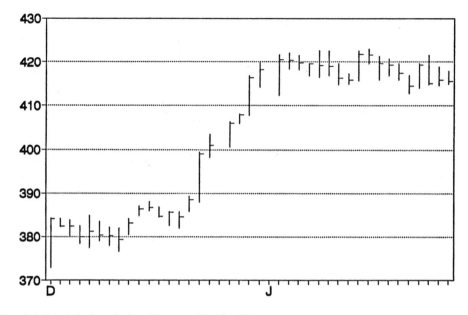

FIGURE 17–2.   Major Market Index Futures Daily Charts.

Compatibility

The futures and their respective indexes tend to trade at values which are both close to each other and in similar patterns. Figure 17–2 illustrates the Major Market Index as well as the futures contract. Figure 17–3 is a graph of the S&P 500 and the S&P futures contract. In each of these figures, it can be seen that the futures contract and the value of the stock index creates similar patterns. If the future contract does not keep in tandem with the value of the underlying index, professional arbitrageurs will step in and take advantage of the disparity in prices by either purchasing the futures contract and selling the basket of stocks or selling the future and purchasing the basket of stocks, as in the program trades described earlier. This is similar to the conversion and reversal strategies outlined in Chapter 13.

Differences Between Futures Contracts

Like stocks and indexes, there are several differences between the use of different financial futures contracts. While it is not in the scope of

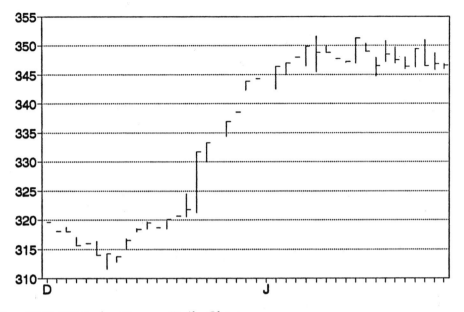

FIGURE 17–3.   S&P 500 Index Futures Daily Charts.

this book to go into the details of these differences, it is important to know what types of differences exist.

The first difference is in the margin requirements. Each exchange sets margin requirements for its own products. Based on the liquidity, volume and volatility of both the underlying index and the futures, the exchanges determine the margin required for futures. Therefore, the margin requirement between indexes which seem similar may not be the same, making it difficult to constantly switch between the use of two or more futures. In addition, the margin requirement for one index may not offset the requirement of another index, making it difficult to spread between two different financial future instruments.

The second difference between the futures is in their multipliers. Some contracts may represent 100 shares of stock while others may represent 150 shares. The trader or investor should carefully note to the difference between the index multipliers. In addition, the multiplier has a bearing on the principal value of the trade, the margin requirement and ultimately the commission which will be paid for the trade.

A third difference is in the settlement. The future contract may be settled for cash or for delivery of the basket of underlying stocks. If the trader has offset the future position with the basket of stocks, and the contract is settled for cash, the trader might encounter a problem at settlement. In such a case, early close-out or rolling to another future contract before expiration is highly suggested. The settlement of the futures contract may be subject to certain restrictions, such as based on the close of the previous day (the night before). This can make adjustments to the position difficult as well as unprofitable to the trader.

The larger the basket of stocks which the index represents means more frequent adjustments. Traders who trade futures on an index with more than 20 stocks rarely purchase or sell the entire basket, but merely use a small group of stocks which duplicate the movement of the index. It is not practical to purchase 500 different securities to duplicate the S&P 500 when the purchase of the largest 100 will make more sense.

Finally, the trading volume and open interest between different futures can provide easier execution of orders as well as greater opportunities for adjustment to positions. This plays a major role for traders when deciding which contracts to follow and utilize. Work-sheets 17–1 and 17–2 at the end of the chapter will assist in the computation of both buy and sell programs.

Most professional traders will utilize the Major Market Index (20 stocks) or the S&P 500 Index (500 stocks). Money managers as well as fund managers will utilize the S&P 500 as well as the Value Line Index. There are also financial futures available on the New York Stock Exchange Composite as well as other futures.

More

The use of financial futures in conjunction with both stocks and options can provide opportunities for both investors and professionals. Those who are unable to trade futures contracts or unable to take advantage of the sophisticated strategies detailed in this chapter can still benefit from understanding when such trades will take place. This opportunity may allow for the purchasing of a stock or option at a lower level, or the sale of the stock or option at a higher level. The information outlined here will also benefit those who trade index options, by providing insight into price movements.

Those who are interested in additional information on the use of futures should read *Futures: A Personal Seminar,* (New York Institute of Finance, 1989).

Summary

1. Financial futures are another instrument for use in investment decisions.
2. Futures, like index options, allow the user to take action on a bullish or bearish market opinion.
3. Program trading allows the user to take advantage of price discrepancies between futures contracts and the basket of underlying stocks.

WORKSHEET 17-1:

Buy Program

Quoted Index Value...........................		
Index Multiplier.............................	×	
Amount of Shares............................	×	
Commission Charges on Stock Purchases	+	
Debit Cost................................	=	

Debit Cost................................		
Interest Rate...............................	×	
Days Until Expiraton.........................	×	
Divided by 365.............................	÷	365
Interest Charges.............................	=	

Debit Cost................................		
Interest Charges.............................	+	
Dividends Collected..........................	−	
Amount of Shares............................	÷	
Futures Fair Value...........................	=	
Commission on Futures (per share)................	+	
Buy Program Break-Even Point..................	=	

WORKSHEET 17-2:

Sell Program

Quoted Index Value...............................		
Index Multiplier	×	
Amount of Shares.................................	×	
Commission Charges on Stock Purchases	+	
Credit	=	
Credit		
Interest Rate	×	
Days Until Expiraton..............................	×	
Divided by 365...................................	÷	_____ 365 _____
Interest Charges	=	
Credit		
Interest Charges	+	
Dividends Collected...............................	−	
Amount of Shares.................................	÷	
Futures Value	=	
Commission on Futures (per share)	−	
Sell Program Break-Even Point	=	

18
Long-Term
Options Contracts

Option contracts provide investors and traders with short and intermediate vehicles for trading, hedging, speculation, and portfolio management. The use of such contracts has changed the way many investors determine the amount of risk they are willing to accept and has provided another means of increasing potential profits. Greater leverage on higher priced stocks is still another reason why many use option contracts, yet the stock objective has been limited to a maximum of nine months. In 1990, the Chicago Board Options Exchange introduced a new option product: *Long-term Equity AnticiPation Securities* (**LEAPS**[R]).

The American Stock Exchange, Philadelphia Stock Exchange, and Pacific Coast Stock Exchange are now also trading in LEAPS. The use of LEAPS is limited to more active stocks which already trade listed option contracts. LEAPS are option contracts, both puts and calls, which trade with a longer period until expiration. LEAPS have been listed with three years until expiration, allowing the investor to mimic the purchase of a high price security for a fraction of the price, and hold that option for several years before the contract expires.

The longer-term option contracts are usually listed with two or three exercise prices. The spacing for the exercise prices is usually the difference of the stock and exercise price, between 20 and 25 percent in-the-money and out-of-the-money. Some LEAPS are also trading one at-the-money exercise price. As the price of the stock moves up or down additional exercise prices will be added, as needed. When an exercise price is added on a LEAP, the exchange will usually look for a price which is 20 to 25 percent away from the current value of the stock, rounded to the nearest five-point interval, keeping within the standards set for option contracts.

There are several advantages to purchasing LEAPS over short-term option contracts. When purchasing a call leap which is in-the-money, in many cases the time-premium is low, especially when compared to its shorter-term counterpart. For example, assume that MZZ's stock is trading at 105 points. A two year LEAPS on MZZ with an exercise price of 85 is trading at 22 points ($2,200 per contract). The time-premium on this contract would be two points or 1.9 percent of the value of the underlying stock. This is a fairly low time-premium. The option premium (22) is only 20.9 percent of the value of the actual stock.

When purchasing such an option, the investor is realizing an additional benefit. The capital which is not to be used may be invested in a risk-free instrument, such as a T-bill. Assume that in this example, the difference between the funds needed to purchase 100 shares and purchase 1 call ($8,300) is invested into a T-bill yielding 7 percent, for two years. The return on the T-bill would be $1,162 which is more than half of the option premium paid. This lowers the break-even point from 107 to 96⅝, or 8 percent below the current level of the stock.

Purchasing a call which is out-of-the-money can also be benefi-cial. Instead of purchasing the call with the 85 exercise price, we purchase a two-year call with an exercise price of 110 for a premium of four points. To break-even at expiration, the stock must be at 114. In keeping with our investment scenario, let us take the difference between the current stock price and the option premium and invest it in a T-Bill yielding 7 percent. The interest earned during the two-year period would be $1,414. Using this scenario, it is not possible to realize a loss. If the stock drops to zero, the investor would still have a gain of $1,014, aside from the fact that the capital which would have been invested in the stock would be lost. In this case, LEAPS provided not only the same opportunity as owning the stock (except for dividends) but also aided in capital preservation.

However, if the stock rose 8 percent per year for the two year holding period, the new value of the stock would be almost $122 per share. The value of the LEAPS would be 12 points for a gain of $800 per contract or 200 percent. Imagine the idea of earning 200 percent on an option contract, 7 percent on the value of the capital not

TABLE 18-1.   In-The-Money Leaps versus Out-of-the-Money Leaps

Stock = 91
Call LEAPS with 85 Exercise Price = 10
Call LEAPS with 105 Exercise Price = 4

	85 Exercise Price	*105 Exercise Price*
Position	+1	+1
Cost	$1000	$400
Stock at		
Expiration	*Profits and Losses*	
80	<$1000>	< $400>
85	<$1000>	< $400>
90	< $500>	< $400>
95	-0-	< $400>
100	$500	< $400>
105	$1000	< $400>
110	$1500	$100
115	$2000	$600
120	$2500	$1100
Break-Even Point	95	109

invested on the stock, and the knowledge of knowing that your capital is preserved. LEAPS can provide not only the flexibility of an option contract, but also the ability to limit capital loss while allowing the investor to speculate on the underlying stock. Table 18–1 evaluates the use of an in-the-money LEAPS and an out-of-the-money LEAPS. Figure 18–1 graphically depicts the returns of the evaluation of Figure 18–1.

Going Short: Longer Term

The purchase of a longer term put option has many advantages. For the first time investors can take a long-term bearish view of a stock and take a position which reflects on that view with the risks of selling the stock short or rolling puts on a consistent basis. One of the major advantages in this situation is that a would-be short-seller of

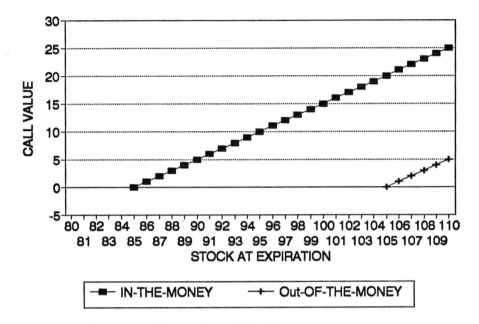

FIGURE 18–1. Leaps: In-the-Money Versus Out-of-the-Money.

the underlying stock would have to fear being bought in, which is highly probable over a length of time. In addition, a 50-percent margin requirement on the short-stock position would be a lost opportunity as the funds would be tied up.

Instead of the problems involved with selling a stock short, the investor could take a long put position and invest the balance of the funds into a T-bill. Assume that SHT's stock is trading at 82. A three-year put with an exercise price of 90 is trading at 9½ ($950 per contract). Instead of selling the stock short, the investor purchases the above mentioned put. In evaluating the results, we see the difference between the required margin for the short sale position and the purchase of the put is 35½ points. If the difference is invested in a T-bill which might be earning 7 percent, the income from that investment would be $745.50 for the three years. That recaptures 78 percent of the capital invested in the put and raises the break-even price on the put from 80½ points on the underlying stock to almost $88 per share or 9.3 percent. If the stock rises, the maximum loss on this position would be just over 2½ points.

As with calls, the purchase of an out-of-the-money put can provide a greater amount of leverage while allowing for additional capital preservation. For example, using the SHT's stock, assume that a put with an exercise price of 75 is trading at two points is purchased. In this case, the investor is only committing 4.9 percent of the capital that would have been required if the stock were sold short. The maximum loss to the put buyer would be $200 per contract as compared to a potential unlimited loss for the would-be short-seller. In addition, the purchaser of the put could invest the difference between the margin requirement and the put cost into such a vehicle as a T-bill. If such action is taken, the put buyer would gain $819, more than offsetting the $200 per put contract. In such a case, even if the stock rose to 500 and the put expires worthless, the investor could not lose all of the capital which would have been lost plus some, if the stock were sold short.

Protecting Stock

The use of married or protective put strategies is not only common but encouraged. Many investors hold stocks for years and years. Employees purchase the stock of the firms for which they are employed through employee stock ownership programs or in the open market. Once the stock is purchased, the employees tend to hold the stock until a merger or until retirement. This can provide a little nest egg in a company with which the employee feels secure.

At times, companies hit hard times and the value of the stock drops. While many rationalize that the stock will not only recover the loss but will show gains once again, these employees are not only missing an opportunity, but their retirement capital is at risk. Another reason why these stock holders refuse to sell their holdings is the tax implications they might face.

Purchasing a put for a long period of time does not obligate the holder to sell the underlying stock, but allows him to make a decision at a later time, allowing for a sale at a more favorable price. If the purchaser of the put does not wish to sell the shares, the put may be sold and the profit which is received can be applied toward the unrealized loss in the stock or may be captured purely as a gain. For those who are worried about selling the stock for tax reasons, the purchase of the put will allow them to offset most of the loss without selling the underlying shares. Before using this strategy for tax reasons, it is highly recommended that a tax adviser or accountant be consulted as not all strategies which defer or change tax liabilities are appropriate for all individuals.

An employee who purchases stock through an employee stock purchases plan can realize another advantage of purchasing a LEAPS put on the stock of the firm for which they work. Most employee stock purchase plans require that the stock which is purchased be held for a certain period of time, say 18 months. If the stock drops, the employee must still hold the restricted stock, and is therefore unable to take the invested money out of the stock. If the put is purchased, while additional capital must be spent on the put, the amount of the loss would be primarily, if not entirely, offset from the gain in the value of the put contract. This is especially true, since in most cases the amount which is paid for the shares through an employee stock benefit program is less than the market value at the time the shares are purchased.

In a worst case scenario, the firm for which a person works goes out of business: the employee's job is lost and the stock is worthless. While it is bad to lose your investment, and it is bad to lose your job, it is much worse to lose both, especially since most people will look to offset the loss of one situation with the other situation. If this were the case, the put contract would allow for the sale of the underlying stock at the exercise price. In such a situation, careful planning today could save some of the financial heartache two or three years down the road should the unimaginable happen.

The protective put strategy can also help those investors who purchased the underlying stock at an earlier date and are looking for a hedge to offset any downturn in the price of the stock. If the stock does drop, the investor may sell the put for a profit, which might be used to offset the loss of value in the stock. In this situation, the investor may actually be able to protect profits in the stock which have not been realized, allowing the investor to continue holding the stock without risking all that has been worked for. Should the stock drop, the investor may sell the puts at any time and take advantage of a decrease in the stock. If the investor believes that the stock will continue dropping, the put might be exercised and the capital will be removed at the higher level, allowing the investor to use the capital in another investment. If the stock continues to rise, the rise in the stock will be partially offset by the premium paid for the put contract.

The married put using LEAPS has become another favorite strategy among investors. Purchasing a stock today for a long-term investment is a popular investment technique. However, if the stock drops in price and continues to drop, the investor may not be able to recapture the loss of capital. It is therefore suggested that the married put be utilized. If the stock drops in price, the investor would be able to sell those shares at the exercise price. If the stock rises in value, the investor can just adjust the cost of the purchase of the stock by the amount paid for the put contract.

For those who wish to use either the married put strategy or the protective put strategy, the worksheets in Chapter 5 may be used, just as with the short-term options. Note: Stock purchased in a margin account should adjust the formula to correctly reflect the holding period for interest charged.

Long-Term Spreads

The use of LEAPS in spreads can provide investors additional opportunities and extra time for being correct on their assumption of the price on the underlying stock. Users of spread techniques such as the bull spread using puts and bear spreads using calls, which result in an unprotected contract, should pay special attention to the use of these strategies with LEAPS. Special attention should be paid on all spreads with respect to stock price and dividend payments. If the option is in-the-money and a dividend is paid, the short option position might be exercised against (assigned to) the investor, leaving the investor with exposure to a short stock position and the dividend which must be paid.

Spreading techniques can be very profitable for long holders of LEAPS contracts. If an investor purchases a long term option and writes a shorter-term option which is out-of-the-money the investor may realize substantial gains. This is especially true, since the spread position is covered and there is no additional risk to the holder. In addition, once the short option expires, the investor would have the opportunity to write another contract, maximizing the use of the time decay of options contracts. Another benefit of such a strategy is that it forces the investor to maintain and evaluate the position upon the expiration of the short option contract.

Investors who spread options will also find a benefit of rolling at least the long option position into a longer-term position. The cost of rolling the options contract will probably be small compared to constant rolling of shorter-term contracts. The investor, however, must also realize that the exercise prices for the roll may also have to be adjusted as there are not as many exercise prices on the LEAPS as there are on the shorter-term option contracts. On a theoretical basis, investors should also be aware that the pricing of short-term option contracts may not be compatible with the longer-term contracts.

Which Way?

For those who are confused about the direction of the stock, the purchase of a straddle or combination using longer-term option contracts may be beneficial. An investor who believes that a stock will have a major move over a longer period of time, should examine the purchase of a combination. If the stock does make a substantial move, the investor will have the opportunity to profit with risking a great deal of capital.

For example, assume that XXX's stock is trading at $118 per share. The investor believes that over the next year or so the stock will either be at $170 or $50 per share. This is a confusing scenario but it does arise. The investor may wish to purchase a two year call with an exercise price of 125 at 6 and a put with the same expiration and an exercise price of 100 at 4. The total cost is 10 points or $1000 per combination. If the stock rises to 170 during the period, the call should be sold for at least the intrinsic value of 45 points, realizing a gain of $3500 per combination or 350 percent. If during that period the stock drops to 50, the put would have an intrinsic value of at least 50 and, if sold, a gain of $4000 or 400 percent.

In many cases over a period of years, a stock will move in one direction and then in the opposite direction. If one contract is sold and the other is held for the turn around, there is the possibility that the investor could realize a grand slam and benefit from owning both contracts. While this scenario does happen frequently, there is a possibility of its occurrence.

Purchasing combinations using LEAPS can hold extra value, if the investor is willing to trade against the long option positions. Writing out-of-the-money shorter-term contracts against the leaps can offset the cost of the longer-term contracts and allow the investor to take in premium as frequently as every month until the spot month of the LEAPS is reached. The investor's position would be either two diagonal time spreads (both bull and bear), one diagonal time spread and one horizontal time spread or two horizontal time spreads. Frequent collection of these premiums can allow the investor to possibly recapture the entire premium which was paid for the combination.

The same technique can be used when the LEAPS straddle is purchased. Writing out-of-the-money shorter-term contracts can help to offset the higher cost of the at-the-money options which were purchased. By taking this action and adjusting on a monthly basis, the investor can decrease the distance to break-even while holding the position. It should be cautioned that a large movement in the stock price shortly after the positions are initiated could lock the investor into a loss situation since the premium for the contracts purchased may exceed the difference in the exercise prices plus the premium collected from writing the shorter-term options.

Tables 18–2 and 18–3 compare the purchase of a LEAPS combination to the purchase of a LEAPS combination with writing shorter-term options. The break-even levels of the LEAPS at expiration are

TABLE 18-2. Leaps Combination versus Leaps Combination and Shorter-Term Call Write

Stock = 112¾
LEAPS Call with 115 Exercise Price = 5¼
LEAPS Put with 95 Exercise Price = 2⅛
Call with 120 Exercise Price = 2⅝

	Leaps Combination	Leaps Combination and Shorter-Term Call Write
Position	+ 1 LEAPS Call + 1 LEAPS Put	+ 1 LEAPS Call + 1 LEAPS Put − 1 Call with 120 Exercise
Debit	7⅜	4¾
Stock at Expiration of Shorter-Term Call	*Profits and Losses*	
85	7	9⅝
95	2⅝	5¼
113	3⅛	5¾
120	6⅝	4
125	10¾	¼
130	15⅛	¼

TABLE 18-3. Purchase of a Group of Leaps versus Purchase of One Stock

Stock	Price	Two Year Call Price	Exercise
Sears (S)	37⅝	5	35
Walmart (WMT)	49	7½	50
KMart (KM)	43¾	5	40
Woolworth (Z)	26¼	2	30

	Group of Leaps	Walmart Stock
Position	+ 1 of each	+ 100 Shares
Debit	19½ or $1950	49 or $4900
At expiration of LEAPS		
Group down 10%	<$1950>	<$500>
Group up 10%	<$162>	$500
Group up 20%	$1075	$1000
Group up 20% w/o WMT	$375	-0-

closer to the price that the stock was at when the LEAPS were originally purchased, the profit potential is greater and the capital at risk is less. The tables show the returns at expiration for both strategies.

Naked Put Writing

Chapter 4 outlined the use of writing naked puts when bullish on a stock. A quick review shows that the investor writing the put would not mind owning the stock at the exercise price of the put less the premium received. Imagine using the same strategy for a year or two, with an exercise price which is 20 percent below the current value of the stock.

Imagine the LPS's stock is worth $100 with a put with two years to expiration and an exercise price of 85 is trading at four points. If the investor writes the put, and the stock remains above the 85 exercise price, the entire premium would be captured. If the stock declined below 85, and the put was assigned against the writer, the cost of the stock position would be $81 per share or 19 percent below the value of the stock when the put was written. The break-even point would be $81 a share as well.

If the stock accumulates value, the value of the put will decline, allowing the investor either to repurchase the put for a profit or to let the put expire worthless. If there is time left until expiration, it is suggested that the put be repurchased. The repurchase of the put allows the investor to realize a profit without further risk and elimi-nates the responsibility of keeping up the margin required on the position, freeing the capital for other ventures.

The Put Writers Worksheet in Chapter 4 allows the investor to view potential gains, cost of owning the stock if put, and the break-even point. This worksheet may also be used in conjunction with LEAPS. The Worksheet provides the investor with a tool which will aid in an educated decision whether this strategy is appropriate. Note that the difference between the current stock price and the price at which the stock would be put to the investor may be a great distance from the current value of the stock. While the possibility of being put might be remote, based on the investor's opinion of the stock, the possibility does exist. If the possibility of being put was null, the put would have virtually no value.

Covered Call Writing

The purchase of a covered write is an attractive strategy, especially for conservative investors. The covered writing strategy allows the investor to be bullish while taking advantage of the decline in option premium. In most cases, the covered call writer will benefit and even profit if the value of the stock remains unchanged until expiration, as the decay in the time value allows the investor to still have some profit, however limited. Should the stock rise, the investor will bene-fit until the exercise price is reached. The benefit is limited in ex-change for the collection of option premium when the call is written. This strategy may not be as appealing to the investor when used with LEAPS.

The use of LEAPS when utilizing the covered writing strategy may have two disadvantages. The value of an underlying stock *generally* tends to appreciate as time passes. Even in bear markets, stocks might rise, although not as quickly as in bull markets. As the price of the stock rises, the investor's opinion of the company, of the industry and/or the market may change. At that point, the investor may be forced to repurchase the call, if the investor believes that the stock will rise substantially above the exercise price of the call which was written. The repurchase of the call might be substantially higher than the premium collected when the call was written, lowering and possibly negating the unrealized gain on the value of the stock which was purchased. This is especially true, if there is still plenty of time until the option expires.

A second disadvantage is time. When the stock is purchased, whether for all cash or margin, the investor has made a capital commitment for the time in which the stock will be held. If the stock is to be held for two years, the writing of a two year option contract can reduce some of the initial cost. This capital requirement may inhibit the investor from making further capital commitments when investment opportunities arise in the future. Within that capital commitment comes the cost of borrowing money if the stock is purchased in a margin account. The longer the period in which the stock is held, the greater the dollar amount of interest which the investor will be charged, lowering the return on the investment. In addition to the interest charge, the investor runs the risk of additional charges to interest if the rate of interest rises during the holding period.

The covered call writing strategy might be attractive when the premiums are high and the appeal of the married put strategy is low because of the high premiums. If the married put strategy appears unattractive, the covered call write might be attractive. Use of LEAPS for limited gain, however, may prove unattractive since the holding period is longer than in shorter-term option contracts. In addition, the longer holding period until expiration does not allow for effective use of the time decay of the option contracts.

Combining Stock, Put and Call

There are several strategies which hedge the position of a stock through the use of both puts and calls. These strategies involve either the purchase of the underlying stock, the purchase of a put and the writing of a call or the sale of short stock, the writing of a put and the purchase of a call. While the gains and losses of such positions are both limited, in many instances the use of LEAPS for such strategies will prove to be a disservice to the investor, especially over the long term.

The hedge wrapper, which involves the purchase of the underlying stock, the writing of an out-of-the-money or at-the-money call and the purchase of an out-of-the-money put locks the investor into a limited risk/limited reward trading range. The use of long-term contracts here is neither appropriate nor practical. It does not make good investment sense to purchase a stock and hold it for a long period of time to lock into a narrow trading range. In addition, with the stock limited to a narrow range, the cost of carrying the position and the commitment of capital to maintain the position will keep any potential reward small, especially after commissions and other transaction charges.

Other strategies such as conversions and reversals, lock the investor into a closeout price without the opportunity for further profit. In addition, the use of such strategies which involve high capital commitment and interest charges to carry the positions as well as other transaction charges, can easily lock the investor into a loss, which might even be a greater loss if the position is closed prematurely, since there will be additional commission charges and premium paid for repurchase of the option contract. It is suggested that investors avoid such strategies when using LEAPS.

What Went Wrong?

Chapter 19 discusses the uses of option contracts to repair damage to a stock position as well as to option positions. The use of LEAPS in such strategies can provide the investor or trader with a long-term repair strategy, which might be the only suitable strategy when a substantial loss is a possibility. In such cases, if the value of the underlying stock has declined by 25 percent or more, the use of a long-term repair strategy may be feasible and required. It is important that the user of the repair strategy be convinced that the stock will recover over the long period of time and have evidence to substantiate that claim. Thinking that a stock will recover and enacting a repair strategy may not be a prudent move since the position might have to be held for a period which is longer than desired. In such an instance, it is usually best to replace the stock with an option or to bite the bullet (see Chapter 19) and take the loss.

If a repair strategy is needed for a shorter-term option position, the use of other shorter-term options should be explored before the use of LEAPS. This is prevalent since the original purchase or writing of the contract was for an anticipated short-term holding, which the investor/trader should attempt to maintain. If the use of the shorter-term contract does not provide for ample opportunity, the use of LEAPS may provide the necessary level for repairing the position and should not be overlooked.

While LEAPS may provide an opportunity which is not available in shorter-term option contracts, to repair the damage to a position being held, the user of such a strategy should pay special attention to the price movements of the underlying stock and the LEAPS and shorter-term option contracts. As the value of the underlying stock moves or as time ticks on and the value of time changes the level of option premium, the user of the LEAPS for repair may have additional opportunities to reduce risk or loss while exchanging the LEAPS for a shorter-term option contract. Repair strategies, since they are not long-term investments, should be limited to as little time as possible so that if the strategy does not work, the investor might close the entire position and take the loss or attempt to duplicate the repair strategy a second or even a third time.

Synthetically Creative

Chapter 12, discussed the use of puts and calls in creating different stock positions. The creation of a synthetic stock position can be extremely beneficial through the use of LEAPS. The longer the term until expiration, the greater the possibility for success in holding a synthetic stock position. Capital requirements for holding a synthetic stock position are lower, in most cases, than purchasing the actual stock. This is especially true when the price of the underlying stock is high.

Creating a stock using LEAPS involves the purchase of a call, usually in-the-money, and writing a put with the same exercise price (which is out-of-the-money) and the same expiration date. The investor is required to pay for the call in full, and additional capital for the margin on the short put position. If the stock appreciates, the call should rise and the put should decline, almost point for point with the change in stock price. If the stock declines, the call will decline and the put will rise, leaving the synthetic stock purchaser with a loss almost the same as if the stock were purchased. While the percentage changes are greater for the synthetic position as opposed to the stock position, the dollar gain or loss is approximately equal. See Chapter 12 for further discussion.

The creation of a synthetic short-stock position is another benefit which is provided through the use of LEAPS. The creation of a synthetic short stock position involves the purchase of an in-the-money put and the writing of a call with the same exercise price and the same expiration date. As with the synthetic stock position, the synthetic short requires that the long option, the put, be paid for in full and that the capital requirement is met for the margin on the short call. If the underlying stock declines, the put will increase and the call will decrease, resulting in almost a point for point gain compared to the stock being sold short. If the stock rises, the loss of the put and call combination should be equivalent to that if the stock were sold short. While the gains and losses are almost the same dollar wise, the percentage change will be much greater since the margin requirement for the short stock position should be greater than the requirement for the option positions.

One of the great uses of synthetic option strategies allows for the use in combining other option strategies which would have required a stock position. For instance, if the synthetic long stock position were purchased, the investor may wish to write either a short-term call or a long-term call against the synthetic stock position, creating a synthetic covered write strategy. This strategy can have greater benefits than a covered write using LEAPS. **Note:** The user of the synthetic stock strategy does *not* collect dividends paid by the underlying corporation and therefore should *not* figure them into the returns in such a strategy as a covered write.

A strategy similar to that used for the synthetic covered write can be utilized for a synthetic short-stock position. The creation of a synthetic short-stock position coupled with a naked put position allows the investor to repurchase the stock (synthetic stock) position. This will allow for the investor to take advantage of excessive put premiums while creating a synthetic short stock position. If the stock drops below the exercise price of the put which was written, the investor would purchase the stock at that exercise price. At that point, the investor may wish to close the synthetic short or exercise the put and repurchase the call, completely closing the positions, and hopefully realizing a profit.

Synthetic strategies can be useful in creating synthetic call and synthetic put positions, however, this book will not examine them.

The use, risk and reward possibilities of synthetic options are almost the same as regular option contracts, except that the holding period is longer-term, which can be beneficial for long positions while an additional liability for short positions.

TABLE 18-4.   Leaps Purchase versus Stock Purchase

Stock = 92⅜
LEAPS Call with 85 Exercise Price
and Two Years Till Expiration = 13¼

	Leap Position	*Stock Position*
Position	+ 1 LEAPS Call	+ 100 Shares
Capital Requirement	$1325.00	$9237.50
*Stock Price in 1 Year		
80	*Value = $ 200	$8000
	Loss = $1125	$1237.50
	% Loss = 84.9%	13.4%
85	*Value = $ 425	$8500
	Loss = $ 900	$737.50
	% Loss = 67.9%	8.0%
92	*Value = $1150	$9000
	Loss = $ 175	$237.50
	% Loss = 13.2%	2.6%
100	*Value = $1950	$10,000
	Gain = $ 625	$762.50
	% Gain = 47.2%	8.3%
110	*Value = $2775	$11,000
	Gain = $1450	$1762.50
	% Gain = 109.4%	19.1%
Maximum Profit	Unlimited	Unlimited
Maximum Loss	$1325.00	$9237.50
Stock Break-Even Point at Expiration	98¼	92⅜

*Note: Denotes that value is based on the theoretical value of the LEAPS and not the intrinsic value of the LEAPS.

Industry Focus Using LEAPS

Through the use of LEAPS, investors can obtain better leverage over a longer period of time. Many investors do not limit their holdings to just one stock, but purchase a variety of stocks. LEAPS allow the investor to purchase a variety of stocks while limiting downside risk and increasing returns. Those investors who purchase a group of securities or an industry group of securities can benefit from purchasing LEAPS as an alternative. In many cases, an investor can purchase a quantity of LEAPS as a substitute for stock, with a total cost for all of the contracts at the price of what the highest stock would have cost to purchase. This allows the investor to find alternative investments. Substituting LEAPS for stocks can be extremely rewarding not only in an upward market but also in a downward market, as the amount of risk will be much lower, saving the investor substantial capital risk during the holding period.

Table 18–4 compares the use of a group of LEAPS to the purchase of the underlying stock. As can be seen in the table, the purchase of the LEAPS will allow the investor to realize substantial profit if the prices of the underlying stocks rise while limiting poten-

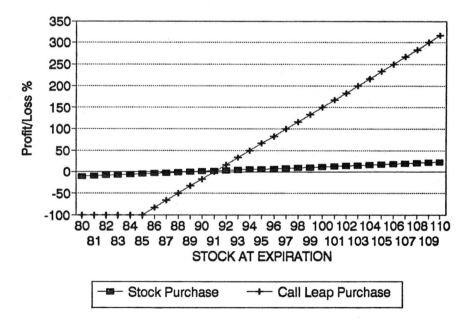

FIGURE 18–2. Leaps Versus Stock.

tial loss if the underlying stocks decline. The percentage returns are also greater compared to both the purchase of the stocks for all cash or in a margin account. Figure 18–2 is a graphic representation of the comparison in Table 18–4.

Summary

1. Through the introduction of LEAPS, investors can benefit from some of the many option strategies over a longer-period of time.

2. The use of LEAPS is not limited to longer-term options, as the writing of shorter-term options against their longer-term counterparts can be extremely rewarding and beneficial.

3. Hedging stock positions using LEAPS can provide a great amount of protection. Protective and married put strategies are taken to greater lengths as investors can purchase a substantial amount of protection for a small premium. This can be a great benefit to investors who wish to use LEAPS in an individual retirement account or a KEOGH.

4. Protective put contracts can provide security for those who purchase stocks through an employee stock benefit program or other comparable program. This limited risk does not just protect their investment as an investment but can provide for additional security if the firm in which they are employed falls on hard times.

5. Creation of synthetic stock and synthetic short stock positions provides some additional leverage while mimicking the movement of the underlying stock. Synthetic positions can also provide the investor with the opportunity to take advantage of covered call writing and covered put writing strategies.

6. The use of longer-term put and call strategies allows for the purchase of a portfolio of stocks for a substantially lower amount of capital. The gains on such positions may be greater than those on the purchase of the underlying stocks, and the investor can also realize a lower dollar risk potential compared to an out right purchase of the stocks.

19
Repair Strategies

What do you do when things just aren't going your way? If your car breaks down, call your mechanic. If a pipe in your house springs a leak, call your local plumber. If you have a toothache, your dentist becomes your best friend. Many people keep the names and numbers of emergency services next to their telephones. Those numbers usually include their doctor, the Fire Department and the Police Department. Then, there are those who add other "emergency" telephone numbers, such as boyfriend/girlfriend, pizza delivery, television repair shop and horoscopes, just to name a few. These may be some of the most important numbers, depending upon the priorities of the individual. But who are you going to call when your investments don't work out like you have planned?

It is bad enough when the stock you purchased on the anticipation that it would rise 10 percent does not move. It is even worse when that same stock declines. No matter how you fight for gains, every once in a while, there is a very good chance that a loss is possible. No one makes money all of the time. The idea is to keep the frequency and the dollar value of the losses to a minimum. It is very possible that the amount of a loss can be reduced to as low as nothing. The main thing to remember in such a situation is to avoid panicking and take some time to evaluate the current situation.

This chapter focuses on using option contracts to repair both stock and option positions. While it is not always possible to turn a situation around completely, sometimes a partial recovery can lead to a break-even situation for the investor utilizing an option repair strategy. There are times, however, that no matter what you do, there is no way to avoid a loss. This situation may occur if the repair strategy is initiated, but the stock continues to move against the investor, or if there is no possible way to initiate the repair strategy based upon the mathematics.

The first process in attempting to repair a position is to evaluate what possible choices the investor can make. These choices include:

Do nothing.

"Bite-the-bullet" and close the position for the loss.

Average the position downward.

Prevent further damage while holding the position.

Initiate an options repair strategy.

To do nothing is a common practice among individuals who await the recovery of the position. This is a form of rationalization in that there is strong belief that the stock will not only turn around, but that a full recovery is possible. Biting the bullet is a plausible strategy if the investor believes that losses will continue to mount and the investment opinion cannot be met. Averaging down on a position is one of the worst ideas: this is throwing good money after bad into what may be a further eroding situation. This technique is favored by many investors who try to lower their break-even point and cost by taking the average of the original price and the new price and trying to adjust the original effective price of the trade. This is similar to replacing all of the parts in a 10-year old car. The worst part is that when reality sets in, the owner finds the car must still be replaced.

Creating an options repair strategy allows the investor minimal further investment while attempting a partial recovery in the stock. If the stock does not move as expected by the investor, the repair will not work, but the addition of capital will be kept to a minimum. It is strongly suggested that the investor evaluate the movement of the stock *before* the repair strategy is enacted. If the stock continues to move against the investor, further losses might be realized. The use of option repair strategies will not perform miracles, and the cooperation of the stock is required for the strategy to work. One further caveat: the repair strategy is meant as just that; to repair a position which the investor is losing money in. At times, it is possible that the repair strategy will turn a loss into a profit, however, this is *not* to be expected.

Repairing a Long Stock Position

The purchase of a security without any option position assumes that the investor is bullish on the stock and expects a gain which she may not wish to limit or which she believes needs no protection against the possibility of a decline. The naked stock position can leave the investor subject to a limited loss of 100 percent of the investment, should the company go out-of-business. While the chances for this are remote, total loss is always a possibility. However, even a small decline in the price of the stock can lead to a loss of capital for the investor. For example, if 1,000 shares of stock are purchased for $41 a share, and the stock drops four points, the investor faces the situation of losing $4,000 or 9.6 percent. Accumulation of such losses will not only hurt the investment objective but also erode the original capital investment.

The objective of the options repair strategy is to lower the break-even point, with little or no additional cost. The major technique for repairing a long position is to initiate a set of two option positions simultaneously. To do this, the investor will look to purchase 1 call option with a low exercise price for each 100 shares of long stock, and sell two calls with a higher exercise price expiring in the same month. The difference between the purchase of the one call and the sale of the two calls should be virtually zero. If it is possible to obtain a credit, the strategy will work a little better.

Once the "spread" is enacted, the investor has basically two separate investment strategies. The first is a 1 for 1 bull spread (long one call with low exercise price, short one call with higher exercise price) and a covered write (long 100 shares of stock, short one call with the higher exercise price). The goal is for the stock to rise to or above the higher exercise price by expiration, allowing the spread to be closed for its maximum and the stock to be called away.

The following example will help to show the use of this strategy. Assume that Texas Instruments (TXN) stock was purchased for $40 a share and has dropped to $31 a share over a two month period. The investor evaluates the situation and decides to enact an options repair strategy. Table 19-1 is a display of available option contracts for TXN stock. Assuming that today is October 1, the investor will evaluate the options on a month by month basis. The call which the investor will look to purchase in this situation is in-the-money and the calls which will be written should be out-of-the-money. In this

TABLE 19-1. Texas Instruments (TXN) Option Display

Call Bid	*Call Ask*	*Call Last*	*Call Volume*	*Option Series*				*Put Bid*	*Put Ask*	*Put Last*	*Put Volume*
6½	6⅝	6¼	16	IE	SEP	25	UE		1/s	1/s	1
¾	15/s	⅞	132	IF	SEP	30	UF	5/s	⅜	⅜	18
	⅛			IF	SEP	35	UG	4⅞	5⅛	5⅛	20
7⅛	7¼	7	36	JE	OCT	25	VE	3/s	5/s	¼	10
2⅛	2 3/s	2⅛	46	JF	OCT	30	VF	⅞	1		
15/s	1⅛	1	41	JG	OCT	35	VG	5⅛	5⅜	5¼	46
	1/s			JH	OCT	40	VH	9⅞	10⅛	9¾	2
7¾	7⅞	7¾	3	LE	DEC	25	XE	⅜	7/s		
2¾	2⅞	2¾	108	LF	DEC	30	XF	1¼	1 7/s	1⅜	14
1⅜	1⅝	1½	31	LG	DEC	35	XG	5½	5¾	5⅝	26

situation, the investor decides to purchase the December 30 call for three points and write December 35 calls for 1½ points. There is no additional cost to the investor, since the premium collected on the two calls equals the cost of the call which was purchased. Once this trade is completed, the investor will have the following positions:

Bull Spread	Covered Write
+ 10 calls Dec 30	+ 1000 shares
− 10 calls Dec 35	− 10 calls Dec 35

Table 19-2 shows this repair strategy for the unrealized loss on the TXN stock. If the stock rises to the 35, the spread position can be closed for a five-point profit. At the same time, the 1000 shares will be called at expiration at the exercise price of 35. In this situation, the stock will have an overall loss of five points since the original purchase price was $40 per share. However, the five-point gain in the spread will offset that loss, and the investor will break-even, excluding any dividends paid during the holding period. This assumes that the stock rises above 35 (a four-point gain from the price of the stock when the repair strategy was initiated) versus a nine-point gain. This allows the investor to break-even with only a 13 percent move in the stock versus a 29 percent move. In addition, many technicians believe that the stock may retrace a decline to 50 percent of the downward move before the stock begins to turn lower again.

If the investor had purchased the stock in the example for a price of 39 instead of 40, the break-even point for the options repair strategy would be 34 and if the stock rose above the 35 exercise price, a one-point gain might be realized. If the stock were purchased at 41, the investor would still have a loss if the stock rose above 35, but that loss would be one-point instead of six points.

The break-even point for the options repair strategy is easily calculated by equating the loss in the stock to the gain in the spread, less any dividends collected during the holding period.

Some people will state that the same goal can be accomplished if the stock position is averaged down (an equivalent amount of shares purchased at the lower price). There are two reasons why the options

TABLE 19-2. Texas Instruments (TXN) Repair Strategy

Original Purchase of 1000 Shares TXN at 40 = $40,000
Current Value of 1000 Shares TXN at 31 = 31,000
Unrealized Loss of 1000 Shares TXN   9 = $ 9,000

Strategy: Purchase 10 calls TXN Dec 30 at 2⅞ = $2875.00
              Write 20 calls TXN Dec 35 at 1½ = 3000.00
              Credit on Position(s)   ⅛ = $ 125.00

New Positions:

Covered Call Position—   Bull Spread Using Calls—
   + 1000 Shares TXN   + 10 Calls TXN Dec 30
   − 10 Calls TXN Dec 35   − 10 Calls TXN Dec 35

Stock Price at Expiration	Stock Value	+ Dec 30 Call Value	− (x2) Dec 35 Call Value	= Net Value	*Profit/Loss
29	$29,000	-0-	-0-	$29,000	<$10,875>
31	31,000	$ 1,000	-0-	32,000	<7,875>
33	33,000	3,000	-0-	36,000	<3,875>
35	35,000	5,000	-0-	40,000	125
37	37,000	7,000	−$ 4,000	40,000	125
40	40,000	10,000	− 10,000	40,000	125

repair strategy is better than the average down method: first, the break-even point on the average down strategy would be 35½; second, and far more important, the average down technique requires the commitment of additional capital. In this example, the investor would have had to invest an additional $31,000 plus commission charges. If the stock continued to decline, the average down technique would have capital which is in excess of the original investment at risk, compared to no additional capital risk through the use of the options repair strategy.

Long stock positions which have slim losses, usually do not require the use of the options repair strategy, but may be repaired using options. The investor may reduce the break-even point through the writing of a covered call which is at-the-money or out-of-the-money. The amount of premium collected by writing the call will partially offset the loss in the stock. If the call is out-of-the-money and the stock rises above the exercise price, the stock will be called and an additional gain offsetting the loss in the stock will be realized, which might even provide the investor with a marginal profit.

There is another possibility for repairing a long stock position, if the other techniques do not meet the needs of the investor. The investor may sell half of the stock position, and write combinations which are out-of-the-money. The credit received will help to reduce the cost of owning the stock position and may offset the stock which was sold. If the stock rises above the exercise price of the call, the remaining stock will be sold, hopefully at or above the price for which it was originally purchased. If the stock drops below the exercise price of the put, the shares which were sold will be repurchased, automatically averaging down the cost of the entire position, and the investor is no worse off than if the stock were held.

As the options near expiration, the investor should begin to think about adjusting positions. This is especially so if the long calls are in-the-money and the calls which were written are out-of-the-money. If this is the case, the investor should contemplate rolling the position by repurchasing the short calls and selling the long calls for a profit. Once that is done, the investor may wish to enact the same or similar strategy in another month. In addition, this is an opportunity for the investor to adjust the exercise prices. If the investor does not wish to make an adjustment, the repurchase of the short calls alone may be desired. In any event, the value of the calls and the stock price should be monitored. If the stock drops, the investor may wish to take a loss in the stock and repurchase the calls which were written while holding the long call position in case of a sudden rise in the stock.

There are several guidelines for using option repair strategies on long stock positions. First, the investor must be convinced that the stock will turn and appreciate during the period for which the options will be utilized. Next, the price paid for any repair strategy should be kept extremely low, usually under ⅜ of a point, since paying for the repair strategy would defeat the use of using options. Third, the use of the repair strategy should be more than 30 days to allow for the stock to make a move, but be less than 180 days so that it does not tie up the position indefinitely. The exception to this rule is using LEAPS, which will be discussed at the end of the chapter. Finally, the break-even point for the break-even strategy should be at least 5 percent lower than the original price paid for the stock. The Long Stock Repair Worksheet (Worksheet 19-1 at the end of the chapter) will aid in the formation of this repair strategy.

Repair for the Short Seller

Unlike the purchaser of stock, the seller of a short position has additional risks. The main risk is that the potential loss is unlimited. As long as the price of the stock rises, the loss to the short seller accumulates. Another risk is that the short seller can be bought-in, requiring that the stock be repurchased before the short seller is ready. This possibility can undermine the use of a repair strategy: therefore, the positions should be monitored with extreme care. And third, the short seller must pay any dividends which are payable during the holding period.

The short seller enacts a strategy with similar positions and characteristics to those of the repair strategy for long stock positions, except using put contracts. The conventional repair strategy for the short seller involves purchasing one put contract for each hundred shares of stock sold short, with a high exercise price and writing two puts with a lower exercise price expiring in the same option month. Once the trade is done, the investor has two basic positions. The first is a bear spread using puts and the second is a short put position versus a short stock. The goal for the investor is for the stock to drop to or below the exercise price of the short puts. The investor will attempt to implement this strategy for little or no additional cost.

If the stock continues to rise, the investor will continue to lose, but not as much as if additional stock were sold in a so-called average up technique. (Table 19-3 compares the use of a repair strategy for a short stock position against averaging up.) If the stock, on the other hand, begins to decline, then the options repair strategy for the short position will begin to work, raising the break-even level. Once the stock drops below the lower exercise price, the spread should be worth its maximum of the difference between the exercise prices, and the stock should be repurchased at the exercise price of the short put. The profit on the spread will be applied against the loss on the short stock position, which hopefully will result in a break-even position.

Let's evaluate the options repair strategy on a short sale position through the use of an example. Assume that a stock was sold short at 65 and has risen to 75, leaving the investor with an unrealized loss of 10 points or $10,000 on 1,000 shares of stock. The investor decides to implement a repair strategy using options by purchasing 10 puts with three months (December) until expiration and an exercise price of 75 for 3½ points and writing 20 puts with an exercise price of 70 for 1¾ points. The net cost for this trade is zero since the two puts which are being written equal the value of the put to be purchased. Once the trade is complete, the investor will have the following positions:

Bear Spread	Short Stock/Short Put
+ 10 Dec 75 Put	− 1,000 stock
− 10 Dec 70 Put	− 10 Dec 70 Put

If the investor is correct, and the stock drops to the lower exercise price, the spread should be worth its maximum five points, and the stock should be repurchased for 70. The gain of five points in the spread will offset what would be a five-point loss in the stock, and the investor will break-even. However, if any dividend is paid during this period, the investor would be required to pay that dividend, lowering the break-even level by the amount of that dividend. If the investor had sold an additional 1000 shares short, as an alternative to the repair strategy, the position would have the same break-even level, except that additional risk would be present if the stock continued to rise.

If the stock does not drop and actually rises, the investor would

TABLE 19-3.   Repair Short Stock versus Averaging Up

Original Short Sale = 19½
Stock Now = 24   Unrealized Loss 4½ Points or $4500
Put with 25 Exercise Price = 3
Put with 22½ Exercise Price = 1¾

	Repair Strategy	*Average Up*
Action	+ 10 Put with 25 Exercise − 20 Put with 22½ Exercise	− 1000 shares
Additional Capital	$500 credit	$24,000 credit
Additional Margin	-0-	$12,500

Stock at Expiration	*Profits and Losses*	
30	<$10,000>	<$16,500>
25	<$ 5,000>	<$ 6,500>
22½	-0-	<$ 1,500>
20	-0-	$ 3,500
18	-0-	$ 7,500
Break-Even Point	22½	21¾
Additional Risk	None	Unlimited

have no additional risk except for the short stock position already being held. If the investor sold an additional 1000 shares short, and the stock continued to rise, the investor would have double the risk as before. If the stock remains unchanged, the investor would have no additional risk from the repair strategy. Worksheet 19-2, the Short Stock Repair Worksheet, provides a tool for developing this strategy.

If the loss on the short sale position is not that great, the investor may look into writing an at-the-money or out-of-the-money put contract, taking in premium to offset the loss. If the stock drops through the exercise price of the put written, the stock would be repurchased for an effective buy back price of the exercise price less the premium received for the put. If the stock remained unchanged and the position was not repurchased, another put may be written against the position once the first put expires. Another alternative to repairing the short stock position requires that the investor re-purchase one-half of the short position and write an out-of-the-money combination on the remaining short shares. In such a case, if the stock rises above the exercise price of the call, the investor would wind up short the original amount of shares, with a higher short sale price. Averaging the two short sale prices and adjusting for the repurchase and the premiums received, the investor should have an equivalent share position to the original position with a short sale price above the original short price. If the stock should decline below the exercise price of the put contract, the investor would repurchase the remaining shares at the exercise price for an effective price on the original position of an average of the exercise price of the put plus the price of the buy back of the first half of the shares less the premiums. The formula for this is:

Repurchase = (Put Exercise Price + Repurchase of first half) /
2 − (Call Premium + Put Premium).

The use of the repair strategies for the short stock position attempts to avoid taking an additional short stock position, which the averaging up strategy entails. Shorting additional stock requires the investor to take the risk of borrowing additional stock, awaiting the up-tick rule, the payment of any dividends and the risk of being bought-in prematurely. Using options as an alternative usually is a benefit over the shorting of additional shares, and usually requires less capital commitment from the investor.

Following up the repair strategy is very important. As the options begin to near expiration, the investor should contemplate the next move. If the strategy has been partially successful, the investor may wish to repurchase the short option contracts, if they have a low premium, and sell the profitable contracts. At the same time, the investor may wish to roll that position out for an additional month or two, adjust the exercise prices or simply close the position and take the remaining loss as an alternative to maintaining the position further. In addition, the investor may wish to purchase an at-the-money or out-of-the-money call to protect the short position if the options repair strategy is rolled out for additional time.

There are certain guidelines which the investor should consider when using an options repair strategy for short stock positions. The first and most important is that as little additional capital should be required. Paying a high price for a repair strategy defeats its purpose and limits its effectiveness, especially if the stock refuses to cooperate. Next, the use of the strategy should require that the *new* break-even point be at least five percent higher than the original break-even point. Third, if the investor is not convinced that the stock will drop, the short stock should be repurchased and the idea of using the repair strategy should be abandoned. Fourth, the positions of the options and the underlying stock should be monitored carefully, allowing for both adjustment of the positions as the time till expiration and the price of the stock change.

Stock positions are not the only investments which can get into difficulty. Options are subject to the same type of risks and more. If the value of the stock remains static from the time an option is purchased till expiration of that contract, the time premium of the contract will erode, leaving the investor with a loss even though the stock did not decline. In fact, it is possible for a call to lose if the underlying stock rises and a put to lose if the underlying stock declines, simply because the movement of the stock does not outweigh the movement of time against the option purchaser. Naked writers of option contracts can also lose money if the price of the stock moves in the wrong direction. Investors who utilize option contracts also need to repair damage to a position from time to time. Through the use of option contracts, investors might be able to construct a strategy which will allow them to break-even, similar to those constructed for the stock positions outlined earlier.

Repairing a Long Call

There are two circumstances which can lead to a loss in the value of a purchased call. The first is that the stock declines in value, decreasing the worth of *all* of the calls on the underlying stock. The second is that time continues and even a stock which has appreciated will be subject to the decrease in time value, especially as the time to expiration grows near. In either case, the investor is losing value as the option premium declines. Option strategists have developed certain techniques which adjust the option positions and either lower the break-even point or buy the investor additional time. Therefore, all may not be lost. It should be noted that the investor or trader should not wait until the value of the call is virtually nil, as the repair strategy would not be feasible.

In the first scenario, the value of the underlying stock has depreciated since the purchase of the call option. In so doing, the value of the call deteriorates as well, and not just from the decline in the stock but also from the movement of time. In this situation, it is the goal of the investor to lower the break-even point, allowing for a better opportunity to break-even. At the same moment, it is in the best interest of the investor to attempt to extend the life of the position, if possible, allowing for the maximum chance.

Since the stock has declined, the call which the investor holds is no longer considered to be a favored call since it is out-of-the-money. An in-the-money or at-the-money exercise price should be sought as a call which the investor would wish to purchase at this time. The premium for the desired call should be approximately two times the value of the losing option. Once the exercise price is selected, the investor should attempt to find such a call with a longer period to expiration, if it is possible. Once the correct option contract is selected, the investor will purchase a quantity of one contract of the new option for each losing option being held and sell the losing contracts *twice*: once to close the position being held and once to open a new position. Once the transaction is completed, the investor will be holding either a diagonal bull spread using calls (if the expiration months are different) or a bull spread using calls (if the expiration months are the same). The cost of initiating this strategy should be kept as close to zero as possible. Note: If the original call cost is greater than the difference between the strikes, it is very difficult to break-even if the new position is a diagonal spread and impossible to break-even if the spread is a simple bull spread using calls.

If the new position is a diagonal bull spread, it would most benefit the investor if the stock held until after the short call position failed to gain value. The reason for this is that the long call would not be limited in the gain by a short call above it. If the stock rises above the exercise price of the short call position before expiration, the investor will probably have to close the position for a credit value of the difference between the strikes, maybe a little higher, since the long call has greater time premium. If the price of the original call is equal to or less than the difference between the exercise prices, the strategy would be a success. Computing the new break-even level for the repair strategy is done using the following formula:

New Break-Even Price = Lower Exercise Price + Original Cost of the Call + Additional Cost for Repair Strategy

If the repair strategy position has the long call and the short call expiring in the same month, the formula above will also calculate the new break-even point. The only difference between the two is that the bull spread using calls position will not have the opportunity of an unlimited gain during the life of the options since both contracts will expire at the same time.

Figure 19-1 shows the movement in Texas Instruments (TXN) stock from August through December. When TXN was at 30¼, an investor purchased 10 TXN October 30 calls for 3½ points. During the month of September, the stock declined to $27 per share, and the October 30 calls dropped to one point. At this time, the investor decided to take advantage of this repair strategy and purchase 10 TXN November 25 calls for 2½ points and sell 20 October 30 calls (10 from the original position and 10 new options) for a cost of ½ point. The new cost of owning the options for this investor is 4 points. If the stock remains below 30 until the October 30 call expires, and then begins to rise, the investor may not just break-even but may actually turn a losing proposition into a profit. If the stock rises above 30 before the October expiration, the position should be closed for at least the difference between the exercise prices or in this case five points. Since the cost of the original options plus the additional cost for the repair strategy was four points, the investor will still make money. If the stock remains at 29, the investor will break-even. The break-even point, using the formula above, requires the stock to be at 29 at the expiration of the November 25 call. In this example, the investor paid an additional ½ point for an extra month's opportunity to correct a trade which would have resulted in a loss otherwise.

The use of the option repair strategy for long calls may have also prevented the investor from making a common mistake of averaging down calls. Lowering the cost of owning calls by purchasing additional contracts at a lower price is a bigger mistake than averaging

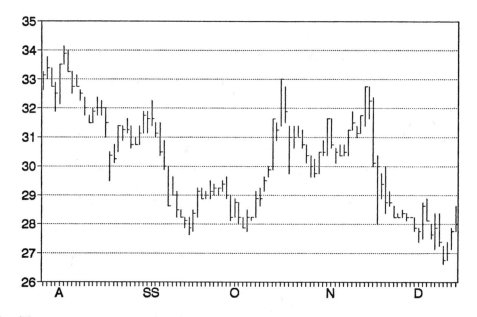

FIGURE 19-1. Texas Instruments Daily Chart.

down on stock, since the calls are going against time. There is little opportunity to break-even using an average down technique in conjunction with long option contracts. This technique not only requires a favorable move in the value of the underlying stock but also requires that the move occur in a very short period of time, and really does not effectively lower the break-even price of the position. The comparison of these two strategies are shown in Table 19-4.

In this example, if the investor would have purchased an additional 10 October 30 calls for one point, the new break-even price would be 32½ or 3½ points higher than the break-even point for the repair strategy. This would require an upside move of more than 10 percent in less than a months time as opposed to no rise in a two-month period for the repair strategy.

There are some important guidelines to remember when attempting to repair a long call position. First, never purchase another option which expires before the contract which is losing. This limits the time to expiration while also opening the position to a high margin capital requirement on the *naked call* position. Next, try to select an option for purchase which would give additional time to be correct. Third, the purchase of the new call should utilize a contract with an exercise price which is either at-the-money or in-the-money. The break-even point should be relatively near the current price of the stock, re-

TABLE 19-4. Repair Long Call versus Averaging Down

Long 10 Calls with 65 Exercise Price at 4
Call now at 2⅛   Unrealized Loss = 1⅞ Points or $1875
Jan Call with 60 Exercise Price = 4⅛

	Repair Strategy	Average Down
Action	+ 10 Jan 60 Call − 20 Jan 65 Call	+ 10 Jan 65 Call
Additional Capital	⅛ Credit or $125	$2125
Total Risk	$3875	$6125
Stock at Expiration	Profits and Losses	
60	<$3,875>	<$6,125>
62	<$1,875>	<$6,125>
63½	<$ 375>	<$6,125>
65	$1,125	<$6,125>
70	$1,125	$3,875
Break-Even Point	63⅞	68⅛

quiring little movement for the investor to break-even. The investor should also continue to have faith that the stock will rise, and if there is no faith, the long call should simply be sold and the loss realized. Finally, the time to make a decision is both before losing contract expires and before the contract has no value which would be usable in setting up a repair strategy. To assist, Worksheet 19-3, The Long Call Repair Worksheet, has been provided at the end of the chapter.

If the call has deteriorated in value due to time and not a decrease in the stock, all is not lost. If the stock has remained virtually unchanged from the time in which the call was originally purchased, the goal is to increase the length of time until expiration. Implementing this strategy requires that the original call be sold and a call with a longer term till expiration be purchased. Rolling this position should be attempted for as little additional cost as possible. If the call is out-of-the-money, the investor may wish to sell twice as many of the original contract, initiating a forward time spread, and collecting a credit which would help to offset any possible loss. Use of this strategy allows for the purchase of additional time, costing the investor *no* additional capital.

If the time spread is used, the investor has a certain disadvantage if the stock rises above the exercise price before the expiration of the short call. If the stock does rise before the expiration of the short option, the spread should be closed since the long call will have a greater value than the short call since there is a longer period until expiration. If the short call expires worthless, the investor should close the long option once the value rises to or above the price of the original option less any credit received on the calendar spread. The investor must take special care to monitor the position for any further opportunity, such as another roll for extra time or the opportunity of creating a bull spread using calls by writing an out-of-the-money call against the long call being held. Table 19-5 compares use of the repair strategy for calls against the holding of the position.

Repairing a Short Call

The writing of naked calls has been a very profitable method of trading during bear and neutral markets and has even been profitable during bull markets. Time is on the side of the naked writer and the closer the option comes to expiration, the more the time premium deteriorates. For the naked call writer the benefit of time can often outweigh an upward movement in the price of the underlying stock or index. However, there are those instances when the call rises due to a greater rise in the stock or index than the trader anticipated. There is a strategy which will help to raise the break-even point for the trader.

The trader must still be convinced that the stock/index is gong to decline. If the opinion of the trader/investor is that the market or company is going to continue to rise, the trader should repurchase the call and take the loss. If the trader continues to believe that a decline is imminent, an equivalent amount of contracts should be written with a lower exercise price and twice the amount of calls with the original exercise price should be purchased. The net difference between the two premiums should cost the trader no additional premium. The result is a bear spread using puts. If there is little time until expiration, this idea should be abandoned.

If the stock declines below the exercise price of the short call by expiration, both calls should expire worthless. If the stock rises

TABLE 19-5.   Stock Repair Strategy Using Options versus Holding Stock Position

Purchased 1000 Shares of Stock at 44
Current Price = 35
Call with 35 Exercise Price = 3
Call with 40 Exercise Price = 1½

	Repair Strategy	*Hold Position*
Action	+ 10 Calls with 35 Exercise Price − 20 Calls with 40 Exercise Price Even Money	-None-

Stock at Expiration	*Profits and Losses*	
30	<$14,000>	<$14,000>
35	<$ 9,000>	<$ 9,000>
38	<$ 3,000>	<$ 6,000>
40	$ 1,000	<$ 4,000>
44	$ 1,000	-0-

above the exercise price of the long call, a maximum loss of the difference between the exercise prices less the original collected premium should be realized. The new break-even point for the trader is figured by adding the original premium collected less any debit paid for the repair strategy to the exercise price of the new short call.

The use of this repair strategy still holds some risk, which is basically the same as the risks associated with a bear spread using calls (Chapter 6). While some risks do exist, this position is far less risky than holding a naked call position while the value of the underlying instrument continues to rise. The risk of a bear spread using calls is limited: the person using this strategy knows from the beginning what his maximum dollar loss can be.

It is extremely difficult to repair a strategy which is losing money if the strategy has a risk which is unlimited. One of the reasons behind this is that the trader utilizing a strategy with such high risk as the naked call write, usually is losing due to a move in the stock which was totally unexpected. An unexpected movement in the price of the underlying instrument usually adds volatility, raising the option premium even further. A combination of an unexpected stock direction and high volatility usually adds additional strength through increased volume and more investors jumping on the bandwagon.

There are few guidelines for the user of an options repair strategy for naked call writers. The main suggestion is that if the stock rises with great intensity, the writer of the naked call should either repurchase the contract and take the loss or purchase a call with a higher exercise price and limit the loss potential. A stock that has a strong price accumulation may be subject to a reversal: this may cause the purchaser to reevaluate his position. Another suggestion is that any position being selected to repair a naked call should be kept short in time to expiration. A third consideration is that the repair strategy have adequate protection with a limited loss position, not exposing the position to continued unlimited loss. Finally, if the loss is shrunk to a small amount, the position should be closed and the use of an additional unlimited risk position should be avoided on this stock or index.

Repairing the Long Put

Use of the long put position is very similar to that of the long call, except that the opinion of the investor is different. Like the long call, the investor who purchases a put has a disadvantage in that time is not in favor and the investor is attempting to play "Beat the Clock." Even if the value of the underlying stock or index declines, the amount of that decline may not be enough to offset the loss of time value. This is especially true if the option is out-of-the-money. Thus, the purchaser of the put does not face defeat just from the incorrect opinion of the stock direction but also if the desired downward movement does not happen in a relatively short period of time. Just as with the long call, the investor may have several opportunities to correct the situation.

If the value of the stock has risen since the put has been purchased, there is little doubt that the investor is losing money. If the stock were to turn and drop, the investor may continue to lose money since time has eroded and the depreciation in the value of the stock or index may not be enough for the position to break-even. In such a situation, it would be practical for the investor to attempt rolling the long put for another put with a higher exercise price and possibly some additional time. To enact such a strategy, the investor should consider purchase of a put which is in-the-money or at-the-money and a cost which is approximately double the value of the put which is currently being held. Then, for each put which the investor is holding, one of the new puts should be purchased and two of the old puts should be sold, one which closes out the position and one which opens a new short put position. This will establish either a bull spread using puts (both contracts have the same month) or a diagonal bull spread using puts (if the expiration months are different). As with the repair on the long call position, the goal is to initiate the strategy with very little or no additional cost, or with any luck a credit. In doing so, the investor continues to believe that the price of the stock is going to decline.

If the bull spread using puts is established, the maximum value which the investor will be able to recoup will be the difference between the two exercise prices. This is possible only if the price of the underlying instrument drops below the level of the lower exercise price. If the underlying instrument continues rising, however, then the maximum loss might be realized if the value reaches the higher exercise price. The maximum loss of the position would be calculated using the following formula:

Maximum Loss = Original Premium + Cost for repair Strategy.

The investor may also calculate the new break-even point for the stock or index using the following formula:

Break Even Point = Higher Exercise Price − Maximum Loss.

The maximum which this repair strategy may be worth to the investor can be figured using the following formula:

Maximum Worth = Difference in Exercise Price − Maximum Loss.

These calculations are formatted in Worksheet 19-4 at the end of the chapter, the Long Put Repair Worksheet. Table 19-6 compares the use of this repair strategy for the losing put to the averaging down technique.

TABLE 19-6.   Repair Long Put versus Averaging Down

Purchased 1 Put with 55 Exercise Price at 4½
        Currently, this put is at 2 Unrealized Loss = 2½ pt or $250
Put with 60 Exercise Price = 4

	Repair Strategy	*Averaging Down*
Action	+ 1 Put with 60 Exercise − 2 Put with 55 Exercise	+ 1 Put with 55 Exercise
Additional Capital	$100 Credit	$250
Total Capital	$350	$750
Stock at Expiration	*Profits and Losses*	
62	<$350>	<$750>
60	<$350>	<$750>
58	<$150>	<$750>
56	$ 50	<$750>
55	$150	<$750>
53	$150	<$250>
51	$150	$100
Break-Even Point	56½	51½

If the investor utilizes the diagonal spread, there is greater potential, due to the unhedged position of the long put *once* the short put expires. If the stock or index drops below the lower exercise price before the short put expires, the same ultimate results should be realized since the position must be closed. While this may seem like a defeat in utilizing this strategy, there is the possibility that the long put would still hold additional time value, allowing the investor to close the spread for a credit which is higher than the difference between the exercise prices. If the stock or index does not drop below the lower exercise price before that put expires, the investor will hold a long put with a higher exercise price and additional time for basically no additional cost, assuming that no additional capital is paid for the repair strategy. This can give the investor almost unlimited potential. Remember that the purpose of this strategy is to turn a losing position into a break-even situation and that gains should *not* be the primary concern of the investor. If the position can be closed at break-even, such appropriate action should be taken. In addition, if the short put expires worthless, another out-of-the-money put may be written against the long put, allowing the investor to accumulate premiums and further offset any losses. The use of the new short put position will limit the potential of the long put so the investor must decide if use of this strategy is prudent. The value of the premium collected should be taken into account.

In some cases it is time, not the direction of the stock, that plays against the long put position. If this is the case, the investor may choose to roll the position into another month, allowing for additional time to be correct. In doing so, the investor should purchase one put with a longer period to expiration and sell two puts which are expiring (one which was being held and one additional contract), creating a horizontal time spread. There should be no additional costs for this strategy and actually a credit should be collected.

If the stock remains above the exercise price until the put with the least time to expiration expires (the short put), then the long put may have a basically unlimited potential. If the stock drops below the exercise price after that point, the long put may be sold, and the investor may even receive a slight profit out of the strategy. The new break-even point for this strategy will be calculated as follows:

$$
\text{Break Even Point} = \text{Exercise Price} - (\text{Cost of Original Put} - \text{Credit for Repair Strategy}).
$$

If the price of the underlying security drops below the exercise price before the short put expires, then the time spread should be closed. The investor should remember that the value of the long put should be greater than the value of the short put contract since the long put has a greater amount of time until expiration.

Another alternative if the value of the stock drops below the exercise price of the put, the investor may wish to be put the stock at the exercise price, if the opinion of the stock has turned bullish. The long put may continue to be held giving the investor a new position which is similar to that of the married put strategy, outlined in Chapter 5.

It is urged that the investor avoid the temptation in either case of averaging down the cost of the puts and raising the break-even point through the purchase of additional put contracts. This is just another instance of throwing good money after bad. The use of the option repair strategies is to avoid the risk of additional capital exposure, which the averaging down strategy will not do.

When using the repair strategy techniques for long put positions, the investor should follow the following guidelines. The first is that a bearish opinion on the stock should still be in the mind of the investor. If not, the long put should be closed and the loss should be taken. Second, the price paid for the repair strategy should be virtually nil as the repair strategies have been designed to limit the use of additional capital. Third, the break-even point should be raised and there should be no more than a 4 percent decline needed in the stock to break-even. In addition, if the repair strategy being used is to offset an upward move in the stock, the new break-even point should not be more than half way between the current stock price and the level from which it rose from. This helps to account for the 50 percent retracement rule.

Repairing the Naked Put Position

Chapter 4, which discusses the writing of the naked put position, states that the writer of the put contract should be willing to purchase the underlying stock with an effective price of the exercise price of the put less the premium collected for writing the put. However, sometimes the opinion on the underlying stock or even index changes. This change is usually due to a sudden and vigorous drop in the price of the underlying security. At this point, the trader is no longer confident in the bullish opinion once held. If the opinion of the underlying instrument has truly changed to bearish, then the put should be repurchased, the loss taken. If the opinion remains bullish, then there might be some help.

As with the writing of naked calls, there is additional difficulty in trying to correct a problem with a strategy which basically has an unlimited risk. At this point, the trader may have to realize some type of loss, however, sometimes this loss may be reduced. The put which was written should be repurchased plus an additional put with the same exercise price but a longer term till expiration and a put which has a higher exercise price and a longer term till expiration (same as new put purchased) should be written. Once the trade is completed, the new position will be a bull spread using puts and the original short put will no longer be part of the picture. This should be done for as little additional capital as possible.

If the price of the stock or index begins to rise, then there is a chance that the position might realize a break-even, especially if the instrument rises above the exercise price of the put which was sold in the spread. If this does happen, the spread might expire worthless. In such a case, the worth of the strategy would be computed using the following formula:

$$\text{Worth of Repair} = \text{Original Premium} - \text{Cost for Repair.}$$

If the worth of repair result is a negative number, then regardless of what happened, the best situation for the repair would result in a loss. If the number is positive, then the best result would still return some profit. The trader should not complain if the loss is less than the potential of the original short put position. The trader can also calculate the new break-even point using the following formula:

$$\text{Break-Even Point} = \text{Higher Exercise Price} - \text{Worth of Repair}$$
$$\text{subject to the Worth of Repair being positive.}$$

The maximum loss for the repair strategy occurs when the stock or index drops below the lower exercise price. The calculation for the maximum loss is:

$$\text{Maximum Loss} = \text{Difference of Exercise Prices} + (\text{Cost for}$$
$$\text{Repair Strategy} - \text{Put Premium Received}).$$

It is especially important that the user of the naked put strategy *not* attempt to average up. Averaging up on the naked put strategy will put additional risk on the trader. This is equivalent to putting ones head into the lion's mouth.

Naked option positions should be approached with *extreme* caution, especially when attempting to repair the situation. The trader or investor should consider the accepting of the loss for sake of simplicity and to avoid further risk or complication involved with creating a repair strategy for such a situation.

Repairing Spreads

Bull and bear spreads which result in the investor paying a debit (bull spreads using calls or bear spreads using puts) have a limited risk which is tied to the debit price paid for the spread (see Chapter 6). Since the potential return is also limited, there is usually a very small range in which the stock may trade: this range is between the two exercise prices. The break-even points also fall between the two exercise prices. Now there is a question of what to do if the strategy is not working the way in which the investor had planned.

Repairing spreads of any type is difficult since the value of the existing spread is very close to null when the investor runs into the problem, since the debit which was paid for the spread was less than half of the difference of the exercise prices. Once the stock violates the exercise price of the long contract, the investor is usually faced with a potential loss situation. There are times, when there is still some time left till expiration, that the investor may be able to pull a rabbit out of a hat and create a repair for the spread.

One technique which *might* work would be to roll the existing spread into a diagonal ratio calendar spread. This entails several trades taking place at the same time. One of the major disadvantages to using this repair technique is that there is usually a large amount of commission which must be paid to adjust the positions. Also, the investor must maintain the opinion on the underlying stock and believe that the stock will turn around. We shall evaluate two situations, a bull spread using calls and a bear spread using puts, using examples.

Assume that BUL's stock is selling for $46. Since we believe that the stock will rise to at least $50 per share in the next three months, a three-month call is purchased, which we shall state expires in October, with an exercise price of 45 and write a call expiring in the same month with an exercise price of 50 for a debit of two points per spread. The quantity of this spread was ten contracts on each side.

In September, the stock dropped to $43 per share and the October 45 call dropped to 1⅛ points while the October 50 call dropped to ⅛ of a point. In the November options, the November 40 calls are trading at 4½ points. The investor can repurchase the short call and sell the long calls twice (total of 20 contracts). Once this is done, the investor purchases 10 of the November 40 contracts. The new position is as follows:

+ 5 BUL Nov 40 calls   − 10 BUL Oct 45 calls

The total cost (excluding commission and other transaction charges) for this transaction is calculated as follows:

+ 10 BUL Oct 50 calls .... close transaction ..... ⅛ $125.00
− 10 BUL Oct 45 calls .... close transaction .... 1⅛ $1125.00
− 10 BUL Oct 45 calls .... open transaction .... 1⅛ $1125.00
+ 5 BUL Nov 40 calls ... open transaction .... 4½ $2250.00
         * * TOTAL COST $125.00

The investor must put up the additional margin on the naked call position. As long as the stock remains under 45 until the October expiration, there is a possibility that the investor can break-even. If the stock does rise above 45, the spread should be closed. The November option should still have more time value than the October contract so if the position is closed when the stock is under 46, the spread position should still return a profit. If the stock remains at 44 until the October options expire, then the five November 40 calls will be worth at least four points or $2000. Since the cost of the *original* spread was $2000, then a loss of $125 (cost of repair strategy) might be realized.

It is cautioned that if the stock starts to gain value quickly and the October contracts have not expired, there is a possibility of unlimited loss because of the naked short call position. Any investor utilizing this strategy should take extreme care in monitoring the position.

Bear spreads using puts may be repaired in a similar method, except using puts. Once again, the situation requires the use of a new spread which is a diagonal ratio put spread using puts. Should the price of the stock drop below the exercise price of the puts written before they expire, there is potential for a substantial loss.

The repair strategy for spread positions should be used with extreme caution. This type of strategy is not for the faint hearted or people who cannot take on extreme risk. In most cases, the investor will sleep better at night by selling the original spread and taking the loss or by letting the options expire and taking the loss.

Summary

1. It is possible to turn a losing situation into a break-even or even a small profit.

2. The investor or trader should not wait until the the last minute to attempt to correct a bad position. It might be too late.

3. The aim of repair strategies is simply to break-even. The person utilizing these strategies should not expect to make a profit from them.

4. The repair of long call or put positions should be undertaken before the value of the contract becomes virtually worthless.

5. The repair to short option positions will still require that some risk be taken, however the new positions should attempt to limit the risks.

6. The use of option strategies to repair positions might require the use of the stock. All possibilities should be carefully evaluated and plotted using both the value of the stock and the time until expiration.

7. To repair certain positions, the investor/trader may need to use ratio spreads. These spreads should not be overlooked, but the careful implementation of such spreads requires careful evaluation and monitoring.

WORKSHEET 19-1:

Long Stock Repair

STOCK			SHARES	PRICE	—52 WEEK—		RATING	PIE RATIO	YIELD
					HIGH	LOW			
OPTION CONTRACT		CALL	CONTRACTS	PREMIUM	EXPIRATION DATE		DAYS TILL EXP.		
OPTION CONTRACT		CALL	CONTRACTS	PREMIUM	EXPIRATION DATE		DAYS TILL EXP.		
QUART DIVID	DIVIDS TO EXP	TOTAL DIVID COLLECT		DEBIT	REG. T RATE		MARGIN INT RATE		
INTEREST CHARGES:		INT RATE ×	DAYS ÷ 365 ×	DEBIT BAL =	$		TODAY'S DATE		

STOCK LOSS

Original Purchase Price of Stock..................		
Amount of Shares...............................	×	
Commission on Stock Purchase..................	+	
Original Stock Cost............................	=	
Current Stock Price		
Amount of Shares...............................	×	
Current Value.................................	=	
Original Stock Cost............................	−	
Unrealized Loss................................	=	
Amount of Shares...............................	÷	
Unrealized Loss Per Share.......................	=	

REPAIR STRATEGY

Premium on Lower Exercise Price................		
Amount of Shares...............................	×	
Purchase Call Commission	+	
Call Purchase Cost.............................	=	
Premium on Higher Exercise Price		
Amount of Shares...............................	×	
Multiplied by 2........................	×	
Sale Call Commission	−	
Call Proceeds.................................	=	
Call Proceeds.................................		
Call Purchase Cost.............................	−	
Credit (Debit)	=	
Amount of Shares...............................	÷	
Credit (Debit) ÷ Share.........................	=	

BREAK-EVEN POINT

Unrealized Loss Per Share.......................		
Lower Exercise Price	+	
Credit ÷ Share................................	−	
*Break-Even Point.............................	=	

*Break-even point only if at or less than higher exercise price.

Short Stock Repair Worksheet

STOCK		SHARES	PRICE	—52 WEEK—		RATING	PIE RATIO	YIELD
				HIGH	LOW			
OPTION CONTRACT PUT		CONTRACTS	PREMIUM	EXPIRATION DATE		DAYS TILL EXP.		
OPTION CONTRACT PUT		CONTRACTS	PREMIUM	EXPIRATION DATE		DAYS TILL EXP.		
QUART DIVID	DIVIDS TO EXP	TOTAL DIVID COLLECT	DEBIT	REG. T RATE		MARGIN INT RATE		
INTEREST CHARGES:	INT RATE ×	DAYS ÷365 ×	DEBIT BAL =	$		TODAY'S DATE		

STOCK LOSS

Original Sale Price of Stock . . . .

Amount of Shares. . . . . ×

Commission on Stock Sale . . . . +

Original Stock Sale. . . . . =

Current Stock Price . . . .

Amount of Shares. . . . . ×

Current Value . . . . =

Original Stock Sale. . . . .

Current Value . . . . −

Unrealized Loss. . . . . =

Amount of Shares. . . . . ÷

Unrealized Loss Per Share. . . . . =

REPAIR STRATEGY

Premium on Higher Exercise Price . . . .

Amount of Shares. . . . . ×

Purchase Put Commission. . . . . +

Put Purchase Cost . . . . =

Premium on Lower Exercise Price. . . . .

Amount of Shares. . . . . ×

Multiplied by 2. . . . . ×

Sale Put Commission . . . . −

Put Proceeds . . . . =

Put Proceeds . . . .

Put Purchase Cost . . . . −

Credit (Debit) . . . . =

Amount of Shares. . . . . ÷

Credit (Debit) ÷ Share. . . . . =

BREAK-EVEN POINT

Unrealized Loss Per Share. . . . .

Higher Exercise Price. . . . . −

Credit ÷ Share. . . . . , +

Dividends Paid ÷ Share . . . . +

*Break-Even Point. . . . . =

*Break-even point only if at or higher than lower exercise price.

WORKSHEET 19-3:

Long Call Repair Worksheet

STOCK			SHARES	PRICE	—52 WEEK—		RATING	PIE RATIO	YIELD
					HIGH	LOW			
OPTION CONTRACT			CONTRACTS	PREMIUM	EXPIRATION DATE		DAYS TILL EXP.		
OPTION CONTRACT			CONTRACTS	PREMIUM	EXPIRATION DATE		DAYS TILL EXP.		
QUART DIVID	DIVIDS TO EXP	TOTAL DIVID COLLECT		DEBIT	REG. T RATE		MARGIN INT RATE		
INTEREST CHARGES:		INT RATE | DAYS | ÷ 365 ×		DEBIT BAL | $ =			TODAY'S DATE		

CALL LOSS

Original Purchase Price of Call . . . .

Equivalent Amount of Shares.   ×

Commission on Call Purchase . . . .   +

Original Call Cost . . . .   =

Current Call Price . . . .

Equivalent Amount of Shares.   ×

Current Value. . . . .   =

Original Call Cost . . . .   −

Unrealized Loss. . . . .   =

Equivalent Amount of Shares.   ÷

Unrealized Loss Per Share. . . . .   =

REPAIR STRATEGY

Premium on Lower Exercise Price. . . . .

Equivalent Amount of Shares.   ×

Purchase Call Commission . . . .   +

Call Purchase Cost. . . . .   =

Premium on Original Exercise Price. . . . .

Equivalent Amount of Shares.   ×

Multiplied by 2. . . . .   ×

Sale Call Commission . . . .   −

Call Proceeds. . . . .   =

Call Proceeds. . . . .

Call Purchase Cost. . . . .   −

Credit (Debit) . . . .   =

Amount of Shares. . . . .   ÷

Credit (Debit) ÷ Share. . . . .   =

BREAK-EVEN POINT

Unrealized Loss Per Share. . . . .

Lower Exercise Price . . . .   +

Credit ÷ Share. . . . .   −

*Break-Even Point. . . . .   ±

*Break-even point only if at or less than higher exercise price.

WORKSHEET 19-4:

Long Put Repair Worksheet

STOCK			SHARES	PRICE	—52 WEEK—		RATING	PIE RATIO	YIELD
					HIGH	LOW			
OPTION CONTRACT			CONTRACTS	PREMIUM	EXPIRATION DATE		DAYS TILL EXP.		
OPTION CONTRACT			CONTRACTS	PREMIUM	EXPIRATION DATE		DAYS TILL EXP.		
QUART DIVID	DIVIDS TO EXP	TOTAL DIVID COLLECT		DEBIT	REG. T RATE		MARGIN INT RATE		
INTEREST CHARGES:		INT RATE	DAYS	DEBIT BAL	$		TODAY'S DATE		
		x	÷ 365 x		=				

PUT LOSS

Original Purchase Price of Put..............		
Equivalent Amount of Shares....................	×	
Commission on Put Purchase...................	+	
Original Put Cost...........................	=	
Current Put Price		
Equivalent Amount of Shares....................	×	
Current Value................................	=	
Original Put Cost............................	−	
Unrealized Loss..............................	=	
Equivalent Amount of Shares....................	÷	
Unrealized Loss Per Share......................	=	

REPAIR STRATEGY

Premium on Higher Exercise Price		
Equivalent Amount of Shares............... ...	×	
Purchase Put Commission......................	+	
Put Purchase Cost	=	
Premium on Original Exercise Price.............		
Equivalent Amount of Shares....................	×	
Multiplied by 2............................ .	×	
Sale Put Commission..........	−	
Put Proceeds	=	
Put Proceeds		
Put Purchase Cost	−	
Credit (Debit)	=	
Amount of Shares............................	÷	
Credit (Debit) ÷ Share........................	=	

BREAK-EVEN POINT

Unrealized Loss Per Share......................		
Higher Exercise Price.........................	−	
Credit ÷ Share..............................	+	
*Break-Even Point...........................	=	

*Break-even point only if at or higher than lower exercise price.

20
Option Pricing

Chapter 1 discussed what is involved in the pricing of calls and puts. Chapter 13 discussed options arbitrage and how conversions and reversals are used to keep the price of option contracts in line. This chapter will further examine the pricing of options and the determination of option premiums and will then investigate strategies for the selection of option contracts.

There are several formulas which option professionals have developed to determine the value of an option contract. Some of these formulas may be familiar. Formulas such as the Black-Scholes Option Pricing Model, Cox-Ross Pricing Model, or the Bi Nomial Option Pricing Model return a theoretical option price. The theoretical value (T.V.) is a value which the formula returns based on the input of several variables. The value is used by professionals as a comparison between the current price of the option contract and the theoretical price. The comparison is also carried between the use of different option contracts, allowing for the determination of an option which is believed to be overpriced and a contract which is believed to be underpriced.

The determination of a T.V. is based upon the price of the underlying stock, the relationship of the exercise price to the stock price, time until expiration, the volatility of the stock, annual dividend and the risk-free interest rate, and whether the option contract is a put or call. The relationship among all of the above variables plays a big part in the valuing of an option contract. As the value of any of the variables changes, the T.V. will change. In this chapter we shall explore the effects upon the T.V. as the variables change.

Hedge Ratio

The Black-Scholes Option Pricing Formula will be the focus of discussion for this chapter. One of the benefits of the Black-Scholes formula is the calculation of delta or hedge ratio (H.R.). Delta is the Greek letter which represents change. The H.R. is the theoretical change in the T.V. of an option in relation to the change in the price of the stock. Therefore, if a call has a H.R. of 40, the call should increase 40 percent of the change in the stock if the stock rises, or decrease 40 percent of the stock move if the price of the stock decreases. Therefore, if the price of the stock rises 1 point, the T.V. of the call will increase .4 of one point. If the stock drops one point, the T.V. of the call should drop .4 of one point. If the stock drops one point, the T.V. of the call should drop .4 of one point. The value of the delta is usually good the first one point move in the stock over a short period of time.

The delta of a put contract has a negative value. Therefore, the put H.R. has a negative relationship to the movement of the underlying stock. If a put contract has a H.R. of −55, then if the stock rises one point, the value of the T.V. of the put should decrease by .55 of a point. If the value of the stock declines by one point, the T.V. of the put should rise by .55 of a point. Like the delta of the call, the delta of the put is usually good for the first point move in the underlying stock over a short period of time.

When the absolute value (positives) of the H.R. of both put and call with the same exercise price and same expiration month are added together, their value should be approximately 100 percent. As discussed in Chapter 13, the total movement of put and call should equal a one-point move in the underlying stock.

A change in the delta occurs if the stock moves one point or if time changes. The change in the delta is known as the gamma. The gamma is not provided by the Black-Scholes model. The gamma is a percentage of how much the delta will change. Option arbitrageurs will use the gamma to help in creating positions and determining the risks involved in positions which are not fully hedged.

A call with a theoretical value of 4.25 and a delta of 45 will have a T.V. of 4.70 if the stock rises one point. If that same stock drops one point then the new T.V. will be 3.80. The corresponding put with a T.V. of 1.08 will have a delta of −65. Thus if the stock rose one point, that put will have a T.V. of .43. If the stock drops one point, the new T.V. of the put will be 1.70. Therefore, if the underlying stock rose one point, the combination of the call rising and the put declining will result in an equivalent one point change in the options, 45 percent accumulation of the call and 65 percent declining of the put.

An option with a high hedge ratio is usually a better purchase than a write, since the value of the option will have a greater percentage movement with the price of the stock, and little time value erosion as compared to a contract with a low hedge ratio. This allows the purchaser of an option greater leverage. Contracts with a lower hedge ratio make for better writes than purchases since they are usually high in time premium and have a lower intrinsic value. Options which have a high delta are usually in-the-money and contracts which are out-of-the-money usually have a low delta. A call with a high delta will result in the corresponding put having a low delta and vice versa.

As the value of the underlying stock rises, the T.V. of the call and the H.R. increase while the time value of that call decreases. If the stock declines, the T.V. and the H.R. decrease while the time value increases. Put contracts hold opposite values.

Comparing Values

This section will evaluate and discuss how the changes to different variables effect the theoretical value and hedge ratios of puts and calls. Some of the changes will have a positive effect on both put and call while others will have a positive effect on one and a negative effect on the other. Tables have been included to show the actual changes and compare the new values to the old values. The modified theoretical value (M.T.V.) and the modified hedge ratio (M.H.R.) are labeled and show the what those values would be based upon the change on *that* variable. In many instances, a change in one of the variables may result in the change on another. These examples will analyze the change in one variable at a time.

Table 20-1 is a display of option contracts utilizing the following variables:

TABLE 20-1. Option Contracts for Warner-Lambert Stock

Stock Price: 70⅜   Date: 9/30   Ann Divd: 1.76   Riskless: 9
Volatility: 25

Calls				Option	Puts			
T.V.	H.R.	M.T.V.	M.H.R.	Series	T.V.	H.R.	M.T.V.	M.H.R.
5.80	93			Oct 65	.12	−7		
1.97	58			Oct 70	1.29	−43		
.32	16			Oct 75	4.71	−84		
6.27	88			Nov 65	.57	−11		
2.88	57			Nov 70	2.17	−44		
1.00	27			Nov 75	5.32	−74		
7.91	79			Jan 65	1.29	−22		
4.75	60			Jan 70	3.10	−41		
2.57	40			Jan 75	6.05	−61		
1.26	24			Jan 80	9.94	−77		
9.61	76			Apr 65	2.12	−25		
6.61	63			Apr 70	4.02	−39		
4.33	48			Apr 75	6.79	−53		

Stock Price 70⅜
Today's Date ....Sept 30
Annual Divd 1.76
Riskless Interest Rate 9%
Volatility 25
X-Div Dates ....11/4, ⅔

These variables were taken from Warner-Lambert (WLA) stock. The T.V.s and the H.R.s in Table 20-1 are the result of the preceding variables being input into a computer model of the Black-Scholes Option Pricing Formula.

Changes in the Stock Price

Raising the value of the underlying stock by approximately 10 percent, results in the theoretical value of the calls rising and the theoretical value of the puts declining. Simulating the price of the stock at

TABLE 20-2. Display of Option Contracts Comparing T.V. and M.T.V.

Stock Price: 77⅜   Date: 9/30   Ann Divd: 1.76   Riskless: 9
Volatility: 25

Calls				Option	Puts			
T.V.	H.R.	M.T.V.	M.H.R.	Series	T.V.	H.R.	M.T.V.	M.H.R.
5.80	93	12.68	99	Oct 65	.12	−7	.00	−0
1.97	58	7.76	97	Oct 70	1.29	−43	.06	−3
.32	16	3.42	74	Oct 75	4.71	−84	.71	−26
6.27	88	12.95	99	Nov 65	.57	−11	.05	−2
2.88	57	8.18	93	Nov 70	2.17	−44	.39	−11
1.00	27	4.33	68	Nov 75	5.32	−74	1.59	−33
7.91	79	14.01	93	Jan 65	1.29	−22	.35	−7
4.75	60	9.83	83	Jan 70	3.10	−41	1.10	−18
2.57	40	6.37	67	Jan 75	6.05	−61	2.60	−35
1.26	24	3.79	49	Jan 80	9.94	−77	5.06	−51
9.61	76	15.45	89	Apr 65	2.12	−25	.83	−11
6.61	63	11.64	80	Apr 70	4.02	−39	1.84	−21
4.33	48	8.41	68	Apr 75	6.79	−53	3.55	−33

77⅜, Table 20–2 compares the difference between the original theoretical value and the modified theoretical value. The theoretical value of the November 70 call rose 5.30 points or 184%, while the T.V. of the corresponding put dropped 1.78 points or 82% of its value. At the same time, the M.T.V. of the January 75 call, which was originally out-of-the-money rose 149%. The January 75 put, which was originally in-the-money and now is out-of-the-money dropped 57% of its value.

In addition to the theoretical value of the calls rising, the hedge ratios on all of the calls also rose. The M.H.R. of the January 70 call rose 38 percent, giving the new value of that call an 83% correlation rate to the movement of the stock. The January 70 put's hedge ratio dropped 23 points to −18, meaning that the movement of the stock would not have as great effect on the put as it did when the H.R. was at −41.

As shown in this example, the value of a call will rise when the stock rises. The more the stock becomes in-the-money, the stronger the delta factor on the call will be. As the value of the calls rise with the appreciation of the stock price, the value of the puts will decline.

TABLE 20-3.   Option Contracts for Stock at 63⅜

Stock Price: 63⅜   Date: 9/30   Ann Divd: 1.76   Riskless: 9
Volatility: 25

| Calls | | | | Option | Puts | | | |
T.V.	H.R.	M.T.V.	M.H.R.	Series	T.V.	H.R.	M.T.V.	M.H.R.
5.80	93	.89	37	Oct 65	.12	−7	2.25	−63
1.97	58	.08	5	Oct 70	1.29	−43	6.63	−96
.32	16	.00	0	Oct 75	4.71	−84	11.63	−99
6.27	88	1.68	43	Nov 65	.57	−11	3.06	−59
2.88	57	.44	16	Nov 70	2.17	−44	6.85	−86
1.00	27	.08	4	Nov 75	5.32	−74	11.63	−97
7.91	79	3.29	51	Jan 65	1.29	−22	3.89	−50
4.75	60	1.57	31	Jan 70	3.10	−41	7.30	−70
2.57	40	.66	16	Jan 75	6.05	−61	11.64	−86
1.26	24	.25	7	Jan 80	9.94	−77	16.63	−92
9.61	76	4.93	56	Apr 65	2.12	−25	4.70	−46
6.61	63	3.00	48	Apr 70	4.02	−39	7.89	−52
4.33	48	1.72	27	Apr 75	6.79	−53	11.86	−54

As puts decline, so does the delta relationship between the stock and the put contract. Therefore, an upward movement in the value of the stock will lead to a greater disparity between the put and the call. The price relationship between put and call is usually opposite, when measured by a price move in the underlying security, but in this case the values of the hedge ratios also have a differing effect.

To show a contrasting view, Table 20-3 changes the price of the stock to 63⅜, down 7 points or almost 10%. As the price of the shares declined, so did the theoretical value of the calls. The November 70 calls lost 85% of their value with the stock declining 10%. The value of the complementing put rose 216%. Looking further, the April 65 put, which was out-of-the-money, more than doubled and is now in-the-money, while the complementing call dropped from 9.61 to 4.93, and went from being in-the-money to being out-of-the-money.

The modified deltas also had a similar reaction. For example, the October 65 call's delta dropped from 93 to 37 while the put rose from −7 to −63, or nine times the original hedge ratio. The delta on the January 75 call dropped from 40 to 16 while its respective put rose from −61 to −86. As seen here, the hedge ratio of a put will have greater significance if the value of the stock declines while the hedge ratio of the call will decline, resulting in less relevance in the relationship between the stock price and that of the call.

Just as there was a relationship between the T.V. and the H.R. in the first example, there is a similar relationship in this example. As the value of the stock declines, the value of the call also declined and so did the call's H.R. The opposite held true for those values on the corresponding puts. As the value of the stock declined, the put's T.V. and its H.R. rose.

Time as a Pricing Factor

Some investors find it difficult to believe that if the price of the underlying stock remains unchanged, the value of the options will still change. In the world of options, this is very far from being the truth. The closer to expiration, the greater the decrease in the time value of the option contracts. The relationship between time and option premiums is a fundamental basis for options trading. The time-decay curve in Chapter 3 shows the change in the value of time as expiration grows near.

Table 20-4 changes the current date from September 30 to October 30. Since the October option contracts have expired, most investors would have their focus upon the November and January puts and calls. The at-the-money November 70 put lost just over 50 percent of its T.V., even though the value of the stock has not changed. The January 70 call also lost, with the T.V. dropping 17 percent in one month. The value of time does not just present a potential opportunity for a writer, it is also a factor on which calculations are based. This fact will become clearer shortly when we explore the interest rate factor and the dividend factor.

The change in the value of time also has its effect on the hedge ratios. The decrease in time till expiration results in the hedge ratios of the in-the-money options rising. This is true for both put and call. While the in-the-money deltas rise, the out-of-the-money deltas decline, since there will be less opportunity for the option to become in-the-money. At-the-money contracts are little effected by the movement in time.

TABLE 20-4. **Option Contracts—Effect of One Month Change in Current Date**

Stock Price: 70⅜   Date: 10/30   Ann Divd: 1.76   Riskless: 9
Volatility: 25

Calls				Option Series	Puts			
T.V.	H.R.	M.T.V.	M.H.R.		T.V.	H.R.	M.T.V.	M.H.R.
5.80	93	N/A	N/A	Oct 65	.12	−7	N/A	N/A
1.97	58	N/A	N/A	Oct 70	1.29	−43	N/A	N/A
.32	16	N/A	N/A	Oct 75	4.71	−84	N/A	N/A
6.27	88	5.46	96	Nov 65	.57	−11	.12	−2
2.88	57	1.67	64	Nov 70	2.17	−44	1.06	−37
1.00	27	.21	12	Nov 75	5.32	−74	5.08	−89
7.91	79	7.15	80	Jan 65	1.29	−22	1.00	−21
4.75	60	3.93	59	Jan 70	3.10	−41	2.74	−43
2.57	40	1.85	36	Jan 75	6.05	−61	5.84	−64
1.26	24	.75	18	Jan 80	9.94	−77	10.04	−83
9.61	76	8.97	77	Apr 65	2.12	−25	1.90	−25
6.61	63	5.95	61	Apr 70	4.02	−39	3.83	−41
4.33	48	3.72	46	Apr 75	6.79	−53	6.64	−55

One of the reasons why the out-of-the-money contract's hedge ratio declines is because the complementary contract's hedge ratio is rising. Remember what was stated earlier: the absolute value of the call's delta and the put's delta should roughly equal 100. If the value of the in-the-money put's hedge ratio rose while the out-of-the-money call's hedge ratio remained the same, the absolute value of the two hedge ratios would be over the 100 percent limit.

Pushing ahead in time, Table 20-5 explores the theoretical values and hedge ratios of the options as an additional month has passed. With 60 days gone by, the value of the at-the-money January 70 calls has dropped from 4.75 to 3.20, resulting in a decline of almost 33 percent. The days left till expiration on this contract have been modified to 48 from 108, so as can be seen the decrease in value still does not match the difference in the amount of time. The out-of-the-money Jan 75 call dropped approximately 54 percent. Since the call is out-of-the-money, there is less of an opportunity for the option to become in-the-money. The in-the-money calls declined only 16%,

TABLE 20-5. Option Contracts—Effect of Two Month Change in Current Date

Stock Price: 70⅜   Date: 11/30   Ann Divd: 1.76   Riskless: 9
Volatility: 25

| Calls | | | | Option | Puts | | | |
T.V.	H.R.	M.T.V.	M.H.R.	Series	T.V.	H.R.	M.T.V.	M.H.R.
5.80	93	N/A	N/A	Oct 65	.12	−7	N/A	N/A
1.97	58	N/A	N/A	Oct 70	1.29	−43	N/A	N/A
.32	16	N/A	N/A	Oct 75	4.71	−84	N/A	N/A
6.27	88	N/A	N/A	Nov 65	.57	−11	N/A	N/A
2.88	57	N/A	N/A	Nov 70	2.17	−44	N/A	N/A
1.00	27	N/A	N/A	Nov 75	5.32	−74	N/A	N/A
7.91	79	6.67	85	Jan 65	1.29	−22	.53	−15
4.75	60	3.20	59	Jan 70	3.10	−41	2.05	−42
2.57	40	1.18	30	Jan 75	6.05	−61	5.12	−75
1.26	24	.33	11	Jan 80	9.94	−77	9.63	−91
9.61	76	8.62	78	Apr 65	2.12	−25	1.54	−23
6.61	63	5.50	62	Apr 70	4.02	−39	3.38	−42
4.33	48	3.25	44	Apr 75	6.79	−53	6.20	−62

since most of that contract is intrinsic value. The time value portion of the January 65 call dropped from 2.54 to 1.30 or 51%.

The theoretical value of the put contracts also showed a decline. The January 70 put lost 1.05 or 34% while the in-the-money January 80 put (9⅝ points in-the-money) lost all of its time premium and is now valued at its intrinsic value. The out-of-the-money January 65 put lost .76 of a point or 60% of its T.V.

Once again, the relationship between the in-the-money options and the stock became closer as time moved on. The delta of the out-of-the-money options continued to decrease, further separating the relationship between option and stock. The at-the-money options continued to basically maintain a constant stock/option price relationship.

To further illustrate the influence time has on the value of options contracts, let us compare the in-the-money, at-the-money and out-of-the-money January puts and calls using elapsed time of both 30 and 60 days. The original T.V. and H.R. were based on a term till expiration of 108 days. The T.V. of the in-the-money calls lost 9.6% in the first month and 6.7% in the second month. The complementary put options (out-of-the-money) lost 22.5% in-the-first month while losing 47% in the second 60-day period. The at-the-money calls lost 17% during the first 30 days while losing 18.5% during the second 30 day period. The January 70 put dropped 12% in the first month and 25% in the second month. Moving on, the out-of-the-money January 75 call lost 27% during the first 30 days and 36% during the second month. The in-the-money January 80 puts fell 3.5% in the first 30 days and 12% during the second 30-day period.

As can be seen, the in-the-money option contracts lose a greater percentage of time value in the first month than in the second month. The at-the-money puts and calls lose approximately the same percentage of time value during both 30-day periods. The out-of-the-money options lose a greater percentage of time value during the second 30-day period as opposed to the first period. In addition, the T.V. of the put contracts declines more than the T.V. of the calls.

Rising and Falling Interest Rates

Interest rates play a major role in investment decisions. As interest rates rise, the market usually declines and vice versa. This interest rate/stock price relationship adds a bias to the valuation of option contracts. As the rate of interest rises, the cost of holding a position which was purchased in a margin account goes up, making the break-even point on the purchase of stock higher. For professional traders, who may not be subject to the same margin requirements as an investor, the change in cost for holding the position will also be greater. This causes many to abandon the idea of purchasing securities as investors and traders believe in the trend effect.

When interest rates rise, covered call writers require additional premium for their positions to break-even. Married put purchasers have an additional burden from the cost of holding a stock and therefore are unwilling to pay high premiums for the put contracts, causing the time value of the puts to decline. The cause and effect relationship can also be seen in the computation of conversions and reversals (see Chapter 13) as the cost-of-carry is a major contributor.

If interest rates decline, so will the premium of calls. Covered call writers will not require high premiums since the cost-of-carry will be lower, lowering the break-even point. Married put purchasers will

TABLE 20-6.   Option Contracts—Relation of T.V. and Increased Riskless Interest Rate

Stock Price: 70⅜   Date: 9/30   Ann Divd: 1.76   Riskless: 11
Volatility: 25

T.V.	H.R.	M.T.V.	M.H.R.	Option Series	T.V.	H.R.	M.T.V.	M.H.R.
5.80	93	5.86	94	Oct 65	.12	−7	.12	−7
1.97	58	2.01	59	Oct 70	1.29	−43	1.26	−42
.32	16	.33	16	Oct 75	4.71	−84	4.69	−86
6.27	88	6.38	85	Nov 65	.57	−11	.54	−16
2.88	57	2.98	58	Nov 70	2.17	−44	2.09	−43
1.00	27	1.05	28	Nov 75	5.32	−74	5.21	−74
7.91	79	8.20	80	Jan 65	1.29	−22	1.21	−21
4.75	60	4.98	62	Jan 70	3.10	−41	2.97	−39
2.57	40	2.73	42	Jan 75	6.05	−61	5.87	−61
1.26	24	1.35	25	Jan 80	9.94	−77	9.79	−76
9.61	76	10.09	78	Apr 65	2.12	−25	1.95	−23
6.61	63	7.03	65	Apr 70	4.02	−39	3.80	−36
4.33	48	4.66	50	Apr 75	6.79	−53	6.51	−51

not have as great a burden with respect to the cost-of-carry, and can therefore pay additional premium for the positions.

The changes in theoretical value can be seen in Table 20-6, raising the riskless interest rate to 11%, and in Table 20-7, lowering the riskless interest rate to 7%. As the interest rate rises, the theoretical value of the November 70 call rose from 2.88 to 2.98, the January 70 call rose from 4.75 to 4.98 and the April 70 call rose from 6.61 to 7.03 or 6.4%. The November 70 puts dropped in T.V. from 2.17 to 2.09, the January 70 put from 3.10 to 2.97 and the April 70 put dropped to 6.51 from 6.79 or 4%. As can be seen, there are greater changes for the calls than there are for the puts.

During periods of rising interest rates, the hedge ratio on calls rises slightly while the hedge ratio for puts has a slight decline. When interest rates decline, the delta of the calls declines slightly while the puts rise slightly.

The theoretical values of calls fall during declining interest rates, as can be seen in the figures. If the riskless rate falls to 7%, the theoretical value of the November 70 call declined 3%, the January

TABLE 20-7. Option Contracts—Relation of T.V. and Decreased Riskless Rate

Stock Price: 70⅜   Date: 9/30   Ann Divd: 1.76   Riskless: 7
Volatility: 25

Calls				Option	Puts			
T.V.	H.R.	S.T.V.	S.H.R.	Series	T.V.	H.R.	S.T.V.	S.H.R.
5.80	93	5.74	93	Oct 65	.12	−7	.13	−7
1.97	58	1.93	57	Oct 70	1.29	−43	1.31	−43
.32	16	.31	15	Oct 75	4.71	−84	4.74	−86
6.27	88	6.16	88	Nov 65	.57	−11	.60	−14
2.88	57	2.79	55	Nov 70	2.17	−44	2.24	−45
1.00	27	.96	26	Nov 75	5.32	−74	5.44	−75
7.91	79	7.63	78	Jan 65	1.29	−22	1.38	−23
4.75	60	4.53	59	Jan 70	3.10	−41	3.25	−42
2.57	40	2.42	39	Jan 75	6.05	−61	6.24	−62
1.26	24	1.17	22	Jan 80	9.94	−77	10.13	−83
9.61	76	9.13	75	Apr 65	2.12	−25	2.29	−27
6.61	63	6.21	60	Apr 70	4.02	−39	4.28	−42
4.33	48	4.01	46	Apr 75	6.79	−53	7.09	−54

70 call dropped 4.6% and the April 70 call losses 6%. At the same time, the November 70 put rises 3.2%, the January 70 put rises by 4.8% and the April 70 put gains 6.5%. The changes to the in-the-money options is not as great as to those contracts which are at-the-money. The out-of-the-money options have a greater change than those contracts which are at-the-money. Options with greater time till expiration will also realize a greater effect from the changes in interest rates, as the cost-of-carry over a period of time will be greater than the cost-of-carry over a short period of time.

Market Activity and Volatility

The upward and downward movement of a stock presents opportunity for profit and loss. The amount of these movements can determine the value of profits or losses. The frequency of such movement is known as the volatility. The greater the frequency and the greater the degree of the movements, the higher the volatility. If the frequency and degree of the stock movements decline, so will the volatility of that stock. The direction of the movement in the stock price has no bearing on the volatility. As the volatility in the stock rises, the greater the probability that the stock will rise or fall through an exercise price. A decrease in the volatility will lower the probability of the stock moving through an exercise price.

Volatility has a tremendous effect on the value of both put and call premiums. As the volatility rises, so will the premiums of the options. The inverse relationship is also true: the premiums of the contracts will decline as the volatility declines. During periods of high volatility, the premiums rise making the use of a strategy such as covered call writing more attractive than the purchase of married puts. During periods of declining volatility, the drop in option premiums would make the use of a married put more attractive than a covered call writing strategy.

Volatility may be determined through one of two methods. The first method is based upon the movement of the stock over a period of time. This is known as historic volatility. Historic volatility provides a long-term view of the trading in the underlying stock or index option, and is best used with a large sampling of prices. Some programs utilize the high, low and closing prices of a security while other programs only use the closing price. The use of high, low and closing data can provide a more detailed volatility which would be slightly higher than the closing price method, especially if the stock has violent swings during the trading day. The second method for measuring volatility is known as the implied volatility method. Implied volatility (I.V.) is based on the Black-Scholes Option Pricing Model: the option premium is substituted in the calculation and it is solved for volatility. Once the volatility of all of the options has been calculated, a complicated average is calculated based upon the distance that the stock is from the exercise price and the volume of contracts traded on that option contract. The implied volatility is the volatility resulting from the perception which option traders have upon the stock. Since options are purchased for the use of short term trading, the I.V. should be used for valuation of short term trading. A one day violent price movement in the stock will result in a greater I.V. than a volatility which is measured historically.

A look at Table 20-8 shows the changes in theoretical value and hedge ratio if the volatility rises from 25 to 35. As can be seen in the figure, the longer the period to expiration, the greater the rise in the premium of both puts and calls. The in-the-money, at-the-money and

TABLE 20-8.   Option Contracts—Effect of Rise in Volatility

Stock Price: 70⅜   Date: 9/30   Ann Divd: 1.76   Riskless: 9
Volatility: 35

	Calls			Option		Puts		
T.V.	H.R.	M.T.V.	M.H.R.	Series	T.V.	H.R.	M.T.V.	M.H.R.
5.80	93	6.08	86	Oct 65	.12	−7	.41	−14
1.97	58	2.60	57	Oct 70	1.29	−43	1.91	−44
.32	16	.77	24	Oct 75	4.71	−84	5.11	−77
6.27	88	6.94	77	Nov 65	.57	−11	1.29	−23
2.88	57	3.87	56	Nov 70	2.17	−44	3.15	−45
1.00	27	1.89	34	Nov 75	5.32	−74	6.20	−66
7.91	79	9.11	73	Jan 65	1.29	−22	2.53	−28
4.75	60	6.24	59	Jan 70	3.10	−41	4.57	−42
2.57	40	4.08	45	Jan 75	6.05	−61	7.47	−56
1.26	24	2.55	32	Jan 80	9.94	−77	11.06	−71
9.61	76	11.28	72	Apr 65	2.12	−25	3.88	−29
6.61	63	8.57	62	Apr 70	4.02	−39	5.98	−40
4.33	48	6.39	51	Apr 75	6.79	−53	8.82	−50

out-of-the-money exercise prices seem to have approximately the same increase in points relative to the stock price, but the out-of-the-money has a greater percentage increase than both the in-the-money and at-the-money options. The premium changes in the puts are not as great as the changes in the calls. In addition, the price relationship between the in-the-money, at-the-money and out-of-the-money contracts is not as close as the calls.

The hedge ratios on the calls tend to rise on the out-of-the-money calls and decline on the in-the-money calls when the volatility increases. The at-the-money calls are virtually unchanged. The increases in the out-of-the-money hedge ratios are slightly greater than the decreases for the in-the-money calls. While the same relationship is true for the hedge ratios on the puts, the decline in hedge ratios for the in-the-money puts is greater than the increase for the H.R. on the out-of-the-money puts.

Just as option premiums rise when volatility increases, they decline as volatility drops. Table 20-9 shows the drop in option premiums as the volatility drops from 25 to 15. The in-the-money call

TABLE 20-9.   Option Contracts—Effects of Drop in Volatility

Stock Price: 70⅜   Date: 9/30   Ann Divd: 1.76   Riskless: 9
Volatility: 15

Calls				Option	Puts			
T.V.	H.R.	M.T.V.	M.H.R.	Series	T.V.	H.R.	M.T.V.	M.H.R.
5.80	93	5.68	99	Oct 65	.12	−7	.01	−1
1.97	58	1.35	62	Oct 70	1.29	−43	.67	−39
.32	16	.04	4	Oct 75	4.71	−84	4.63	−96
6.27	88	5.97	97	Nov 65	.57	−11	.09	−4
2.88	57	2.47	66	Nov 70	2.17	−44	1.69	−35
1.00	27	.28	15	Nov 75	5.32	−74	4.66	−87
7.91	79	6.97	90	Jan 65	1.29	−22	.31	−11
4.75	60	3.29	64	Jan 70	3.10	−41	1.65	−37
2.57	40	1.13	32	Jan 75	6.05	−61	4.82	−72
1.26	24	.27	10	Jan 80	9.94	−77	9.63	−91
9.61	76	8.21	87	Apr 65	2.12	−25	.63	−14
6.61	63	4.69	67	Apr 70	4.02	−39	2.10	−33
4.33	48	2.28	43	Apr 75	6.79	−53	5.06	−58

premiums drop slightly compared to the out-of-the-money calls which have a greater drop. The November 75 call dropped from 1.00 to .28, a decrease of 72% while the November 65 calls dropped only 4.8%. The longer the period till expiration, the less the effect on the call premiums. The April 75 call dropped 47% compared to the November calls.

Put premiums have a more violent reaction to the drop in volatility than the calls do. The out-of-the-money November 65 puts lose 84% of their theoretical value when the volatility is lowered compared to the out-of-the-money November 75 calls. The in-the-money November 75 put loses 12.4% of its value compared to the out-of-the-money November 75 calls. The further the period until expiration, the less the effect upon the put premiums.

The hedge ratios of the in-the-money option contracts (put and calls) rise, making the relationship between the options contract and the stock stronger. The out-of-the-money contracts see the hedge ratios drop, decreasing the relationship between the options and the underlying stock. The amount of decline in the out-of-the-money

TABLE 20-10. Option Contracts—Effect of Increase in Dividend

Stock Price: 70⅜   Date: 9/30   Ann Divd: 3.52   Riskless: 9
Volatility: 25

	Calls			Option		Puts		
T.V.	H.R.	M.T.V.	M.H.R.	Series	T.V.	H.R.	M.T.V.	M.H.R.
5.80	93	5.80	93	Oct 65	.12	−7	.12	−7
1.97	58	1.97	58	Oct 70	1.29	−43	1.29	−43
.32	16	.32	16	Oct 75	4.71	−84	4.71	−84
6.27	88	6.27	88	Nov 65	.57	−11	.66	−13
2.88	57	2.68	59	Nov 70	2.17	−44	2.39	−47
1.00	27	.89	25	Nov 75	5.32	−74	5.63	−76
7.91	79	7.57	77	Jan 65	1.29	−22	1.38	−24
4.75	60	4.49	58	Jan 70	3.10	−41	3.32	−42
2.57	40	2.40	39	Jan 75	6.05	−61	6.35	−62
1.26	24	1.15	22	Jan 80	9.94	−77	10.30	−78
9.61	76	8.96	74	Apr 65	2.12	−25	2.35	−27
6.61	63	6.08	60	Apr 70	4.02	−39	4.39	−41
4.33	48	3.93	45	Apr 75	6.79	−53	7.21	−55

contract is added to the complementary in-the-money option, keeping the 1-to-1 relationship between the put and call, with the same exercise price and expiration month in line.

The final variable that was changed in this exercise was the annual dividend. Since the first dividend is after the expiration of the October contracts, there is no effect by the change in dividend paid for that holding period. The longer the position is held, the greater amount of dividends to be collected. The more dividends which are paid during the holding period of the options, the greater the change to the premiums. Therefore, in this example, the April contracts will have a greater change than the November contracts.

The example in Table 20-10 shows that the dividend was doubled to an annual payout of $3.52 per share. The increase in dividend results in the premiums of the calls declining while the put premiums rise. There are two reasons why the premiums have such a relationship to the premiums. The first is that the higher the dividends, the less premium a covered call writer needs to break even. Following the same reasoning, the higher the dividend payout, the more the married put purchaser can afford to pay for the put contract. The second reason for the change in premiums has to do with the action of the stock on the ex-dividend date. On the morning of ex-dividend, the specialist will adjust the price of the stock to reflect the payment of the dividend. This adjustment will lower the stock price by the amount of the dividend paid, rounded upward to the nearest ⅛ of a point. The adjustment in price will lower the stock making the put *seem* more valuable and the call *seem* less valuable. Actually, these contracts are slightly adjusted before the stock goes ex-dividend.

The amount of the reduction in call premiums is usually only a fraction of the value of the dividend. For example, the theoretical value of the November 70 call is reduced by the equivalent of 20 cents when the difference in the dividend during the holding period is raised by 44 cents. This is approximately only 45% of the dividend increase. The April 70 decreases by .53 of a point when only 2 dividends are paid. So, as can be seen the closer-term calls will have a greater move with an increase in the dividend than the contracts with

TABLE 20-11. Option Contracts—Effect of Decrease in Dividend

Stock Price: 70⅜   Date: 9/30   Ann Divd: .88   Riskless: 9
Volatility: 25

Calls				Option	Puts			
T.V.	H.R.	M.T.V.	M.H.R.	Series	T.V.	H.R.	M.T.V.	M.H.R.
5.80	93	5.80	93	Oct 65	.12	−7	.12	−7
1.97	58	1.97	58	Oct 70	1.29	−43	1.29	−43
.32	16	.32	16	Oct 75	4.71	−84	4.71	−85
6.27	88	6.43	85	Nov 65	.57	−11	.53	−15
2.88	57	3.00	58	Nov 70	2.17	−44	2.07	−43
1.00	27	1.06	28	Nov 75	5.32	−74	5.20	−73
7.91	79	8.09	79	Jan 65	1.29	−22	1.25	−22
4.75	60	4.88	61	Jan 70	3.10	−41	3.01	−42
2.57	40	2.66	41	Jan 75	6.05	−61	5.91	−62
1.26	24	1.31	24	Jan 80	9.94	−77	9.82	−76
9.61	76	9.94	77	Apr 65	2.12	−25	2.00	−25
6.61	63	6.88	64	Apr 70	4.02	−39	3.85	−37
4.33	48	4.54	49	Apr 75	6.79	−53	6.61	−59

a longer period till expiration. The in-the-money calls tend to have a greater reduction in points than the out-of-the-money calls.

The rise in the theoretical value of the at-the-money puts is very close to the decrease in the T.V. of the calls on the at-the-money options. The in-the-money puts will rise more than the decline in their complementary calls. The out-of-the-money put contracts will rise less than the decline of their respective in-the-money call contracts.

The hedge ratios on the call contracts tend to have a slight decrease when the dividend is raised. To offset that decrease in the hedge ratios, the hedge ratios on the puts will rise by the amount which the H.R. of the calls drop.

If the dividend is cut, the opposite effect to the theoretical values and the hedge ratios will be evident. Table 20-11 reduces the amount of the dividend by half. The cut in the dividend will require greater call premiums for the covered call writer while lowering the put premiums since the married put purchaser would need a lower cost basis to break even.

Putting It All Together

Changing different variables is a good way to understand how those variables affect the pricing of puts and calls. It is important to remember that a change in one variable usually changes one or more of the remaining variables. For example, if a corporation raises the dividend, the price of the stock will usually rise, and following that rise the stock will probably have less volatility. The change in volatility will also be reflected if the stock makes a sharp move. It is important to understand that some of the changes may add to or offset other changes in the pricing of an options contract.

Table 20-12 is a display of the theoretical values on Consolidated Edison (ED). ED is a utility stock, which historically trades with a high yield. The higher the yield of a stock, the less volatile that stock is. Table 20-13 is a theoretical display on the stock of Sun Microsystems (SUQ/SUNW). SUNW is the manufacturer of computer workstations and pays no dividend. Since the yield is zero, the volatility of the stock is 51 versus 20 for ED.

Comparing the theoretical values of the November 25 calls, the time premium for ED is approximately ½ point while the time premium of the SUNW calls is 1 point. The higher time premium is

TABLE 20-12. Table of Theoretical Values: Consolidated Edison (ED)

Stock Price: 25 Annual Dividend: 1.86 Volatility: 13 Exercise Price: 25

Theoretical Call			Month to Expire	Theoretical Put		
T.V.	0.43	H.R. 56	1	T.V.	0.29	H.R. −43
	0.65	59	2		0.38	−40
	0.83	61	3		0.44	−38
	1.00	62	4		0.47	−37
	1.20	64	5		0.50	−35
	1.34	66	6		0.52	−33
	1.52	67	7		0.54	−32
	1.66	68	8		0.55	−31
	1.80	69	9		0.56	−30
	1.96	70	10		0.57	−29
	2.09	71	11		0.57	−28

due to the higher volatility and lower dividend payout for SUNW. Consolidated Edison has a yearly range of 21 to 26¼ while Sun Microsystems has a range of 15 to 38⅝. The difference between the two ranges is one of the reasons for the higher volatility of SUNW compared to ED. Figures 20-1 and 20-2 show the stock price movement of both of these issues.

TABLE 20-13. Table of Theoretical Values: Sun Microsystems (SUNW/SUQ)

Stock Price: 25 Annual Dividend: 0.00 Volatility: 28 Exercise Price: 25

Theoretical Call			Month to Expire	Theoretical Put		
T.V.	0.84	H.R. 54	1	T.V.	0.71	H.R. −45
	1.23	56	2		0.96	−43
	1.54	57	3		1.14	−42
	1.81	58	4		1.28	−41
	2.11	59	5		1.42	−40
	2.33	60	6		1.51	−39
	2.60	61	7		1.61	−38
	2.79	62	8		1.68	−37
	2.99	63	9		1.75	−36
	3.22	63	10		1.82	−36
	3.39	64	11		1.87	−35

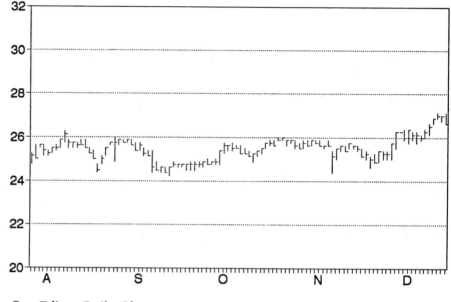

FIGURE 20-1. Con Edison Daily Chart.

Other Derivative Pricing Models

There are certain other pricing models which will be mentioned briefly. The first is known as the Gamma, which measures the change in the delta over a one point move in the underlying stock. Many traders use the gamma to keep their positions neutral. A simple means of deriving the gamma is by dividing the change in the delta by the change in the price of the underlying stock. The result is the gamma or the change in the delta, in relative terms. Like the delta, the value of the gamma will change over time, if the stock has no movement.

Another pricing model is known as the Vega Pricing Model. The vega measures the change in the option premium due to a change in the volatility. Floor and position traders will use the vega to assist in establishing spreads or other strategies which take advantage of changes in volatility during the holding period. Expansion of volatility will cause option premiums to rise, while a decline in volatility will result in a decrease in option premiums. A simple method of calculating the vega is to divide the change in premium by the change in the volatility.

The Theta Option Pricing Model allows a trader or investor to

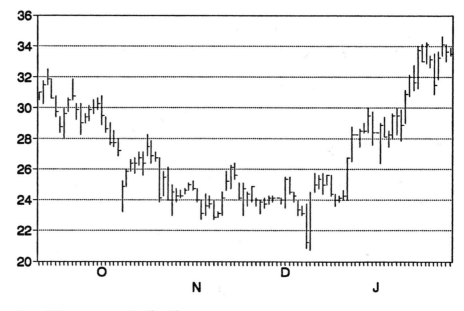

FIGURE 20-2.   Sun Microsystems Daily Chart.

evaluate the change in option premium over a period of time. The options time decay curve, shown in Chapter 3, visually depicts the deterioration of time premium. A decay in time premium can be measured by calculating the theta. The theta is easily calculated by dividing the change in time premium by the change in time. Traders find the comparison of thetas in conjunction with time spreads to be very advantageous.

The three option pricing models shown here also have more complex formulas, which this book will not evaluate. However, the use of these formulas has been made easier through the many different computer option programs which are available to both investors and professional traders. The programming of option pricing models varies slightly among programmers, but the results are generally about the same level. Chapter 21 looks into the use of option programs, including the calculation of different pricing models.

Uses of Option Pricing Models

The use of the delta enables traders to keep positions, when netted together, neutral. This is known as Delta Neutral Trading. By adding delta units to long calls and short puts and subtracting delta units for short calls and long puts, multiple positions may result in a net change of zero value. For example, if a trader purchases five calls with a delta of 40 and purchases 10 puts with a delta of 20, then the position will be delta neutral. As the value of all of the calls rises, the package of puts will decline the same amount, for the first one point move in the stock.

Delta neutral strategies enable the trader to set up several different option positions against one another, keeping the net position flat. These positions may include five or more different option contracts, still allowing the trader to keep little or no risk over a short period of time and over a small movement in the underlying stock price. Traders will periodically adjust their positions to keep the delta neutral or flat positions intact, as the value of the deltas change.

The gamma allows the trader to adjust the delta neutral positions and keep those positions flat with greater control. Since the gamma shows the change in the delta, traders may set up contingent strategies or safer positions which will allow for little change in the deltas with a movement in the price of the stock.

Traders also make use of the vega and theta to evaluate the current and future option positions. Through the day-to-day analysis of the theta, vega, gamma, delta and theoretical value, professional traders can evaluate potential risks and rewards. In addition, market-makers on the exchange floor will have capital requirements adjusted by their clearing firms based on the risk of the positions held. During periods of expanding volatility, market-makers will pay extra attention to the potential risks of positions held. This is especially true for market-makers of highly volatile stocks and index options.

The use of different option pricing models can provide the investor and trader with comparative results. Investors will use theoretical values to compare option premiums for over or under valuation. Hedge ratios provide a comparison of the option contract against a move in the underlying stock price. These pricing models may provide extremely good comparisons, but that is all that these values are. As one variable changes, others will also change, resulting in the changes in the pricing models. While the changes in one set of variables will result in the changes in others, those changes may not be as immediate as the investor or trader would prefer. Due to these changes, the values of the option pricing models should be used for comparison only, and should not be the sole basis for investment decisions by investors.

Summary

1. Theoretical values provide pricing valuation of option contracts based on the value of different variables, such as stock price, exercise price, option type, time till expiration, dividend payments, interest rates and volatility.

2. The hedge ratio or delta provides a comparative valuation between options price movement and the movement of the underlying stock over a one point move in the stock during a short period of time.

3. Pricing models for the gamma, theta and vega provide the investor and trader with tools for evaluating the changes in delta, time value and premium. These models allow for greater control and knowledge of risk.

4. Comparative option pricing can show the investor or trader the potential value of an option contract due to the change in one or more of the variables used to calculate an option's theoretical value. These adjustments will also show the differences in the delta.

5. A change in one of the variables used in an options pricing model will usually result in the change in one or more of the other variables in the model. These other changes should not be overlooked when evaluating the price of an options contract.

6. The use of option models should be used for comparison. These values may not always depict the actual values of the option prices, as unforeseen variables may not be calculated into the formula.

21
Computers and Options

The use of option strategies requires careful planning and thought, not only focusing on the opinion of the underlying stock or index, but on which strategy would be appropriate or which option would be the correct choice. Another situation requires that the appropriate strategy is selected, and a stock is selected based on the strategy. Whatever the method for selecting a stock or a strategy, computers can assist in the selection.

Personal computers have made option analytic programs easy to use. By entering data into a preformatted screen, the use of different strategies may be analyzed. The Best Option Strategy System (BOSS), shown in Table 21-1, allows the user to input the stock, annual dividend, dividends till expiration, option data and commission figures. The input of all of this information allows the investor to formulate an investment conclusion through the returns provided. Table 21-2 is the output of a covered call writing strategy. The output provides the returns if the stock is unchanged to expiration (static), called away at the exercise price, and the break-even points. In addition, the margin returns provide the investor with the interest charged till expiration. The annualized returns are based upon calendar days to expiration with a 365-day year.

Seeing the cash and margin returns side by side helps the investor to decide if the stock should be purchased for cash or for margin. The debit (excluding commission and other transaction charges) is shown at the top of the screen, allowing the investor to enter the order with great ease. When the program is used with an on-line system, the theoretical value of the option, the delta and the stock name are also provided. In addition, when the program is used on-line, the stock

TABLE 21-1. Boss Covered Call Writing Input

Best Options Strategy Selection (BOSS)

COVERED CALL WRITER

OPT101V2.0

TICKER SYMBOL: T	QUANTITY: 500	ANN/DIVD: 1.20	DIV/EXP: 2
STOCK PRICE: 44.125	COMM/CODE: P		VALUE: 20.00

OPTION DATA:

MONTH: OCT	STRIKE: 45.0		OPT-PREMIUM: 2.3750
	COMM/CODE: P		VALUE: 20.00

<ALT-Q> = EXIT   <F10> = ENTER

TABLE 21-2. Boss Covered Call Writing Output

OPT102V2.0

COVERED CALL WRITING
EVALUATION OF DATA

BUY	500 SHARES T AT 44.125	DEBIT 41.750	HI: 0.00	LO: 0.00
SELL	5 OCT 45.0	CALL 2.3750	ANN DIV: 1.20	DIV TO EXP: 2
		T.V. 0.00	H.R. 0	STK YLD: 2.72%	IMP VOL: 13

	CASH A/C					MARGIN A/C		
STOCK	PROFIT	RETN	ANRTN			PROFIT	RETN	ANRTN
44.125	1,251.30	5.9	10.5	STATIC		561.34	5.6	9.9
45.000	1,631.68	7.7	13.7	CALLED		941.72	9.4	16.7
B.E. PT	41.62	5.7%				43.00	2.5%	
REQ. CAP	21,111.20					9,997.55		

CONTRIBUTING FACTORS

COMMISSION ON STOCK PURCHASE: 164.80   ON CALL: 71.40   DAYS TO EXP: 206

COMMISSION IF CALLED: 57.12   COLLECTED DIVIDEND: 300.00

MARGIN INTEREST COMPUTED AT 11.00% =   689.96

VERB SELECTION: GRAPH/MODIFY/NEW/QUIT/+/−:

327

price is provided, based upon the last sale, and the bid price of the option and the dividend information is given, freeing the investor from looking for this information in newspapers.

When the evaluation of the data is shown, the investor has the opportunity to modify any of the variables by depressing the "M" key. Request for modifying the data will bring the investor back to the input screen, filling the fields with the variables already provided. To modify any of those fields, the investor simply types over the values. When the <F10> key is depressed, the program will re-evaluate all of the data, including commission charges (if included).

Depressing the + increases the price of the stock by ⅛ of a point without having to go back to the original input screen. Depressing the − decreases the stock price by ⅛ of a point. This enables the investor to view the evaluation if the trade is done ⅛ better or worse. The N key brings the investor back to a new input screen. The P key directs the output to a line printer, allowing the investor to keep a copy of the trade so that a future evaluation of the position may be viewed. The printout also allows the investor a convenient medium for comparing potential investments.

The Best Options Strategy Selection program allows the investor to evaluate strategies on such strategies as covered call writing, naked call writing, put writing, married put purchases, spreads, straddles and combinations. Future versions are expected to include conversions and reversals, covered combinations, hedge wrappers, butterfly spreads and condors. These evaluations also allow for the same verb usage.

Showing It All

The BOSS program also allows for the display of an entire option display. By depressing the page up, page down, home, and end keys, the user may move through the options display, especially if the display is several pages long. It should be noted that this display is only available if the BOSS program is used through an online service.

The options display shows the bid, offer, last sale, and volume information as well as the theoretical value and hedge ratio for both call and put on the same line. In addition, the display shows the option codes and series information for those contracts.

Table 21-3 shows the option display of calls with covered call

TABLE 21-3.   Boss Covered Call Writing Display

Bid	Ask	Last	Volume	T.V.	H.R.	Series		Call%	Ann%	Unch%	Ann%	B.E.
										Covered Write		
3.25	3.63			0.00	0	KWNOV	17.5	−16.2	−99.9	−16.2	−99.9	20.88
1.13	1.38	1.38	10	0.00	0	KDNOV	20.0	2.6	39.0	2.6	39.0	19.50
0.19	0.31	0.25	50	0.00	0	KXNOV	22.5	9.1	137.9	1.2	18.4	20.63
0.00	0.13			0.00	0	KENOV	25.0	19.7	300.1	0.0	0.0	20.88
0.00	0.06			0.00	0	KFNOV	30.0	43.7	664.3	0.0	0.0	20.88
3.38	3.75			0.00	0	LWDEC	17.5	−16.2	−99.9	−16.2	−99.9	20.88
1.63	1.88			0.00	0	LDDEC	20.0	−4.2	−26.1	−4.2	−26.1	20.88
0.50	0.69			0.00	0	LXDEC	22.5	7.8	48.0	0.0	0.0	20.88
3.50	3.88	3.88	50	0.00	0	AWJAN	17.5	2.9	12.3	2.9	12.3	17.00
1.81	2.06	2.00	2	0.00	0	ADJAN	20.0	5.9	24.9	5.9	24.9	18.88
0.81	1.00	1.00	24	0.00	0	AXJAN	22.5	13.2	55.3	5.0	21.1	19.88
0.25	0.38	0.38	173	0.00	0	AEJAN	25.0	22.0	92.1	1.9	7.8	20.50
0.00	0.06			0.00	0	AFJAN	30.0	43.7	183.2	0.0	0.0	20.88
3.88	4.25	4.25	50	0.00	0	DWAPR	17.5	5.2	10.7	5.2	10.7	16.63
2.50	2.75			0.00	0	DDAPR	20.0	−4.2	−8.6	−4.2	−8.6	20.88
1.50	1.75	1.63	79	0.00	0	DXAPR	22.5	16.9	34.6	8.5	17.4	19.25

<F1> CovWrite <F2> MarrPut <F3> NakCall <F4> NakPut <F5> Simul

AXP 20.88 +0.25 B 20.88 A 21.00 S 5 x 500   AMERICAN EXPRESS
H 21.13 L 20.75 V 378,700 AT 10:11 a

writing returns if the <F1> key is depressed. This display does not compute commission charges but it does include the dividend payments during the holding period. The display shows all of the market information for each call on the left side while displaying the return and annualized return if the stock is unchanged and called away on the right side of the display. In addition, the last column displays the downside break-even point. This display allows the investor to compare the returns for each call option, in order to select the best contract for that strategy. The investor may then elect to view a specific evaluation showing commissions and the amount of shares which the investor may select.

Depressing the <F2> key displays the option series for puts, on the right side of the screen, while showing the evaluation for the married put strategy on the left side of the screen. Table 21-4 shows the output of such a display. This screen allows the user to easily search for the best married put/stock hedge from all of the puts on the stock selected. The returns are based on a one share basis, and do not include commission charges. Investors may use this opportunity as a means for searching for the best put which will protect the position with the greatest valuation. The first column shows the risk in dollar/point value, the second column (RISK%) shows the risk as a percentage, and the third column shows the risk represented as an annual percentage rate, which should be used for comparison only. The fourth column shows the break-even point (B.E.) for the stock and the fifth column shows the percentage move needed by the stock to reach the break-even level.

Depressing the <F3> key shows the evaluation for writing naked call options, as shown in Table 21-5. As with the covered write strategy, the left side of the screen shows the option information for the all of the calls. The right side of the screen evaluates the writing of the naked call position. The first column after the option series is labeled "MAXRTN%." Since the point value of the maximum return per option is already known, it is skipped in the evaluation. The MAXRTN% is the percentage return based upon the margin required per call. The "MAXANN%" is merely the same return shown on an annualized basis. The column "UPBEPT" is the upward break-even point, or the amount the stock can rise in order to break even. The last column shows the amount, in percentage terms, that the stock must rise to reach break-even. This is actually the amount of cushion the writer has. A negative number means that the stock must decline to break even.

TABLE 21-4. Boss Married Put Purchase Display

	Married Put						Puts					
$Risk	Risk%	Arsk%	B.E.	BE%		Series	Bid	Ask	Last	Volume	T.V.	H.R.
3.51	16.7	254.1	0.13	0.6	NOV	17.5WW	0.00	0.13			0.00	−0
1.38	6.5	98.2	0.50	2.4	NOV	20.0WD	0.38	0.50	0.38	26	0.00	−0
0.38	1.7	25.3	2.00	9.6	NOV	22.5WX	1.75	2.00			0.00	−0
0.26	1.0	15.7	4.38	21.0	NOV	25.0WE	4.00	4.38			0.00	−0
0.13	0.4	6.6	9.25	44.3	NOV	30.0WF	8.88	9.25			0.00	−0
3.63	17.2	106.3	0.25	1.2	DEC	17.5XW	0.13	0.25			0.00	−0
1.69	7.8	48.2	0.81	3.9	DEC	20.0XD	0.63	0.81			0.00	−0
0.63	2.7	16.9	2.25	10.8	DEC	22.5XX	2.00	2.25			0.00	−0
3.82	17.9	75.2	0.44	2.1	JAN	17.5MW	0.25	0.44			0.00	−0
2.13	9.6	40.4	1.25	6.0	JAN	20.0MD	1.00	1.25	1.06	25	0.00	−0
1.01	4.3	18.0	2.63	12.6	JAN	22.5MX	2.25	2.63			0.00	−0
0.26	1.0	4.3	4.38	21.0	JAN	25.0ME	4.00	4.38			0.00	−0
0.26	0.9	3.6	9.38	44.9	JAN	30.0MF	8.88	9.38			0.00	−0
4.07	18.9	38.7	0.69	3.3	APR	17.5PW	0.44	0.69			0.00	−0
2.63	11.6	23.8	1.75	8.4	APR	20.0PD	1.50	1.75			0.00	−0
1.51	6.3	12.9	3.13	15.0	APR	22.5PX	2.75	3.13			0.00	−0

<F1> CovWrite <F2> MarrPut <F3> NakCall <F4> NakPut <F5> Simul

AXP 20.88 +0.25 B 20.88 A 21.00 S 5 x 500

H 21.13 L 20.75 V 378,700 AT 10:11 a AMERICAN EXPRESS

TABLE 21-5. Boss Naked Call Writing Display

		Calls				Series			Naked Call Write		
Bid	Ask	Last	Volume	T.V.	H.R.			Maxrtn%	Maxann%	Upbept	%Upbe
3.25	3.63			0.00	0	KWNOV	17.5	77.8	999.9	20.75	-0.6
1.13	1.38	1.38	10	0.00	0	KDNOV	20.0	27.1	411.5	21.13	1.2
0.19	0.31	0.25	50	0.00	0	KXNOV	22.5	7.4	113.1	22.69	8.7
0.00	0.13			0.00	0	KENOV	25.0	0.0	0.0	25.00	19.7
0.00	0.06			0.00	0	KFNOV	30.0	0.0	0.0	30.00	43.7
3.38	3.75			0.00	0	LWDEC	17.5	80.9	500.7	20.88	0.0
1.63	1.88			0.00	0	LDDEC	20.0	39.0	241.5	21.63	3.6
0.50	0.69			0.00	0	LXDEC	22.5	19.6	121.0	23.00	10.2
3.50	3.88	3.88	50	0.00	0	AWJAN	17.5	83.8	351.6	21.00	0.6
1.81	2.06	2.00	2	0.00	0	ADJAN	20.0	43.3	181.8	21.81	4.5
0.81	1.00	1.00	24	0.00	0	AXJAN	22.5	31.7	133.0	23.31	11.6
0.25	0.38	0.38	173	0.00	0	AEJAN	25.0	446.4	999.9	25.25	20.9
0.00	0.06			0.00	0	AFJAN	30.0	0.0	0.0	30.00	43.7
3.88	4.25	4.25	50	0.00	0	DWAPR	17.5	92.9	190.5	21.38	2.4
2.50	2.75			0.00	0	DDAPR	20.0	59.9	122.8	22.50	7.8
1.50	1.75	1.63	79	0.00	0	DXAPR	22.5	58.7	120.3	24.00	14.9

<F1> CovWrite <F2> MarrPut <F3> NakCall <F4> NakPut <F5> Simul

AXP 20.88 +0.25 B 20.88 A 21.00 S 5 x 500
H 21.13 L 20.75 V 378,700 AT 10:11 a   AMERICAN EXPRESS

The writing of naked puts is evaluated by depressing the <F4> key. The right side of the screen, in Table 21-6, shows the information on the puts while the left side evaluates each put for writing. The first column is the maximum percentage that the writing of the put will achieve based upon the margin required per put contract. The point or dollar value is shown on the right side of the screen. The second column shows the maximum return on an annualized basis. The third column shows the cost of owning the stock, should the put be assigned and the stock purchased at the exercise price. The column labeled as "DIFER" is the percentage difference between the current stock price and the cost of owning the stock, if it is put to the writer. The next to the last column shows the amount which the stock can fall to break-even while the last column shows the amount of decline to reach that level.

The evaluations shown thus far use the bid price for the writing of options and the offer or ask price for purchasing options. A choice of either bid, ask, last or average of the bid and ask are often offered to the user. It is suggested that the bid be used for writing and the ask used for purchasing. These choices are also often for the purchase or sale of stock.

Pressing the <F5> key allows the user to compare the theoretical values and hedge ratios with simulated values based upon the changing of one or more variables. The stock price, date, volatility, annual dividend and riskless interest rate may be changed, allowing the investor to simulate the value of an option contract should one or more of these variables change during the holding period.

The BOSS system also allows the investor to simulate the value of a put and call with the same exercise price and same expiration month. The Options Valuation Simulator allows the user to enter the symbol, stock price, annual dividend, riskless rate of interest and month and exercise price. The computer evaluates these variables and returns the put and call values for the theoretical value, hedge ratio, gamma, theta, and vega.

The BOSS system also provides other information. Many traders require the amount of interest per share till expiration. Table 21-7 shows the interest charges per share at each exercise price. By pressing the <F1> key, the user can change the interest rate. Pressing the <+> key, the user can change the interest rate. Pressing the <+> key shows the higher exercise prices while pressing the <−> key returns to the lower exercise prices.

TABLE 21-6. Boss Naked Put Writing Display

		Naked Put Writing					Puts					
Max%	Maxan%	S-Cost	Difer	Bept	BE%	Series	Bid	Ask	Last	Volume	T.V.	H.R.
0.0	0.0	17.50	16.2	17.5	16.2	NOV 17.5WW	0.00	0.13			0.00	-0
11.5	175.3	19.62	6.0	19.6	6.0	NOV 20.0WD	0.38	0.50	0.38	26	0.00	-0
41.9	637.3	20.75	0.6	20.8	0.6	NOV 22.5WX	1.75	2.00			0.00	-0
95.8	999.9	21.00	-0.6	21.0	-0.6	NOV 25.0WE	4.00	4.38			0.00	-0
212.6	999.9	21.12	-1.1	21.1	-1.1	NOV 30.0WF	8.88	9.25			0.00	-0
6.2	38.5	17.37	16.8	17.4	16.8	DEC 17.5XW	0.13	0.25			0.00	-0
19.1	118.2	19.37	7.2	19.4	7.2	DEC 20.0XD	0.63	0.81			0.00	-0
47.9	296.3	20.50	1.8	20.5	1.8	DEC 22.5XX	2.00	2.25			0.00	-0
12.0	50.2	17.25	17.4	17.3	17.4	JAN 17.5MW	0.25	0.44			0.00	-0
30.3	127.3	19.00	9.0	19.0	9.0	JAN 20.0MD	1.00	1.25	1.06	25	0.00	-0
53.9	226.0	20.25	3.0	20.3	3.0	JAN 22.5MX	2.25	2.63			0.00	-0
95.8	401.9	21.00	-0.6	21.0	-0.6	JAN 25.0ME	4.00	4.38			0.00	-0
212.6	892.1	21.12	-1.1	21.1	-1.1	JAN 30.0MF	8.88	9.38			0.00	-0
21.1	43.2	17.06	18.3	17.1	18.3	APR 17.5PW	0.44	0.69			0.00	-0
45.5	93.3	18.50	11.4	18.5	11.4	APR 20.0PD	1.50	1.75			0.00	-0
65.9	135.0	19.75	5.4	19.8	5.4	APR 22.5PX	2.75	3.13			0.00	-0

<F1> CovWrite <F2> MarrPut <F3> NakCall <F4> NakPut <F5> Simul

AXP 20.88 +0.25 B 20.88 A 21.00 S 5 x 500
H 21.13 L 20.75 V 378,700 AT 10:11 a AMERICAN EXPRESS

TABLE 21-7. Boss Interest Rate Sheets

Rate: 10.000%

Options Evaluation System

Date: 10-25-1991

Strike	11–15	12–20	01–17	02–21	03–21	04–18	05–16	06–19	07–17	08–21	09–19	10–17
	22	57	85	120	148	176	204	238	266	301	330	358
5.0	0.03	0.08	0.12	0.16	0.20	0.24	0.28	0.33	0.36	0.41	0.45	0.49
7.5	0.05	0.12	0.17	0.25	0.30	0.36	0.42	0.49	0.55	0.62	0.68	0.74
10.0	0.06	0.16	0.23	0.33	0.41	0.48	0.56	0.65	0.73	0.82	0.90	0.98
12.5	0.08	0.20	0.29	0.41	0.51	0.60	0.70	0.82	0.91	1.03	1.13	1.23
15.0	0.09	0.23	0.35	0.49	0.61	0.72	0.84	0.98	1.09	1.24	1.36	1.47
17.5	0.11	0.27	0.41	0.58	0.71	0.84	0.98	1.14	1.28	1.44	1.58	1.72
20.0	0.12	0.31	0.47	0.66	0.81	0.96	1.12	1.30	1.46	1.65	1.81	1.96
22.5	0.14	0.35	0.52	0.74	0.91	1.08	1.26	1.47	1.64	1.86	2.03	2.21
25.0	0.15	0.39	0.58	0.82	1.01	1.21	1.40	1.63	1.82	2.06	2.26	2.45
30.0	0.18	0.47	0.70	0.99	1.22	1.45	1.68	1.96	2.19	2.47	2.71	2.94
35.0	0.21	0.55	0.82	1.15	1.42	1.69	1.96	2.28	2.55	2.89	3.16	3.43
40.0	0.24	0.62	0.93	1.32	1.62	1.93	2.24	2.61	2.92	3.30	3.62	3.92
45.0	0.27	0.70	1.05	1.48	1.82	2.17	2.52	2.93	3.28	3.71	4.07	4.41
50.0	0.30	0.78	1.16	1.64	2.03	2.41	2.79	3.26	3.64	4.12	4.52	4.90
55.0	0.33	0.86	1.28	1.81	2.23	2.65	3.07	3.59	4.01	4.54	4.97	5.39
60.0	0.36	0.94	1.40	1.97	2.43	2.89	3.35	3.91	4.37	4.95	5.42	5.88
65.0	0.39	1.02	1.51	2.14	2.64	3.13	3.63	4.24	4.74	5.36	5.88	6.38
70.0	0.42	1.09	1.63	2.30	2.84	3.38	3.91	4.56	5.10	5.77	6.33	6.87
75.0	0.45	1.17	1.75	2.47	3.04	3.62	4.19	4.89	5.47	6.18	6.78	7.36
80.0	0.48	1.25	1.86	2.63	3.24	3.86	4.47	5.22	5.83	6.60	7.23	7.85

<F1> Change Rate <+> Higher Strikes <−> Lower Strikes <ESC> Quit

335

Table 21-8 shows the recent price history for the stock AXP. The high, low, close, volume and price change are all shown. On the bottom of the screen, the high and low for the period are shown as well as the amount of days that the data was available for. Through the use of this screen, an investor can historically map the price and volume change of stock, allowing for increased insight and data. In addition, this data can be converted into graph form, which shows the price movement in high, low, close form with 10- and 20-day moving averages. More sophisticated graphs are also available which allow the user to plot relative strength, histograms, volatility, exponential moving averages, stochastic oscillators, on balance volume (OBV) as well as many others.

Still, there are other functions which show the amount of days until expiration or margin interest computation, available for use by both investors and professionals.

Searching the Universe

Many investors and traders will give special precedence to the use of one or two different strategies. In order to use a specific strategy, certain criteria must be met. Due to the high amount of listed puts and calls, the investor usually does not have the time to search all of the options to see which contracts meet the criteria. Computers can search through the universe of option stocks and select which options meet the needs of that user and display those selections through either preformatted screens or customized output. In addition, these programs have the ability to rank the output by a variable selected by the user.

Covered call writing is a strategy which is used by many investors and traders alike. A person looking for certain covered writes can create a table of specifications which the computer will use as a criteria for displaying the results. Table 21-9 is an example of what specifications may be used as a standard search criteria for covered call writing. In addition to the standard criteria, some programs allow users to create their own criteria, in addition to the standard criteria.

Once the criteria have been selected, the user may wish to create a specific output, choosing what data are to be displayed and the order in which they are to be seen. Once the criteria and output have been

TABLE 21-8. Recent Price History of American Express Stock

Stock Symbol: AXP

Date	High	Low	Close	Volume		Date	High	Low	Close	10-23-1991/10:21 Volume
10/22	20.75	20.13	20.63	1392100		9/26	25.88	25.38	25.50	554700
10/21	20.75	19.88	19.88	1929000		9/25	26.25	25.75	25.75	902900
10/18	21.50	20.75	20.75	1996200		9/24	26.25	25.75	26.13	661200
10/17	21.75	21.00	21.00	1942000		9/23	26.25	25.63	25.88	773400
10/16	21.63	21.25	21.50	1722500		9/20	26.25	25.63	25.63	1508300
10/15	21.38	20.63	21.25	2594000		9/19	26.13	25.13	26.13	2353800
10/14	20.88	20.50	20.75	1007400		9/18	25.50	25.13	25.25	675600
10/11	20.75	20.63	20.75	1235900		9/17	25.75	25.25	25.50	1834900
10/10	20.88	20.13	20.50	1714400		9/16	25.63	25.13	25.50	2738100
10/09	21.25	20.63	20.75	1857000		9/13	25.88	25.13	25.50	1226300
10/08	21.13	20.63	20.88	2680900		9/12	25.75	25.25	25.63	1451800
10/07	21.38	20.50	20.75	3792200		9/11	25.63	25.25	25.63	690800
10/04	22.50	21.25	21.63	6272700		9/10	26.00	25.38	25.63	1088500
10/03	24.00	22.88	23.00	6272900		9/09	26.38	25.88	25.88	579900
10/02	26.38	25.38	25.38	804200		9/06	26.50	26.00	26.13	585700
10/01	26.13	25.63	26.13	1167400		9/05	26.38	26.13	26.38	536700
9/30	25.88	25.25	25.63	1755800		9/04	26.13	25.75	26.13	623600
9/27	26.38	25.63	26.13	1342800		9/03	26.63	25.88	25.88	863300

PRESS <RETURN> TO CONTINUE OR <ESC> TO END

PERIOD HIGH: 27.50   PERIOD LOW: 19.88   DAYS COUNTED: 100

337

TABLE 21-9. Sample of Search Criteria for Covered Call Writing

12/02/91	*Covered Call Writing—Ranking—Search Criteria*	*Page 001*
File Name: Sample	*Created: 12/02/91*	

STOCK PRICE USES:	ASK
STOCK PRICE MINIMUM:	10.00
STOCK PRICE MAXIMUM:	50.00
CALL PRICE USES:	BID
CALL PRICE MINIMUM:	1.00
CALL PRICE MAXIMUM:	6.00
EXERCISE PRICE RELATION MINIMUM:	− 10.00%
EXERCISE PRICE RELATION MAXIMUM:	20.00%
ANNUAL MINIMUM STANDSTILL RETURN:	9.00%
ANNUAL MINIMUM CALLED RETURN:	18.00%
DISTANCE TO BREAK-EVEN POINT:	2.50%

established the user may request that the computer run all of the cover writes in the universe or against a user-defined data base of stocks or against one individual stock. If the criteria of a specific covered write is not met, that option contract will not be displayed. If the user requests the computer to rank the contracts in some user defined order, the computer will wait till all of the options in the universe (or data-base) have been examined and then proceed to put them in order according to the variable chosen by the user.

In addition to the covered call writing strategy, similar programs are available on the following strategies:

Married Put	Hedge Wrappers
Bull Spreads	Bear Spreads
Butterfly Spreads	Combinations
Conversions	Reversals
Naked Option Writing	Time Spreads

Gathering Information

Selecting and monitoring a stock involves more than just watching the price of the underlying security. News services disseminate information about hundreds of different corporations every day. Information, such as new products, earnings, dividends, law suits, legal requirements, new legislation, industry developments and even competitor actions can influence the movement of the price of a stock. Timely information can be found on the screens of many data vendors. News organizations charge for their news services, many of whom are excellent. Services such as Dow Jones, Dow Jones Professional Investor Report, Capital Markets, Reuters, Reuters Worldwide, United Press International, Business Wire and Fed Filings are just some of the services carried for use by investors and professionals. The use of such information can provide the user with important insight and timely decision making information.

Summary

1. The use of option programs allows the investor a quick method of calculating profits, losses, and risks.

2. Option programs allow investors to carefully plan the use of certain strategies in significantly less time than it would take them to perform manual calculations.

3. On-line programs can be used to evaluate specific strategies very quickly.

4. Programs are available which allow the user to search the options universe or a specific data-base of stocks and select the right candidates for a certain strategy.

5. These programs can also aid the user by ranking the selections on a user defined variable.

6. Criteria selections and customized outputs allow the user to select the option contracts and display the information which the user determines as necessary.

7. News services provide the investor and trader with important market and stock developments which gives the user the ability to make quick decisions.

22

Portfolio Management

Option strategies must be selected very carefully. The more complicated a strategy becomes, the greater the chance for risk or miscalculation. Once a strategy is implemented, it may become difficult to reverse out should the stock move in the wrong direction. This is usually the case if the strategy is implemented incorrectly, adding further to the original mistake. While some of these problems may be avoided, others may not. This is where portfolio management techniques become necessary. While many investors and traders believe that they can effectively pick the movement of a stock or option contract, there are factors which they may not be able to judge effectively.

First, it is important to anticipate the unexpected. Day-to-day as well as unusual events in the market can change the direction of the market instantaneously. In 1981, the attempted assassination of President Reagan, changed the movement in the market. Before the announcement that the president had been shot, the Dow Jones Industrial Average was up eight points. Within seconds of the announcement, the market was down eight points and trading was halted. If the President had died that evening, chances are the market would have opened much lower. It is very difficult to figure the shooting of the president into a decision making process, such as buying a call option on IBM. While this may be an extreme case, these situations do pop up from time to time. It is important to limit the impact of such problems.

Diversification

One of the chief rules of portfolio managers and market strategists is that "all of one's eggs should not be in one basket." Should the one stock that the investor purchased go bankrupt, all of that investor's money might be lost. In the same way, it is important to spread the risk not only among stocks but among different industries. If an investor purchased shares of different stocks in the automobile industry, that portfolio might be severely damaged during a recession. Risk should be spread as far as possible.

In Chapter 2 one of the suggested guidelines stated that purchase of option contracts should be limited to an equivalent amount of shares which the investor would be able to purchase. It was further stated in that chapter that the difference in investment capital should be invested into a vehicle with lower risk, such as government bonds or T-bills. Investing with this method provides the opportunity for excellent returns while limiting the risk of purchasing that option contract. If the stock does not perform in the manner which the investor expects, only a small fraction of the original capital might be lost.

An investor who uses the purchase of option contracts as leverage should diversify in both the stocks and industry groups, as if the shares of the underlying corporations were being purchased. If the risk is effectively spread among different groups and different stocks, the chance for a total loss is reduced unless there is a major market correction.

The next rule regarding diversification is that when purchasing contracts, select contracts that do not all expire at the same time. Risk spread over time usually yields less danger. If the market has a major decline during one month, the next month might prove to be surprisingly bullish. Even if the next month is not, the options which are expiring later down the road, might have the opportunity for repair using one of the techniques outlined in Chapter 19.

In addition to avoiding a bad month as far as market movement goes, the investor or trader can also benefit through more effective control if the positions are not all expiring during the same period. This allows for greater flexibility and thought as to the adjustment of positions. It becomes much easier to manage and modify option positions if only a portion of those positions is expiring at the same time. Positions which are expiring in the following month can receive greater attention once the current positions have been attended to.

Diversification should also be taken into account when developing strategies. The use of one strategy may require more attention and monitoring than another. The purchaser of a covered write has less risk than the writer of a naked call. The naked call writer, therefore, should spend more time and resources monitoring the position, since there is a possibility of an unlimited loss. In addition, the spreading of risks over time as well as spreading them over strategies will help to limit potential loss. A mixture of aggressive and conservative strategies will allow for substantial growth, assuming the investor is correct, while helping to limit capital loss if the investment decisions are not correct. An investor who is very aggressive may wish to utilize one or two aggressive strategies as well as one moderate or conservative strategy. A mixture of a married put purchase may be complemented with the use of a well-chosen long call purchase, allowing the investor further profit if the stock rises and limited loss if the stock falls.

Open-Ended Risk

One of the most troubling situations is when an investor's or trader's entire portfolio is open to unlimited risk. This might be in the form of writing naked calls or naked puts. In such a case, individuals may realize a substantial loss should the stock or the market move suddenly against them, leaving them with absolutely no protection. Some type of hedge strategy should be utilized to help limit or offset potential runaway losses.

As an options strategist, I have seen customers write naked puts and naked combinations on many stocks. One of the favorite situations is the use of these strategies on stocks which are expected to be taken over. One common line after the announcement of a takeover is "the deal is done . . . nothing can possibly go wrong." After several successes, this individual believes that the high put premiums are merely a gift from the market-makers. Nothing can be further from the truth. If there is a high premium there is a reason behind it. At some point, one of these situations will go wrong, and the investor/trader stands the chance of losing all of the gains from previous endeavors, and possibly more. This was the case for many in the attempted takeover of UAL Corp. When the company announced that the takeover at 300 (the stock was in the 280s) was not going to happen, the stock immediately fell. Writers of the puts were crushed as this jet seemed to nosedive. If that writer would have also purchased a put with an exercise price, even 20 points lower, the loss would have been limited.

Hedging positions such as long call or put purchases can help reduce the amount of capital at risk. While the purchase of an option contract may not be considered an open-ended risk, the possibility of losing 100 percent of investment capital stands to be the closest thing to unlimited loss. The use of different spread techniques, as outlined in Chapter 6, offers the investor or trader many opportunities. It should also be noted that long option positions may be adjusted as time goes on, which will be further discussed shortly.

Substantial risk is also possible in both long and short stock positions. Volatile changes in stock prices may put the investor in a position of greater loss than originally anticipated. For example, if a stock were purchased at $90 per share and the market suddenly turned lower, a decline of 45 points may provide more risk than the investor was willing to accept when the original transaction was made. Short stock sellers face an unlimited risk should the price of the stock suddenly rise. These stock positions can be replaced with option strategies which are lower in risk or in conjunction with different option techniques to help limit potential risk.

Which Strategy Is Best?

The use of one strategy versus another is dependent on several factors. Determining any investment requires thought into stock expectation. Option strategies require a little bit more. Such factors as time, risk and opportunity as well as premium levels are part of the decision making process.

While the investor or trader may have an idea as to the anticipated direction of a stock's movement, determining the amount of movement is an important factor. If the investor realistically believes that the stock is going to have a major rise over a short period of time, the purchase of a call might be an appropriate strategy. However, if it is believed that the stock might only rise 5 points, the use of a covered write or spread might show more prudence.

Time is a major factor in creating option strategies. The purchase of an option is not just an investment decision on the underlying stock, but a bet that the anticipated stock movement will happen during a certain period of time. Naked option writers are contemplating that the stock will not make such a move and that time is on their side. There are many times when the stock makes a move one day before option expiration or one day after option expiration. Such a move may not only hurt the buyer or writer financially but may scar the investment ego for a long period of time.

Determining the amount of risk which an investor is willing to accept is another factor to be considered when putting together a strategy. The greater the risk, the greater the potential reward. The covered call writer and the call purchaser both believe that the value of the underlying stock will appreciate. The covered call writer has greater downside protection while the call purchaser stands to make a lot of money if correct. The difference between these two investors is their view of risk as well as the amount in which they expect the stock to move. The married put purchaser has the same view of the underlying stock as the person who purchased the call. The married put buyer simply wishes to protect the stock position while the call purchaser may be looking for greater leverage which is accompanied by greater risk.

The amount of possible profit is another driving force behind the determination of a strategy. Investors seeking great profit through what they believe to be high opportunity stocks may write naked option positions while the investors who believe that the opportunity is not as great may also seek the option time premium advantage. Through the use of different strategies, investors may adjust the potential rewards and risks as they see fit.

Option premium levels can change the potential for reward and also change the risk factors. During periods of high premiums, investors may seek the return and lower capital requirement connected with writing covered calls. If option premiums are low, that same investor may purchase a married put as an alternative, since there may be little opportunity for profit on the covered call strategy. Option premiums are a function of different variables and while the premiums for one type of strategy may not be great, another might be better.

Once all of the above has been determined, the investor can begin to put it all together. Determination of a stock target should be contemplated as well as the time frame for this expectation. This will narrow down the possible option contracts which might be used. Next, the investor should determine how aggressive the strategy should be.

Many investors and traders base their investment decisions on their analysis of the underlying stock. There are two types of analysis: fundamental and technical. The fundamental analyst examines the corporation based upon sales, profits and profit margins, new products, legal factors, competition, and so on. The technical analyst bases investment upon the movement of the market, the industry group and the individual stock patterns. Technical analysis does not look at future earnings, growth or competition, but rather the historic price movement. Fundamental analysis works well for longer-term, more conservative strategies such as covered call writing and married put purchases. Technical analysis favors more immediate and aggressive strategies such as option purchases, combinations, straddles, and so on.

In conjunction with all of the variables outlined thus far, an evaluation process should be prepared. This evaluation should look into several strategies which the investor is comfortable in using and understands all of the potential outcomes. Each strategy should first be evaluated on its own merits. Potential reward and risk should be determined. This may be accomplished by determining the values of all positions at different price levels on the stock at expiration, using merely the intrinsic value. The price levels should include both favorable and unfavorable stock price movements. One good test of such movements is moving the stock 10 points in either direction or 5 points in-the-money and out-of-the-money, whichever is greater. Once the risk and reward values are calculated, the break-even points should be determined.

After the potential risks, rewards and break-even points are calculated, the investor may compare the results of two or more strategies to determine which best suits his or her investment requirements. Risk/reward ratios may be calculated by dividing the risk value by the reward value. The lower the ratio, the greater the profit opportunity over the risk opportunity. The return of a high ratio means that the risk potential is greater than the reward. Lower break-even points are desired for bullish strategies while higher break-even points are desired for bearish strategies. The distance between current stock price and break-even point should be compared among the various strategies the investor is looking into.

Before the strategy is implemented, the investor should contemplate the target, the stop out and time out points. A target price for both the option strategy and the underlying stock should be determined. Once the stock or option strategy reaches that point, the position should be closed and the profits realized. Stop out points for both the option strategy and the stock should also be set. If the stock violates that level or a certain loss is being realized in the option strategy, the position should be closed and the loss realized. A time out point should also be set, especially on strategies which involve the purchase of option contracts. Do not let the positions get to a point where they cannot be closed or a repair strategy implemented because there is simply not enough time.

Maintaining Positions on Long Stock

During the holding period, stock and option values will change, reflecting what might be unrealized gains or losses. As the underlying stock changes price, so will the puts and calls. To maximize growth and profit while minimizing risk, the investor must carefully monitor the positions. In addition to watching the values of the positions, movement of the other option contracts should be monitored. The adjustment of positions is a prudent management technique when using options. It is important to follow up on positions and make changes as needed.

A person who owns a stock which has unrealized profits should consider selling the stock and purchasing calls to replace the shares sold. Substituting an option contract for the shares of the underlying security allows the investor to remove the original capital invested plus a portion of the profits, reinvesting the balance of the profits into a call position. This allows the investor to continue holding a bullish position while removing the risk of the invested capital and some of the profits. If the underlying stock should turn bearish, a worse case scenario of losing the premium paid for the call might be realized. Still, the investor has a some profit and has not been subject to a loss from what once was a profit.

Deciding on which call to purchase was discussed in Chapter 2. The investor, however, may wish to explore the purchase of a LEAPS, allowing for the greatest possible time opportunity. This is especially true if the investor is long-term bullish on the underlying stock, and believes that the stock will continue to steadily appreciate. The investor should also be sure to note if the stock is going ex-dividend shortly, and may wish to hold off swapping the stock for options until the dividend has been collected.

Investors should take special caution to realize that the swapping of stock into calls may have unwanted tax implications. A tax adviser, or accountant should be consulted before using this strategy. This is especially true if the stock has a substantial gain.

Since there are so many different option strategies, long stock positions can be protected by using several other methods. One of these methods is writing calls against the long stock position. While the potential gain becomes limited, the premium received will help to protect against an erosion in the stock price. It is suggested that the investor write a call which is not in-the-money and has less than 180 days until expiration. If the option premiums are too low, the investor may opt to purchase a protective put. The put will help to limit loss to a sizable gain in the stock while also protecting the initial investment on the purchase of the stock. The put purchased should be at-the-money and have low premiums.

The investor may combine a covered call and protective put strategy into a hedge wrapper. While the gain might be limited, so will the risk, and the investor still gets to collect any dividends paid until expiration, as long as the stock continues to be held. The investor should pay special attention to the price levels at which this strategy will be enacted so as to limit the chance of locking in a loss due to overpayment of the put or under valuation of the calls.

Another alternative available to the investor is to sell half of the position of the underlying stock and write out-of-the-money combinations against the remaining half. If the stock continues to rise, the remaining shares should be called away at the exercise price of the call. If the stock drops below the exercise price of the short put contract, the shares which were sold will be repurchased at a lower level, and the investor will be long the original amount of shares, but with a lower cost basis. Chapter 14 discusses the use of covered combinations.

Maintaining Positions on Short Stock

As discussed earlier, the use of a short stock position opens the investor to the possibility of unlimited loss should the stock rise. In addition, there is always a chance that the investor can be bought-in, as well as some of the other problems encountered when a stock is sold short. It is especially important that short positions are monitored and adjustments made during the holding period.

An investor who has a profit on a short sale of stock has several opportunities. The first strategy involves the repurchase of the underlying shares and the purchase of a put. If there is already a profit, the repurchase of the underlying shares will remove any risk of loss plus allow the investor to take part of the profit while investing the balance of the profit on the purchase of a put contract. If the stock continues to decline in value, the value of the put will appreciate, allowing the investor to continue to participate on the bearish stock opinion. If the stock begins to appreciate, then the put will decline, maybe even totally. In such a case, the investor may suffer a decline in the overall profit, but this loss will be limited to the premium paid for the put contract. In addition, the risk of being bought-in and the payment of dividends are reduced.

A second strategy for a short seller with an unrealized profit is to purchase a call, with an exercise price above the current price of the stock. If the stock begins to turn around and rise, the stock may be repurchased at the exercise price. This allows the investor to eliminate the risk of loss and protect some of the unrealized profit. If the stock continues to fall, the profit will be slightly reduced by the amount of the premium. The protective call will also protect the short seller in case of a short squeeze, in which the price of the underlying stock rises as short sellers are forced to cover their positions. The greater the amount of short stock interest, the greater the potential loss to short sellers during a short squeeze. Short interest figures are published once a month in periodicals such as *The Wall Street Journal*, *Barron's* and *Investor's Daily*.

A third method for protecting short sales with profits is repurchasing half of the short position and selling out-of-the-money combinations. If the stock continues to decline, the short stock position will be repurchased at the exercise price of the put. If the stock rises, then the short seller will be short an amount of the shares which was repurchased, at the higher exercise price of the call option. If the stock remains between the two exercise prices, both the put and call will expire worthless, allowing the investor to keep the premiums collected. For more information about selling combinations see Chapter 8. If the stock which was sold short remains virtually unchanged, consider writing a put contract which is either at-the-money or out-of-the-money. The premium collected from the put will help to offset any costs, such as dividends, while allowing the short seller some downside movement. If the stock does decline, the investor will repurchase the stock at the exercise price of the put, if the stock is below that level at expiration. Should the stock rise in value, the investor may wish to consider the repurchase of the underlying stock or the purchase of a call, to help protect in case of further stock price appreciation. If the stock rises, the investor will have the opportunity to repurchase the shares at the exercise price of the call, limiting the potential loss. If the loss is significant, the investor may wish to explore the use of one of the repair strategies outlined in Chapter 19.

Maintaining Positions on Long Options

The purchase of an option contract implies that the investor is convinced about the directional movement of the stock, as well as the time period in which the stock will make such a move. During the holding period, the investor should pay special attention to the price of both the underlying stock and the value of the options contract. In addition, the monitoring of prices of other option contracts may provide for opportunity.

In Chapter 2, we discussed the purchase of option contracts. One of the guidelines suggested that if the value of the contract purchased doubles, some action must be taken. In some cases, the use of another strategy may be beneficial, in other cases the closing out of the entire position will be beneficial. Every situation must be evaluated on its own merit.

If premiums are high and the investor continues to feel that the stock will move in the same direction, the writing of an out-of-the-money contract may be advantageous. In such a situation, the investor will have a position equivalent to either a bull spread using calls or a bear spread using puts. The premium collected from writing the contract may help to limit the deterioration of the long option contract should the stock reverse direction or become static. If the stock continues its movement, the spread will reach its maximum value once the exercise price of the contract written is reached and expiration nears. The maximum profit of such a spread can be measured by the following calculation:

Maximum Profit = Difference in Exercise Prices − (Premium Paid
− Premium Collected)

TABLE 22-1. Maintaining Long Call Position by Writing Another Call

Call with 55 Exercise Price Purchased at 2⅞
Current Value of Call with 55 Exercise Price is 5½ with stock at 59⅜
Call with Exercise Price of 60 is 3½ Points

	Maintain Position	*Do Nothing*	*Close Position*
Action	Write Call with 60 Exercise Price		Sell Long Position
Position	+ 1 Call with 55 E.P. − 1 Call with 60 E.P.	+ 1 Call with 55 E.P.	-NONE-

Stock at Expiration	*Profits and Losses*		
53	⅝	<2⅞>	2⅝
55	⅝	<2⅞>	2⅝
56	1⅝	<1⅞>	2⅝
58	3⅝	⅛	2⅝
60	5⅝	2⅛	2⅝
65	5⅝	7⅛	2⅝
Max Profit	5⅝	Unlimited	2⅝
Max Loss	Locked in ⅝ Profit	2⅞	Locked in 2⅝ Profit

The break-even point on the long option will also be changed, allowing for some deterioration to break-even. If the stock becomes static, the premium of the option written will be kept by the investor, and the long option contract may be sold for a gain. Table 22-1 shows an example of maintaining a long call position by writing another call. For more information about the use of spreads, see Chapter 6.

Another method of protecting gains is to swap the long option contract for another contract with an exercise price which is at-the-money. By selling the profitable contract, the investor will remove the initial capital commitment plus some profit from that option while investing a portion of that profit into another contract. If the stock does not continue to perform as the investor expects, the new

TABLE 22-2.   Swap a Call for a Call

Stock = 73
Long 10 Call with 1 Month till Expiration with 70 Exercise
    Price = 4⅛
Call with 4 Months till Expiration with 75 Exercise Price = 2

	Swapping	*Not Swapping*
Action	− 10 Calls with 70 Exercise Price + 5 Calls with 75 Exercise Price	No Action
Position	+ 5 Calls with 75 Exercise Price	+ 10 Calls with 70 Exercise

Stock at Expiration in 1 Month	*Value of Positions*	
68	$ 625	-0-
70	$ 750	-0-
73	$2000	$3000
75	$2625	$5000

contract might expire worthless, but the original investment and some profit will have been taken out. If the stock continues to move as the investor expects, then the new contract will gain value and the investor will reap further profits, without any capital at risk. Table 22-2 shows the use of swapping one call for another call, while Table 22-3 shows the swapping of a long put for another put.

Sizable gains may also be protected by purchasing the opposite type option contract. If the stock has had a substantial move, and the investor is unsure about future stock movement, the purchase of an opposing contract may be warranted. In such a move, the investor holding a call position would purchase an at-the-money put or the investor holding a long put contract may wish to purchase an at-the-money call. If the stock continues on its movement, the new contract purchased may lose value, but the original contract will continue to gain value. If the stock reverses direction, then the loss of the original contract should be somewhat offset by the purchase of the opposing contract. If the stock remains static till expiration, the opposing contract may expire worthless, but the original contract which is in-

TABLE 22-3. Swap Long Put for Longer-Term Put

Stock Price = 86
Put Value with 85 Exercise Price and 1 Month Till Expiration = 2
Put Value with 80 Exercise Price and 1 Year Till Expiration = 4

Investor is Long 10 Puts with 85 Exercise Price and 1 Month Till
    Expiration

	Swap Put for Longer-Term Put	*Hold Put*
Action	Sell 10 Puts with 85 Exercise Buy 5 Puts with 80 Exercise	No Action
Stock in 1 Month	*Value of Positions*	
79	$4,000	$6,000
81	$3,500	$4,000
83	$3,100	$2,000
85	$2,200	-0-

Stock in 6 Months (Assuming Short-Term Option Expired Worthless)

80	$3,000
85	$1,750

the-money, should hold most of its value. Some value might be lost due to the erosion of time. It is stressed that the purchase of an opposing contract be limited to relatively low premium, since the investor still believes that the stock will continue on its original price movement.

Taking a stock position is still another method of maintaining a long option position with gains. The investor may wish either to swap the long contract and buy the stock, in the case of a call, or to sell the stock, in the case of a put. In taking such action, the investor may take advantage of time value still remaining in the option contract, while eliminating the time risk of holding that contract. If the time value is fairly low, the investor may seek to take the stock position through an exercise of the long option contract. The use of swapping is also profitable if the stock is going ex-dividend in a short period of time, allowing the investor to collect the dividend, in the case of a call. Such action on a put contract should be avoided until after the ex-dividend date on the stock.

A common and practical method of maintenance on the doubling in value of the option is to sell half of the position. By taking such action, the investor limits the possibility of loss to nothing since all of the original capital will be removed from the position. The remaining position may be closed when the investor is comfortable or at different price levels. If the stock continues to move favorably, parts of the remaining position may be sold at different levels, allowing the investor to remove profits on a systematic basis. If the stock begins to change direction, the investor may elect to sell the remainder of the position and take the profit.

Finally, the last method of taking a gain on an option contract is simply to close out the entire position. There is no crime in taking a 100 percent profit. If the stock continues to move, the lost opportunity is no shame since a doubling in value is very respectable. It is not prudent to leave the entire position open to a complete wipe out, should the stock suddenly reverse. It is almost a crime to see an investor or trader sustain a loss in capital plus a 100 percent gain.

If the long option contract is losing value, the investor should consider the liquidation of the position. Holding a wasting asset which is also losing value because of an inverse movement of the underlying stock is not a fundamentally sound way of maintaining positions. When a contract reaches a preset stop out level, the investor should close out the holdings and take back a good portion of the original capital invested. If the loss is considerable, the use of an options repair strategy (see Chapter 19) may be warranted. Losing positions may turn around, but allowing for the entire capital to be wiped out is not prudent and can be devastating to the investor.

Gains and losses on long option positions also face the deadline of option expiration. As expiration nears, the holding of positions becomes risky. Investors should consider the sale of the long option and the purchase of another contract with more time until expiration. In addition, the investor may wish to purchase only a portion of the original quantity, adjusting for time value loss or the removal of some profits. This concept should be evaluated at that moment. Table 22-4 is an example of swapping one long contract for another long contract, with a further period until expiration.

TABLE 22-4.   Swap Long Call for Longer-Term Call

Stock Price = 41
Call Value with 40 Exercise Price and 2 Months Till Expiration = 2⅛
Call Value with 45 Exercise Price and 1 Year Till Expiration = 4¼

Investor is Long 10 Calls with 40 Exercise Price and 2 Months Till
   Expiration

	Swap Call for Longer-Term Call	*Hold Call*
Action	Sell 10 Calls with 40 Exercise	No Action
	Buy 5 Calls with 45 Exercise	

Stock in 2 Months	*Value of Positions*	
39	$1,625	-0-
41	$2,062	$ 1,000
45	$3,500	$ 5,000
50	$4,500	$10,000

Stock in 6 Months (Assuming Short-Term Option Expired Worthless)

| 52 | $5,625 | |
| 55 | $6,375 | |

Maintaining Positions on Short Options

The writing of option contracts permits the writer to collect the entire premium if the option remains out-of-the-money. While the potential profit is limited to the premium collected, the potential loss is unlimited. If the option becomes in-the-money, the loss can be substantial. The monitoring of such positions requires more concentration than that of a long option position.

The purchase of an out-of-the-money contract may help to limit the possibility of unlimited loss. By purchasing an out-of-the-money contract, the investor is setting up either a bull spread using puts or a bear spread using calls. In such a case, loss will be limited by the long contract. The maximum loss may be calculated as follows:

$$\text{Maximum Loss} = \text{Difference in Exercise Prices} - (\text{Premium Received} - \text{Premium Paid})$$

If the stock moves as the investor expects, the maximum profit of the premium collected is reduced slightly by the purchase of the out-of-the-money contract. Chapter 6 discusses further the use of option spreads.

Another method of maintaining a short option position is through the use of the underlying stock. Short call positions can be protected by purchasing the underlying stock, turning the position from a bearish opinion to a bullish opinion. In the case of a short put, the short sale of the stock will turn the position from bullish to bearish. In each case, the stock will cover the naked option position. Such a strategy allows the investor to take a losing position and limit the loss or sometimes change that loss to a gain. Chapters 3 and 4 discuss the use of stock and option positions in such situations.

Losing short option positions may not be completely written off. The use of repair strategies (see Chapter 19) may allow the investor the opportunity to break-even. This is not always the case. In addition, before enacting any short position, the investor should determine a stop out point to limit the risk.

Maintaining Positions on Covered Calls and Married Puts

Investors utilizing the covered call strategy as well as the married put strategy believe that the value of the underlying stock will appreciate. The rise and fall of stock prices may require that certain adjustments be made during the holding period. This may include bullish, bearish and neutral stock movements.

If the value of the stock accumulates, the investor who used the covered call writing technique may wish to repurchase the call and write another call, with additional time to expiration but with a higher exercise price. This will allow the investor the opportunity for further gains, should the stock continue to rise. The use of a diagonal movement may also allow the investor to swap option contracts for little or no cost. If the stock remains static at the new level, the investor may only have a time cost. If the stock declines, the break-even point will be virtually unchanged (excluding commissions and other transaction charges).

For the purchaser of a married put, the investor may wish to sell the long put and purchase a put with a higher exercise price and a longer period till expiration. This will result in some additional capital, which may be offset by the unrealized gain in the stock position. This will help the investor to protect not only the stock position but some of the unrealized profits as well. If the cost of the put is too high, the investor may opt to switch the married put position into a covered call position, taking advantage of higher option premiums, while limiting the potential gain to the exercise price of the call.

The investor with a losing covered call position may wish to repurchase the call and write another call with a lower exercise price, with a greater period to expiration. This may allow the position to break-even at the new expiration. Positions with large losses should be closed, avoiding further deterioration in the stock price. Investors who believe that the stock might turn around may seek the idea of selling the stock position and writing a put which is out-of-the-money, if the premium is high. If the stock continues to fall, the stock might be repurchased at the exercise price of the put (less the premium collected for writing the put).

Summary

1. It is important to carefully monitor the price of the underlying stock and option positions.

2. The monitoring of other option contracts can provide the possibility for switching contracts or strategies.

3. Diversification of stocks, industries, strategies and time till expiration is the greatest method of reducing risk.

4. Naked stock positions can prove to be the most dangerous situations. Using puts and calls can help to limit risk and increase returns.

5. Stock positions with gains may be swapped into option positions, allowing the investor to take some profits and the capital investment out of the realm of risk.

6. Option positions with 100 percent gains should take some action, including spreads, closing half or the entire position.

7. Short stock positions with gains can be swapped for puts while positions with losses may utilize the purchase of protective calls.

8. Short option positions should be carefully monitored for opportunity to limit risk or to swap for profits.

9. Strategies involving both stock and options can be adjusted to maximize profits, raise potential and limit losses.

23
Mergers and Acquisitions

During the 1980s, the mergers and acquisitions game seemed to be the main focus of traders. If someone whispered in the ear of another, the stock mentioned was probably purchased since the takeover arena was what many focused upon. The introduction of high yield/ high risk bonds, also known as "junk bonds," allowed for the highly leveraged takeover of corporations with little capital requirement by the firm making the acquisition. The takeover game has slowed in the 1990s, however, there are still some opportunities.

The takeover of a company usually takes place through one of two takeover methods: the **two-tier** takeover and the **one-tier** takeover. There are other methods for taking over companies, but this book will focus on these methods.

It should be noted that no takeover is complete until the stock has been exchanged. Some people believe that once a deal is agreed upon or bidding takes place, the deal is done. In 1990, UAL Corp. was the subject of a takeover which drove the price of the stock from $120 to $280. The deal was supposed to take place at a price of $305 per share, until the acquiring party, led by the pilots union, was unable to obtain all of the financing needed. The stock dropped, triggering what became known as the mini-crash of 1989.

Two-Tier Takeover

The two-tier method of taking over a company involves the purchase of a part of the company at one price with the purchase of the balance of the stock at a lower level at a future date. This allows the company which is taking over to get control of the board of directors by taking a controlling interest (more than 50%) during a hostile takeover, and then lowering the cost of the takeover by purchasing the balance of the stock at a lower level. Since the takeover is usually hostile, the purchase of the first tier of stock is usually at a level which is extremely attractive to holders of the stock. This level may be worth actually much more than the stock is worth. Once the shares have been tendered and accepted for the first tier, the value of the remaining shares will drop since the amount of money which the remaining shares will be tendered for might be much less.

Taking advantage of the two-tier stock deal is relatively easy. The trader holding the stock may purchase a put, expiring after the date for submitting the stock to the takeover company. The amount of puts purchased should be equivalent to the amount of shares which the trader expects to have returned and should be at-the-money. The price of the put may be high, since it is expected that the stock will decline significantly after the completion of the first tier. When the stock is tendered and returned, the trader may exercise the puts, selling the returned shares at the exercise price of the put. Since the stock will probably decline significantly in value, the investor will have very little loss from the put. The trader then does not have to worry about the risk of selling the returned shares at market price or tendering them on the second tier.

For example, a trader purchased 1000 shares of a stock being taken over for $60 per share. The stock is now trading at $80. The company being taken over has made a tender offer of $85 for 70 percent of the shares. The trader decides to purchase 3 puts with an exercise price of 80 for 6 points. The stock is tendered, and 700 shares are purchased at $85 and 300 shares are returned. Thus far, a gain of 25 points is realized on 700 shares. The second tier is announced for the balance of the stock at $60 and the stock immediately drops to $55. If the puts are exercised the 300 shares are sold for an effective price of 74 points (80 exercise less 6 point premium), realizing a gain of 14 points on the 300 shares. If the puts were not owned, the best the trader could do is break-even on the 300 shares.

If all of the shares were accepted, since everyone holding the stock may have not tendered, then the 3 puts could be sold for a profit of 25 points. In this situation, the trader would have made 25 points on the 1000 shares of stock plus 25 points on each of the three puts.

One-Tier Takeover

A one-tier takeover can be hostile or friendly. In such a deal, the acquiring corporation agrees to pay a certain amount in cash, debentures or stock for 100 percent of the company being acquired. Since a deal is not complete until the stock is tendered, the trader has a risk that the deal can fall apart, similar to that of UAL.

To protect against the deal falling apart, the trader can either purchase a protective put or write an out-of-the-money call. Since the premiums on takeover stocks are extremely high, the writing of the calls is preferred. If the stock rises due to another, higher bid, the stock may be called away at the exercise price. While this may not be as high as the new tender price, the sale will be higher than the value of the first tender offer. If the deal does fall apart, part of the decline in the stock will be offset from the premium collected in writing the call.

If the deal is an exchange of stock, the trader should take special care since the option may expire after the tender of the stock, leaving a naked call position, which might be called for the value of the new stock plus any cash in lieu of fractional shares. Many traders fall into this trap, since they believe that the options are no longer valid since the stock is taken over. This misconception can prove to be a very costly mistake.

What Not to Do

Many traders like to take advantage of takeover stock premiums by writing out-of-the-money puts and calls. While the premiums might appear to be attractive, there is usually a reason why they are so high. After all, no one is going to give away something for nothing. The high premium suggests that there is some type of risk in the movement in the stock. If the premium were a give away, the market makers and arbitrageurs would have already taken advantage of it.

Traders believing that a deal is done, may write puts or combinations. If this is done, it is suggested that protective purchases are made against the writing of those positions.

Takeover stocks are more volatile than other stocks especially during periods of negotiations or hostile bids. This volatility could rise further if there is more than one party attempting to takeover that company. Extreme care should be used to protect positions. It might be a disadvantage at this point to open new positions, especially those which might hold a lot of risk for the trader.

Summary

1. It is possible to take advantage of take over situations using option contracts.
2. A takeover is not complete until the stock is exchanged or tendered.
3. High risk positions should be avoided on take over stocks.
4. Nobody gives away something for nothing. High premiums should be the subject of caution.

24
Other Option Products

Options are part of a large group of products which are known as derivative products. Derivatives include certain warrants, commodities, futures and other trading vehicles. This is the fastest growing area in terms of new products. This chapter will highlight some of the other trading vehicles as well as some other option products.

In Chapter 17, we discussed the use of index options and futures contracts. There are futures contracts available on a wide range of commodities from pork bellies to zinc. In addition to the futures contracts, some of these commodities trade options on those futures contracts. Such options allow the buyer to take an action upon the futures contract, as opposed to the underlying stock. In 1991, a five-day option contract was introduced on the gold futures contract. The purchase of the option on the day it was brought out allowed the trader only five days to be correct.

Interest Rate Instruments

The Chicago Board Options Exchange trades options on U.S. Treasury Securities and Bonds. These options allow the investor to hedge or make speculative investments on the value of the instrument. If the value of a bond rises, interest rates drop and vice versa. By purchasing a call, the investor believes that interest rates will fall and bond prices will rise. If the call becomes in-the-money, the investor may purchase a set amount of bonds by exercising the call.

Put buyers believe that interest rates will rise causing bond prices to fall. By purchasing a put option, the investor can hedge bond positions or speculate on rising interest rates. If the put becomes in-the-money, the investor can sell a certain amount of the underlying bonds by exercising the put.

Quantities and descriptions on bond options as well as pricing may be a little confusing. One bond contract may represent $1000 worth of bonds, making one point worth $1000. In addition, the description includes the bonds coupon rate (rate of interest) as well as its term. These descriptions should match the investor's needs. It is suggested that all such option contracts be discussed with an account executive before an investment decision is made.

Like stock options, it is possible to use options on bonds in many different strategies. Covered call writing and married put purchases are just two methods of hedging bond positions. It is possible to purchase or write spreads, create synthetic strategies and even repair bond positions. It is beyond the scope of this book to go into details on these strategies.

Another method of investing on interest rates is through the purchase or writing of puts and calls on interest rate indexes. The CBOE has two different interest rate indexes which are similar to trading index options. The Long-Term Interest Rate Index (LTX) and the Short-Term Interest Rate Index (IRX) are indexes which trade at a 100 multiple of interest rates. The purchase of a call speculates that rates will *rise*, opposite of purchasing a bond option. The purchase of a put implies that interest rates will *fall*. Strategies, such as those used on the index options allow investors to hedge or speculate on the direction of interest rates.

Like index options, the interest rate index options have a multiplier of 100. Therefore the price of one point is equal to $100 per contract.

Currency

Investors and traders sometimes need to hedge certain investments based on the fluctuations of currency rates. The difference between the U.S. dollar and the yen can turn a gain on a Japanese stock into a loss. Some investors purchase or sell goods overseas, requiring some type of stability in currency exchange rates to assure profits. There are methods of protecting against fluctuations in rates or even speculating on those rates.

The Philadelphia Stock Exchange introduced the trading in foreign currency option products. These option contracts allow investors to hedge investments or business dealings against changes in exchange rates between the U.S. dollar and other major currencies, such as the pound, deutche mark, franc, and yen. By purchasing a call on one of those currencies, the investor is speculating on or hedging against an upward move in the foreign currency or a downward move in the dollar. Therefore, an investor who is purchasing goods from a Japanese firm may wish to purchase options on the yen to protect against a rise in the yen versus the dollar. If the yen does rise, part of the additional expense of the goods will be offset through the gain on the call.

The Philadelphia Stock Exchange has also introduced cross foreign currency options, allowing for the speculation or hedging upon one foreign currency rate versus another foreign currency rate. These options allow the investor to take advantage of changes in currency exchange rates between two foreign countries.

Capitalizing

In 1991, the Chicago Board Options Exchange introduced a new product known as CAPS™. CAPS is a product which is very similar to a bull spread using calls or a bear spread using puts, and are currently available on the S&P 100 Index (OEX) and the S&P 500 Index (SPX). The difference between the exercise prices is 30 points and they are initially introduced with four months until expiration. If the index rises through the exercise price of the short call, the CAPS is liquidated the next day for the 30-point difference. If that level is never reached, the CAPS will be closed for the intrinsic value of the spread at expiration. This means that the investor cannot forget to close the position once it reaches the maximum value.

As of the time of this writing, a CAPS cannot be purchased on margin, and must be paid for in full, similar to the purchase of a regular index spread. An investor may not close one side of the spread: the package must be kept together at all times. Therefore, CAPS is its own product.

The writer of a CAPS is subject to the same margin requirements as the writer of a spread. The margin requirement is the difference between the exercise prices of the CAPS (30 points) less the premium received multiplied by the index multiplier. The balance must be deposited in the account. Therefore, an investor selling a 360/390 cap for four points would be required to deposit $2600 per CAPS contract. If the CAPS is assigned at its full value, the investor would

TABLE 24-1.   Example of Use of OEX CAPS

OEX Index at 370
CPO (OEX CAPS) with 360-390 Spread at 13

Buyer purchases 1 CPO with cost of 13
    ($1300) and 3 Months till Expiration.

Index at Expiration	Value of CPO
350	-0-
360	-0-
370	10
380	20
390	30

If the value of the index exceeds 390 any time
    during the holding period, the CAPS will be
    closed for the maximum value of 30 points.

have to deliver the value of the CAPS, 30 points or $3000, realizing a loss of $2600 per CAPS.

Table 24-1 illustrates the use of an OEX CAPS (CPO) for both the buyer and the writer. The example shows the capital requirements and the profit and loss for the positions at different price intervals.

As of the writing of this book, CAPS were not introduced on equity option stocks. It is expected that the use of CAPS will become wide spread among the option stocks, just as LEAPS have become wide spread.

Over-the-Counter Option Contracts

While there are almost 1,000 stocks trading options, at the writing of this book, many more are expected to be added as listing standards are lowered and company standings rise. Although a particular stock does not trade listed options, puts and calls may be purchased on an Over-The-Counter (OTC) basis from put and call dealers. These dealers will create a contract with an exercise price based upon the last sale of the underlying stock. If an investor purchases this contract, the only possible course of action is to exercise the option, since there is not a liquid market for that contract. In addition, the investor can request the period of days or months until the contract expires. The longer the period of time, the greater the premium for the contract.

Put and call dealers also have two other types of option contracts. The first is known as the "Up and Away," a call option contract which is exercised once the price of the underlying stock reaches a certain level. The second type, the "Down and Out," is a put contract that is exercised once the stock drops below a certain level.

Index